ALSO BY ROBERT O'HARROW JR.

No Place to Hide: Behind the Scenes of Our
Emerging Surveillance Society

Zero Day: The Threat in Cyberspace
A Washington Post *ebook*

The Quartermaster

MONTGOMERY C. MEIGS

★

LINCOLN'S GENERAL

★

MASTER BUILDER
OF THE UNION ARMY

Robert O'Harrow Jr.

Simon & Schuster

New York · London · Toronto · Sydney · New Delhi

SIMON & SCHUSTER
1230 Avenue of the Americas
New York, NY 10020

Copyright © 2016 by Robert O'Harrow Jr.

Photo insert: All photos courtesy of the
Library of Congress unless otherwise noted.

First Simon & Schuster hardcover edition October 2016

SIMON & SCHUSTER and colophon are trademarks of Simon & Schuster, Inc.

For information about special discounts for bulk purchases, please contact
Simon & Schuster Special Sales at 1-866-506-1949
or business@simonandschuster.com.

The Simon & Schuster Speakers Bureau can bring authors to your
live event. For more information or to book an event contact the
Simon & Schuster Speakers Bureau at 1-866-248-3049
or visit our website at www.simonspeakers.com.

Manufactured in the United States of America

1   3   5   7   9   10   8   6   4   2

Library of Congress Cataloging-in-Publication Data

Names: O'Harrow, Robert, author.
Title: Quartermaster : Montgomery C. Meigs : Lincoln's general,
master builder of the Union army / Robert O'Harrow Jr.
Description: New York : Simon & Schuster, 2016. | Includes
bibliographical references and index.
Identifiers: LCCN 2016025788| ISBN 9781451671926 (hardcover : alk.
paper) | ISBN 9781451671933 (pbk. : alk. paper) | ISBN 9781451671940 (ebook)
Subjects: LCSH: Meigs, Montgomery C. (Montgomery Cunningham),
1816–1892. | Quartermasters—United States—Biography. | United States—
History—Civil War, 1861–1865—Biography. | United States—History—
Civil War, 1861–1865—Supplies and stores.
Classification: LCC E467.1.M44 O35 2016 | DDC 973.7092 [B]—dc23
LC record available at https://lccn.loc.gov/2016025788

ISBN 978-1-4516-7192-6
ISBN 978-1-4516-7194-0 (ebook)

For my dear Amy

Contents

CHAPTER 20 *Shoddy*   *125*

CHAPTER 21 *"Hard Work and Cold Calculation"*   *132*

CHAPTER 22 *"The War Cannot Be Long"*   *140*

CHAPTER 23 *Gunboats*   *147*

CHAPTER 24 *"His Best Name Is Honesty"*   *154*

CHAPTER 25 *"Vast in Quantity"*   *163*

CHAPTER 26 *Hope Wanes*   *173*

CHAPTER 27 *"Fret Him and Fret Him"*   *181*

CHAPTER 28 *"Exhaustion of Men and Money"*   *190*

CHAPTER 29 *"A Beauteous Bubble"*   *200*

CHAPTER 30 *A Vulnerable Capital*   *209*

CHAPTER 31 *The Refit at Savannah*   *218*

CHAPTER 32 *The Journey Home*   *227*

CHAPTER 33 *"Dogs to Their Vomit"*   *232*

CHAPTER 34 *"Soldier, Engineer, Architect, Scientist, Patriot"* *238*

            Acknowledgments   *247*

            Notes   *251*

            Index   *291*

I do not know one who combines the qualities of masculine intellect, learning and experience of the right sort, and physical power of labor, and endurance so well as he.

—Abraham Lincoln, June 1861

Without the services of this eminent soldier, the National cause must either have been lost or deeply imperiled.

—William Seward, May 1867

The logistical demands of the Union army were much greater than those of its enemy . . . Meigs furnished these requirements in a style that made him the unsung hero of northern victory.

—James McPherson, *Battle Cry of Freedom*

Meigs should be given a place near that of Seward and Stanton, Chase and Gideon Welles.

—Allan Nevins, *The War for the Union*

The
Quartermaster

Prologue

On March 29, 1861, Army Captain Montgomery Meigs, just home from work, found a letter waiting for him. Secretary of State William Seward wanted him to go to a meeting at the White House as soon as possible. President Abraham Lincoln had a problem to solve and needed to talk to a soldier about certain military operations. It was unusual for a president to seek advice from a captain, but these were unusual times, and Meigs was an unusual man. The country stood at the edge of war. Lincoln had been inaugurated on March 4. Six Southern states had formed a separate, provisional government: the Confederate States of America. Virtually all federal operations had been suspended in the South, and only a handful of fortifications there remained under Washington's control.

Lincoln spoke freely. He was determined to keep control of Fort Sumter, in Charleston, South Carolina, and Fort Pickens, on the Gulf of Mexico in Pensacola, Florida. But he worried that the nation's small standing army did not have enough men for such operations. Because he did not want to provoke South Carolina, the most volatile of the Southern states, Lincoln focused on Florida. He told Meigs that General Winfield Scott, the army's elderly leader, thought that reinforcing forts was impossible. Lincoln asked Meigs whether Fort Pickens could be held. "Certainly," Meigs said, "if the navy would do its duty and had not lost it already."

Meigs was an army engineer with no fighting experience, but few could match his mix of creativity and talent for organization. He had built the capital's new aqueduct, including a bridge with the longest masonry arch in the world. He also was the man behind the US Capitol's recent expansion and the ongoing installation of its great dome. His integrity was unblemished. Lincoln knew he had the right man. Without consulting his secretaries of war or navy, he ordered Meigs to prepare an amphibious assault on Fort Pickens.

Meigs and a handful of colleagues sorted out the logistics, chartered fast steamships, and secretly gathered nearly five hundred men and tons of supplies at the Navy Yard in Brooklyn, New York. Before dawn on April 7, the force was heading south. His ship ran into a violent gale at Cape Hatteras, North Carolina. Its crew struggled to keep men and horses from being washed overboard. Meigs had "never seen so magnificent a sight as this roaring, raging sea." The closer they drew to Pickens, the more he hoped the mission would "strike terror into the ranks of rebellion." He believed the country would survive. "I see a bright future in which this great land under a strong and united government will at length again be free and happy," he wrote at the time, "when traitors will have received due punishment for their crimes, and the sin of slavery wiped out by the hands of an avenging God."

Meigs could scarcely imagine that he was about to play a singular role in fulfilling that hope.

PART 1

———————— ★ ————————

CHAPTER 1

Rigid Duty

Montgomery Cunningham Meigs was born on May 3, 1816, in Augusta, Georgia. His father, Dr. Charles Meigs, a recent graduate of the University of Pennsylvania, with his new bride, Mary, had come to Augusta to start his medical career and raise a family in an atmosphere of piety. They lived not far from the Savannah River, optimistic about their prospects. But it soon became clear to the couple they could not stay in the South. The brutality of slavery made Mary ill. So they returned to Philadelphia, a bustling business center quickly filling with schools, churches, and businesses. It retained the charm of a provincial city, giving way quickly to unspoiled countryside. About sixty-three thousand residents relied on wood to heat their homes. Farmers brought food to the city by wagons. The city offered the Meigs family an affordable place to live, study, work, and grow. Montgomery and his six brothers and two sisters explored nearby rivers and forests. He loved to romp along the Delaware River with friends, examining the creatures he found in the mud and water. Sometimes in the summer, he fished until dark on the Schuylkill River. Now and then his family took sailing excursions to nearby farms.

Montgomery was bright and affectionate and "seems to observe everything that passes," his mother wrote in 1822, when he was six. But he also pained his family. He "very soon tires of his play things," she wrote. "Destroying them appears to afford him as much pleasure as their first possession—is not vexed with himself for having broken them. Is very inquisitive about the use of everything, delighted to see different machines at work." When playing, he tended to be bossy. His mother described him as "high tempered, unyielding, tyrannical towards his brothers; persevering in pursuit of anything he wishes."

Meigs's father demanded discipline and excellence from the children. His stories were laden with moral lessons. The children often gathered around him near the fireplace and listened as he told them about their virtuous and industrious ancestors. The stories begin at the great Puritan migration in the 1630s, when the first of the clan arrived in Boston from England. The ancestors were educators, doctors, engineers, soldiers, and public officials. They were ambitious, patriotic, and pious. A certain righteousness also reappeared from generation to generation, much to the annoyance of neighbors and colleagues. Dr. Meigs in his stories underscored the importance of personal honor. He told the children it was their "rigid duty" to protect the family name. They were to "beware lest [they] disgrace that history." In a note inscribed at the end of the family Bible, he wrote: Discard "without mercy every member of their blood line whose conduct might stain" the family reputation.

His father challenged Meigs in other ways. He taught at Jefferson Medical College and became a pathbreaker in the realm of women's health, writing books on obstetrics while maintaining regular hours for patients. He shouldered an extraordinary workload, often snatching only two or three hours of sleep on the family couch before going to work. Charles Meigs didn't seem to mind. He felt called to service and thought his medical work put him closer to God. Montgomery Meigs would credit his mother's influence for much of his success, but he would never lose sight of the model set by his father.

———

As a boy, Meigs watched militia companies march by on Chestnut Street in Philadelphia. He heard how Stephen Decatur, the American naval hero, had offered the toast "My country—right or wrong!" He dreamed of going to the United States Military Academy at West Point, in New York, where he could train as a soldier and engineer. He was accepted in 1832, when he was sixteen, and he was awed by the outpost perched on a bluff in the forested mountains of the Hudson Highlands.

Meigs studied mathematics, engineering, and building. One teacher insisted that every soldier know how to draw for mapmaking, and Meigs was soon able to do so with unusual finesse. Though he thrived as a student, he racked up demerits for cutting against what he later called West Point's "uncompromising devotion to orthodoxy." He complained about the demerit system, saying it impeded enterprising men in favor of "the stolid, the namby pamby, the men having no distinguishing traits or character." In 1836 Meigs graduated fifth in his class and became a second lieutenant in the army, dedicating himself to God, family, country, duty, honor. He joined the artillery corps but gave up that commission a year later to become a brevet second lieutenant in the Army Corps of Engineers, an elite organization that played a primary role in building the young country's roads, canals, bridges, and harbors. Its achievements included the country's longest highway, the Cumberland Road, west of the Ohio River.

In the summer of 1837, one of his first assignments paired him with another West Point graduate, Robert E. Lee, class of 1829. Their task was to find ways of improving navigation on the Mississippi River. Meigs and Lee, his superior, set up headquarters on an abandoned steamboat about 150 miles to the north of St. Louis. Part of the deck was under water, but the staterooms were dry. Meigs drew and painted the countryside as part of mapmaking responsibilities. Lee directed a survey of the river and oversaw preliminary work of laborers to clear the river bottom. Meigs loved nearly everything about the assignment. For a time, the men bunked in a cabin onshore and ate the catfish and pike they caught. Meigs admired Lee, "then in the vigor of youthful strength, with a noble and commanding presence, and an admirable, graceful, and athletic figure. He was one with whom nobody ever wished or ventured to take a liberty, though kind and generous to his subordinates, admired by all women, and respected by all men. He was the model of a soldier and the beau ideal of a Christian man."

With harsh winter weather coming on, Meigs and Lee disbanded their crew. Meigs went back to Philadelphia; Lee, to his wife's plantation at Arlington, Virginia, in the hills overlooking Washington. They would remain fond of each other until a national crisis turned them into mortal enemies.

CHAPTER 2

Patience and Perseverance

Meigs began a long stretch as a journeyman engineer for defense and public works. His new assignment took him to the Delaware River, south of Philadelphia, where he helped improve a stone breakwater that protected the coast and facilitated navigation on the river and bay. He also helped rebuild Fort Delaware, a massive fortification on Pea Patch Island destroyed by fire.

The project posed many challenges. The island had formed from silt over the centuries, and the mud went forty feet deep in places. Meigs and other engineers created an intricate wooden grillage as a foundation, pounding more than twelve thousand wooden piles into the mud, using steam-powered pile drivers. Builders had been using such structures since the days of the Roman Empire. A drawing by Meigs of the grillage looks beautiful, precise, and timeless, with its faint linear depiction of crossbeams layered underneath the outlines of the fort. Though he thrived on practical problems, he did not do as well as a manager. When called on to serve as a supervisor, Meigs sometimes became short-tempered. On Pea Patch, he had control of the federal funding for salaries and supplies. About $75,000 had been deposited in a bank in Philadelphia. Before releasing the cash, bank officials required Meigs to certify the payroll. He took the request as a suggestion that he might be skimming money for himself. The idea that someone might question his integrity was too much to bear. He launched into a letter-writing campaign, pages of complaint that went to officials at the bank and superiors in Washington.

Bank officials were only fulfilling an obligation to guard against a

perennial contracting scheme in which corrupt officials drew pay for
no-show workers. Meigs's behavior embarrassed everyone, though all
agreed to treat it as a misunderstanding, and the episode did no lasting damage to his reputation. He worked hard, and colleagues and superiors could sense his devotion. With his career taking hold, Meigs's
vision for himself evolved. He began thinking of himself as an American patriot and public servant. "I am a citizen of the United States," he
wrote his father, "not of Connecticut where my grandfather lived or of
Georgia where I was born or of Pennsylvania."

———

In 1839 Meigs received orders to report to the Board of Engineers for
Atlantic Coast Defenses in Washington. The board served as a bureaucratic bridge between fortification projects and the army's military
brass. The posting provided exposure to senior officials as well as the
city's ruthless politics. Washington suited Meigs. He liked good conversation and he was soon drawn to a young woman, Louisa Rodgers,
the daughter of Commodore John Rodgers, a naval hero of the War
of 1812. The Rodgers family had been prominent in Washington and
Maryland for decades. Though the commodore had died a few years
earlier, Louisa and her family still lived in a mansion that he had built
on Lafayette Square, near the White House.

Montgomery and Louisa made a handsome pair. Tall, upright, and
proper, Louisa had the firm demeanor of her father. She sang beauti-
fully and enjoyed riding. In addition to attending parties, the couple
rode along the Chesapeake & Ohio Canal through the rugged landscape along the Potomac River north and west of Washington. After
a steady courtship, they married on May 2, 1841, one day before his
twenty-fifth birthday. Their marriage would ground and comfort
Meigs for decades to come, while giving him political and social ties
that would help him through controversy and struggle. They claimed
Washington as their home, but they could not stay for now. Meigs received orders to design and build fortifications, including Fort Wayne
on the Detroit River, near the border with Canada.

The defenses were part of a long campaign to protect against invasion from British forces. Though the significance of the threat in Detroit was debatable, Congress pressed for the work. Because the project depended on the ebb and flow of congressional appropriations, Meigs sometimes had more free time than was advisable for so energetic a person. He filled some lulls by reading the history of engineering. He focused in particular on the work of Sébastien Le Prestre de Vauban, the seventeenth-century French soldier who served as King Louis XIV's chief military engineer. Meigs had heard about Vauban at West Point. His plans for Fort Wayne drew directly from fortifications Vauban had built in France, including thick masonry walls, protected walkways known as sally ports, and an internal parade ground.

––––––

Montgomery and Louisa anchored their lives to their children, with four born in the first five years of their marriage: John, Mary Montgomery, Charles Delucena, and Montgomery Jr.

The family relished the frontier spirit that lingered over Detroit. Because the work there did not demand much of Lieutenant Meigs, he often slept in or took his dog and a gun on long walks through the northern woods. He assumed he would be more motivated when necessary, but that was not good enough for Louisa, who challenged him to find ways to be more productive. In response, Meigs launched a self-improvement campaign that included keeping a journal.

For all his contentment, Meigs felt distant from what was the center of action for the army in the 1840s: Mexico, Texas, and the far West. The country's hunger for that territory became sharp in his first few years in Detroit. It peaked in 1844, during the campaign leading to the election of James K. Polk, who believed America was destined to expand across the continent. In his inaugural speech on March 4, 1845, President Polk underscored his support of the annexation of Texas from Mexico, while making clear his intention to take territory in the Northwest. "The world beholds the peaceful triumphs of the industry of our emigrants," Polk said. "To us belongs the duty of protecting them adequately wherever they may be upon our soil."

The new president was prepared to go to war. For the soldiers who would put his words into action, this meant a chance to earn glory, a rise in rank, and a boost in salary. Meigs had to watch from afar. Soon after taking office, Polk annexed Texas, which became the twenty-eighth state. He accepted a compromise with Britain at the 49th parallel in Oregon. Then, in a series of calculated provocations, he pushed Mexico into war, which began in 1846 after Polk claimed with little evidence that Mexicans had killed Americans near disputed territory at the border. Soldiers moved south, and the conflict soon created a rift in the United States that would only widen in the coming years. Democrats strongly supported their president. The Whig Party—the precursor to the Republican Party—railed against it. One Whig adherent was Abraham Lincoln, a freshman congressman from Illinois who accused Polk of violating the Constitution and called on him to produce evidence of Mexico's culpability.

Meigs followed the far-off fighting through newspaper accounts: the Battle of Buena Vista in northern Mexico, the capture of Mexico City, and the 1848 Treaty of Guadalupe Hidalgo, giving control of California and the entire Southwest to the United States. Many of his army colleagues became famous and received promotions. Among them were Ambrose Burnside, Jefferson Davis, Ulysses Grant, Robert E. Lee, and Thomas Jackson, later known as "Stonewall." The war resulted in appalling casualties, including more than 13,280 American dead, and it ignited a long fuse in Washington over the question of slavery. A lawmaker from Pennsylvania, David Wilmot, offered legislation that declared that "neither slavery nor involuntary servitude shall ever exist in any part of" territory acquired during the war. The House approved Wilmot's proviso. The Senate stood firm against it.

Meigs was unsettled that he had lived safely and comfortably in the northwoods while army colleagues had risked their lives or died for their country. He hoped to redeem himself one day, perhaps by achieving something so beneficial to the country that his name would never be forgotten.

———

As winter descended on Detroit in 1849, Meigs was ordered back to Washington to serve as staff officer to Joseph G. Totten, the army's chief engineer and a hero of the Mexican War. Totten knew Meigs from his earlier days in Washington and would become one of his most important mentors. They had much in common. Totten's family also had roots in England, and he was a West Point graduate who had worked on river and fortification projects. There were also plenty of differences. As a colonel, Totten had controlled engineering operations during the invasion of Mexico City and was made brigadier general for his bravery at the siege of Veracruz. During his rise through the military, Totten made time to study natural history. He focused in particular on sea snails and other Mollusca in New England and the Pacific Northwest. Totten lives on now in the names of some of his discoveries, including one dubbed *Gemma Tottenii*. When Meigs arrived in the capital, Totten occupied a central spot in the capital city's scientific crowd. In addition to being the army's chief engineer, he served as a founding regent of the new national museum known as the Smithsonian Institution. Totten welcomed Meigs into this circle.

There's no overstating the pull that the Smithsonian exerted on certain men. It was the brainchild of James Smithson, the brilliant, illegitimate son of Hugh Smithson, the First Duke of Northumberland. A chemist and mineralogist, Smithson had donated a hundred thousand gold sovereigns to the United States, directing the money to be used after his death for "an establishment for the increase and diffusion of knowledge." Smithson died in 1829, but it was not until 1846 that Congress approved legislation creating the museum. Nothing else like it existed in the country.

At the time of Meigs's return to the capital, the first Smithsonian building, then under construction, was known as the Castle. It was a red sandstone complex modeled on a medieval Norman style. For

Meigs and others, it embodied the spirit of a new era for American engineers and natural philosophers, or physical scientists, who were determined to take part in the tide of technological and scientific advancements sweeping the world, filling cities and landscapes in Europe and the United States with new bridges, buildings, canals, railroads, and telegraph lines. Meigs visited the US Patent Office regularly to study new inventions and engineering techniques, and he bought himself a microscope.

At the same time, he drew and painted. A reunion with Captain Seth Eastman, one of his drawing instructors at West Point, stoked his enthusiasm. Eastman was a talented careerist in the nation's small standing army. He explored, built fortifications, and painted as he moved among posts in Florida, Texas, and Minnesota, becoming a specialist in the depiction of American Indians. In Washington, Eastman focused on illustrations for a multivolume document of native people. With Eastman's encouragement, Meigs began making his own watercolors of local scenes, including the hills west of the city near Great Falls, the unfinished Washington Monument, and buildings in the city's northwest quarter. The paintings spurred him to look at the city in fresh ways. They show the work of a skilled hand and sensitive eye.

Just as he and Louisa settled in, he was ordered to report to Fort Montgomery at the north end of Lake Champlain in New York. It was there, in September 1851, Montgomery and Louisa had their fifth child, Vincent Trowbridge. Now Meigs began to worry about money. Like many fellow officers, he had never made quite enough to feel secure. Fearing he would not be able to pay his bills, he accepted support from his father, who offered him several hundred dollars a year. Meigs thought it was ironic "to be able to buy whatever is proper and desirable for the public works and to be obliged to count sixpence in the management of my family."

The work at least was interesting. It involved planning and constructing walls forty-eight feet high, emplacements to accommodate 125 cannons, and other fortifications. Meigs managed his time well enough to spend many hours tramping through the woods, hunting, and reading about science and engineering. He also made time to sketch and paint, even in the cold weather. He considered all of it as training for something important, something demanding, something big. Even his hunting excursions helped him prepare, or so he argued, because they "gave me, also, patience and perseverance, for the chase of the deer requires all this."

Meigs's chance came sooner than he expected.

CHAPTER 3

Wholesome Water

The fire started somewhere in the bones of the US Capitol, in a recess between the whitewashed walls and the old beams and bricks. Making his rounds near the Capitol's west front, watchman John Jones noticed the flames flickering in the third-floor windows. It was sometime before eight o'clock on the morning of December 24, 1851. The location of the blaze could not have been worse, the reading rooms of the Library of Congress.

Fire in the District at midcentury was almost as common as empty political promises. Just the night before, a nearby hotel had burned down. Fire in the confines of the Capitol could spell disaster. The great pile of wood, brick, and sandstone was more than the center of the government. It also anchored the young country's outsized aspirations to greatness. The building had been under construction or renovation for a half century. Though architects and builders had done their best with the budgets they had, the place had become a grand, handsome tinderbox on a hill. The library itself was especially vulnerable. Established in 1800 with a $5,000 appropriation from Congress, the library received its first shipment from a London bookseller. A room used by the House during the Sixth Congress became its home. The books were secure behind wire netting and locked doors, but nothing could protect the room from fire. In August 1814 flames consumed the library when the British invaded Washington during the War of 1812 and set the chambers in the Capitol ablaze. Thomas Jefferson reseeded the collection by selling the government his personal library—the finest in the land, with nearly 6,500 volumes in all.

Officials took new precautions, including the prohibition of candles and smoking in the reading rooms. But the threat was acute in the winter of '51, when the rooms became nearly as dry as the leaves that skittered over the Capitol grounds. Jones and another man rushed upstairs and broke open the locked doors. For a moment, they had hope. The blaze was contained to a single table and books on shelves in two alcoves, choicest parts of the collection still untouched. With no time to lose, Jones and his comrade dashed off in search of water. In their haste they left the doors open, creating a draft that doomed the library. The flames glided over everything in their path. Volunteer fire companies raced to the scene in horse-drawn engines, the Columbia, Perseverance, Anacostia, and Union. Local toughs who made up the volunteer forces slugged it out over who would have the privilege to fight the blaze, and then they struggled with frozen hoses.

Eventually they pumped water in from a nearby fountain, while a handful of desperate citizens formed a small bucket brigade. The marines rushed in to help. After a daylong battle, two-thirds of the fifty-five thousand books were reduced to gray ash. Lost too were maps, charts, thousand-year-old bronze medals, and busts of Jefferson and George Washington, along with portraits of the first five presidents. Investigators quickly determined the cause. On the floors below, the drafty committee rooms had large fireplaces, which lawmakers had kept stoked in a struggle against the subzero frost that had enveloped the District in those first days of winter. Sparks had ignited a wooden joist jutting into the flue of a poorly constructed chimney. Some residents fumed. "No public building should be erected in these enlightened days which is not made fireproof," one man wrote in his private journal.

The public's anger peaked with the news of how easily the catastrophe could have been averted. Jones told investigators that in the moment he burst into the library, "half a dozen buckets of water would have sufficed to extinguish the fire." Congressional librarian John Meehan told lawmakers they should be grateful that some of Jefferson's books survived. He appealed for action to protect those remaining. "I sincerely hope that the searching investigation Congress will give to the distressing event, which every lover of science and literature must deeply deplore, will lead to a detection of the causes that produced it, and to the adoption of means that will prevent, in all future time, a recurrence of the sad calamity."

———

Pretense and muck marked the capital city midway through the century. The population had soared to more than fifty thousand from about fourteen thousand in 1800, but the District of Columbia remained more provincial than Boston, New York, and Philadelphia. Laborers and clerks were the most common jobs. Washington also had ninety-nine lawyers, fifty engineers, eleven artists, four architects, and one matchmaker. Methodists dominated the ranks of the city's thirty-seven churches. It was politics, not religion, that made the news. Of the eighteen newspapers and magazines published in the District, most of them were political rags.

Though formed as a compromise between North and South, Washington had the look and feel and rhythms of a large Southern town, including almost four thousand slaves and ten thousand free African Americans. To some observers, the District seemed poised between greatness and dissolution. The cobblestone of Pennsylvania Avenue linked Capitol Hill to the White House. The Treasury Department and the US Post Office Building appeared majestic, with their proliferation of columns. Off to the side, the unfinished Washington Monument stood alone in a pasture. The writer Henry Adams, a District resident, remarked famously that when he first saw the government buildings as a boy, they seemed "like white Greek temples in the abandoned gravel-pits of a deserted Syrian city." After his only visit, Charles Dickens described it archly as "the City of Magnificent Intentions," complete with spacious avenues "that begin in nothing, and lead nowhere."

The city was divided by a canal that fed into the Potomac River. It was a sluggish stream that flowed only after sufficient rain. Raw sewage ran from government buildings directly into a branch of Tiber Creek and then on to the Potomac River. Pigs, cows, and chickens wandered on the dirt roads. In the springtime, the smell of stagnant canals wafted on the moist air. The inadequacy of the water supply became more pronounced every year. The system was comprised of a jumble of cisterns, wells, and springs. Though modern cast-iron pipes had been installed in places, primitive pipes made of bored logs also still carried water. (City dwellers tapped into the pipes when no one was looking, supplying their own homes first-come, first-serve style.) The main sources—Old City Spring, Caffrey's Spring, and Franklin Park Spring—fell far short of the demand. Many of the city's residents got their water from pumps on street corners that drew on insufficient supplies below. Others relied on the river, wells, and local ponds, and they often fell prey to typhoid fever and other illnesses. As in many cities at the time, death hovered over the capital like a specter. The onset of a mild illness in a spouse or child triggered a primal dread among even prominent citizens, who fled to healthier terrain each summer.

For decades, Congress had put off the task of creating a sensible water supply system, despite an obvious and growing need. The problem became so compelling that President Millard Fillmore, by temperament a waffler, told Congress that the city should be made clean and safe and "be the pride of Americans."

"And as nothing could contribute more to the health, comfort, and safety of the city and the security of the public buildings and records than an abundant supply of pure water, I respectfully recommend that you make such provisions for obtaining the same as in your wisdom you may deem proper."

Congress's vacillation flowed from an enduring dynamic: every decision was subordinate to the math of politics. Lawmakers simply couldn't divine the benefit of spending millions on work so far from their home districts. But the library fire stirred them to action. They agreed to allocate $5,000, more than ever before, to support the search for a solution. Totten, the army corps engineer, tapped a deputy, Captain Frederick Smith, to lead a study. Then Smith died unexpectedly. So Totten turned to Meigs, who was working on Delaware River improvement projects. Meigs hardly knew what to say. At last a great door was opening for him, giving him a chance to make a name for himself and work among people who mattered.

When he arrived in Washington, at six in the morning on November 3, 1852, Meigs was thirty-six. He was almost six foot two, wore thick side-whiskers, and he often seemed to be scowling. He was optimistic, though, because his simple orders gave him latitude to do great things, or so he thought. He was to conduct a survey and find "an unfailing and abundant supply of good and wholesome water" for the nation's capital and neighboring Georgetown. His days of leisure were over. The hardest three months' work of his life until then had begun.

———

Nearly every day that fall and winter, Meigs trudged to the north and west of the District with an assistant to take stock of available water. He thought that the solution might lay near a stretch of the Potomac River aptly named Great Falls, where water arriving from the west twisted over house-sized boulders. If the river here offered a seemingly unlimited supply of clean water, it also posed titanic challenges. It would take a feat of engineering to master the Potomac's hydraulic power and convey the water to Washington.

Meigs was a man of his time, the great age of engineering. To an almost devout degree, he believed in the power of clear thinking. Technical solutions would come to him, he thought, if only he applied scientific principles and demanded excellence of himself. With discipline and enough money, "any achievement of engineering was possible." He rushed at the work, establishing a pattern for the rest of his life. When he wasn't in the field, he studied, examined maps, and learned what he could about the mystifying dynamics of water. He tallied the cost of every option. No detail was too small to consider. When he came up with ideas for Washington, he compared them to water systems in London, New York, and Boston.

He also rekindled a habit he had developed in Detroit, seeking inspiration from the past. That is how he found Sextus Julius Frontinus, one of the architects of Italy's ancient water system. Frontinus's memoir, *The Aqueducts of Rome*, impressed Meigs. Here in a 1,700-year-old book was a model for the lieutenant's career. Frontinus was a brilliant soldier who committed himself to public service. He wanted little in return except the chance to build great things and a measure of recognition for doing so. His accounts offered insights that applied directly to Meigs's ambitions. The Roman described his vision for a water system that provided not "merely the convenience but also the health and even the safety of the City." He spoke about his practice of immersing himself in the technical details as both a practical matter and a point of honor. The book underscored for Meigs the imperative of will, along with a willingness to make things the right way, even if at great expense. Frontinus wrote that "for this reason, in accordance with principles which all know but few observe, honesty in all details of the work must be insisted upon." The memoir resonated with something else in Meigs. Frontinus wanted the world to remember him, going so far as to order that his name be imprinted on the lead pipe. He also shared this thought: "Remembrance will endure if the life shall have merited it."

CHAPTER 4

An Aqueduct Worthy
of the Nation

Three months after arriving, Meigs delivered his report. It must have come as a surprise to those in power. He had confronted a problem that had languished for years and proposed a solution intended to last lifetimes. Meigs spelled out his ideas in forty-eight pages with clarity and precision. He offered a sweeping view of the city's needs for generations to come, suggesting the capital required far more water than anyone realized.

Great technological, industrial, and demographic shifts were urbanizing cities on the Eastern Seaboard and in England and Europe. From 1830 to 1860, the number of towns and cities in the United States with more than 2,500 people quadrupled to 392. The population soared more than fivefold to 6.2 million. The amount of water used by modern households had soared beyond all expectations. Meigs described how poor planning by other municipalities led to shortfalls, as demand exceeded the supply. New York had created its new aqueduct only a decade before, he said, and already the system each day delivered the last drop it could carry. Meigs noted the problem was particularly acute on Saturdays, due to what New York's water commissioners called "zealous housewifery."

His plan offered a view of the problem that squared with his own devotion to improving the world. Washington had almost eight thousand dwellings, shops, and public buildings, and more under construction. Why not provide so much water that no one had to worry about waste? A near-endless supply would help the people live cleaner, healthier lives. With his system, he said, Washingtonians could open fire hydrants and "cleanse the streets and gutters, and, washing into the sewers the offal of the city, remove at once from sight and smell these offensive and fruitful sources of disease and death."

He reviewed three possible sources of water, including Rock Creek in the District, and Little Falls and Great Falls on the Potomac River. He recommended the last one, by far the most expensive option. The report not only displayed Meigs's grasp of detail but also showed his talent for persuasion. He was a natural lobbyist, and here he was selling a vision—a romantic story of America's future. He called on his readers to consider Washington as part of the great sweep of time. He argued the city needed more than health and protection from fire. To thrive and become one of the world's great capitals, it needed elegance. The system he had in mind would provide enough water to supply in perpetuity fountains that would cool the city "while, by the grace of their sparkling jets, they please the eye, and add beauty to comfort and health." From another man, at another time, it might have sounded fanciful. It resonated with those who read it.

As for the engineering, Meigs described how gravity would carry the water more than twelve miles from near Great Falls into the District. The Potomac water would course through seven-foot-wide conduits made of bricks, dropping on average about nine-and-a-half inches each mile. The minimum cost would be just over $1.9 million. For $350,000 more, Meigs said he could double the capacity by expanding the conduits to nine feet. As he waited to hear how this was received, Meigs hoped that he would be recognized for his vision. "If it is not good & does not give me a standing among engineers," he wrote to his father, "I shall be disappointed for it contains my brains."

———

On March 3, 1853, in the chaos of the last day of the session, lawmakers appropriated $100,000 for the project. After years of vacillation, they finally committed to paying attention to one of the capital's central inadequacies. In one of his first acts, the new president, Franklin Pierce, embraced the project as well. It is not as though Pierce had given the matter much thought. The force behind his decision was Jefferson Davis, the new secretary of war, one of the most formidable men in Washington. Davis had served as the junior senator from Mississippi, where he chaired the Committee on Military Affairs and was a member of the Public Buildings Committee. During army service, he won acclaim in the Mexican War, where he was wounded in his right foot during the Battle of Buena Vista.

Brilliant and tough, with a straight back and piercing blue eyes, Davis would mean more to Meigs's career than almost any other man. Given that Davis was fiercely proslavery, he might have seemed an unlikely supporter of Meigs, who, like his family, opposed slavery. But the two had more in common than was readily apparent. Davis was West Point class of 1828. He too had bucked authority there. As a politician, Davis tempered his suave rhetoric with a grasp of detail, and he had a passion for architecture and new technology. Like Meigs, he was optimistic about the future of the nation's capital and he was driven to impose his will. "Davis excelled in this kind of bureaucratic empire building, and as a major figure in the Pierce administration, he wielded immense power," Guy Gugliotta wrote in a history of the Capitol.

Davis pressed Pierce to transfer control of major public works projects from the new Department of the Interior to the War Department. Davis leveraged his new authority in a decision that baffled and infuriated his critics. On March 29 he handed over control of the water project, to be known as the Washington Aqueduct, to Meigs, still a nearly unknown junior officer who had only just been promoted to captain. What's more, Davis gave Captain Meigs responsibility for enlarging the United States Capitol, an even more prominent plum. It was a fantastic turn for an army officer with no wartime experience, whose career had seemed destined for obscurity. But it would not be the last time that a powerful man, taken by Meigs's intellect and energy, would offer him a hand up.

Meigs took it all in stride, but he was still green and could not know the forces that would stand in his way. As gatekeeper to a fortune in spending, he would be a target for years to come. Under the city's unwritten rules, Meigs would be allowed to succeed only if he directed some of the work to the right people and their friends. To prevail, he would have to master the dark arts of politics and bureaucratic wrangling—while also managing men, overseeing millions in spending, and seeking solutions to mind-boggling engineering problems.

———

Meigs's first lessons in Washington corruption came at the Capitol, a building that epitomized the striving and contradictory character of the republic it represented. From the fields down the hill, Congress's home appeared stately and steadfast. Prints at the time showed it as a romantic vision, cloaked in a gauzy bank of moist air. In reality, it was drafty, damp, and cramped. And that was only the start of the problems. Design flaws made it nearly impossible for lawmakers to understand one another during debates.

When Meigs assumed oversight of the extension project, Capitol architect Thomas Ustick Walter was embroiled in allegations of corruption. Walter was one of the country's leading architects. He had taste, talent, and a fine drafting hand. Before taking on the Capitol post, he had designed hundreds of homes, churches, and prisons. His best-known work was Founder's Hall at Girard College for Orphans in Philadelphia. After the fire in the congressional library, he designed an ingenious fireproof space made of cast iron, a building material that was transforming modern construction. His ink and watercolor drawings stood on their own as beautiful artifacts.

Despite his fine record, Walter was besieged. Certain lawmakers and whistle-blowers claimed he had overpaid for marble and, presumably, pocketed some of the money. They said he used slipshod construction methods. Meigs was asked to weigh these claims. So he dove into the details, poking at the building's foundation, reading through Walter's reports, and examining his accounting ledgers. He figured out what was going on, and it wasn't nice. Contractors, lawmakers, and bureaucrats anxious to control Walter and his budget had spread false allegations. A congressional oversight committee claimed it had evidence suggesting "great irregularities," but it was mostly innuendo, not evidence. Meigs stood by the facts he had unearthed. With a few minor exceptions, he concluded Walter's work was fine. He thought Walter had chosen the "most beautiful specimen of marble" in the United States for the building's outer layer.

The fact that he helped save Walter's job did not mean Meigs would defer to his more famous and experienced colleague. On the contrary, the captain intended to take control. Meigs was on a mission now to do great work and leave a permanent mark in history. Following another man's vision was not the way to make his own name. The two would fight over control of the work at the Capitol for years to come, spurring Walter in a fit of frustration to describe Meigs as "the most tyrannical, despotic, vain, and unscrupulous man the world ever saw."

Meigs soon imposed radical changes in Walter's plans, which called for spare, unadorned spaces. Meigs wanted a building with decoration and details that spoke to the nation's wealth, power, and technical innovation. Meigs's plans, derived in part from an earlier proposal, placed the legislative chambers in the interior of the expanded building. His changes would give lawmakers private rooms and passageways beyond the reach of the public or reporters. To link the building to the outside world, he planned to install a telegraph. His plans included monumental staircases, glazed ceiling panels, and galleries capable of seating 1,200 people. He also called for stained glass set in iron frames in the ceiling and a lobby in the House wing that featured Corinthian columns. Much of what he proposed was modelled on Renaissance painting, architecture, and ambitions. Because he had never traveled abroad, nearly all his ideas came from books.

————

Meigs soon took aim at the building's engineering problems, including the atrocious acoustics and a substandard heating system. In June 1853 he sought help from two luminaries of science he had befriended during earlier spells in the District. One was A. D. Bache, a Smithsonian regent, physicist, and scientific reformer who served as superintendent of the United States Coast Survey, the nation's oldest scientific organization. The other, Joseph Henry, was a pioneer of electricity and the first secretary of the Smithsonian, who had dedicated himself to fulfilling the dreams of James Smithson. They expressed enthusiasm about helping Meigs, and with approval and funding from Davis, the three men went on a whirlwind tour to conduct practical "experiments in sound" at buildings in Philadelphia, New York, and Boston.

The physics of sound had long confounded scientists and builders. Certain churches, theaters, and concert halls over the centuries had just the right angles and proportions to enable speakers to hear one another at great distances, often with amazing clarity. In the best spaces, such as Milan's La Scala opera house, singers and actors could easily cast their voices to the back seats. Obtaining such effects took ingenuity or plain luck. In the legislative chambers in Washington, the result was a fog of sounds. That was a significant defect in a building where talk and debate were the reasons for being. The three men visited concert halls, theaters, churches, and a prison. They spoke from different parts of every room, taking note of the duration, volume, and direction of the echoes. They made drawings showing the general form of the spaces. Meigs was enchanted by the trip. He enjoyed his colleagues and swooned over the art, design, and architecture he saw along the way. In his journal, he exclaimed: "The stairs of the Metropolitan and Saint Nicholas hotels are alone worth the visit to [New York]." When he returned to Washington, he used his insights to reason that both sound and light were essentially waves that rebounded off surfaces. If he could not see sound waves, he thought he could at least assume that they behaved in roughly the same way as light. Predictions could be made. Meigs suggested reforms that seem obvious today, including the installation of draperies on the walls and cushions on chairs to dampen echoes.

In his plans for moving the chambers to the center of the building, he also eliminated windows. Behind this unorthodox idea was a double agenda. Solid walls would eliminate exterior sounds and drafts, which he assumed blocked voices from reaching distant points in the room. Without windows, he also would have to create an unprecedented, steam-powered fan system for pumping air through the legislative chambers. This gave him another chance to leave his mark with something innovative. When news of Meigs's plans surfaced, lawmakers responded with a cacophony of complaints. Who in his right mind would create a room without windows? But Henry and Bache approved, and so did Jefferson Davis and the president. They had faith that his innovations would solve the long-standing problems.

If these were heady times for Meigs, he rarely could rest easy, and just months into his new job, he suddenly faced the prospect of failure. His masons went on strike over their working conditions, and a contractor failed to deliver on a contract for ten million bricks. He worried that even a slight delay would give envious contractors and their allies in Congress the pretext for removing him.

Bricks were vital to his projects. Cast iron and new building methods might be the hallmarks of the industrial revolution, but the homely red baked brick provided its foundation. England had used billions of bricks in the first half of the century. Almost every project Meigs supervised relied on bricks, including the Capitol's inner walls and the aqueduct's culverts and tunnels. Meigs began counting his bricks, tracking the time it took masons to lay them and calculating the per-brick cost to taxpayers. To ensure that he had enough labor, he

traveled to New York and hired bricklayers at $2 per day, while nego-
tiating an end to the strike. Meigs also went in search of other sources
of bricks, finding a million in Baltimore, a million in Philadelphia,
and three million in New York. The bricks varied in quality, size, and
shape, but they sufficed. For now, the crisis was averted.

CHAPTER 5

A Rival to the Parthenon

In just a few months, Meigs had taken on more labor than any other man in Washington. On some days he worked nearly around the clock in an unused committee room at the Capitol, a cluttered space that resembled the nest of a magpie or a mad scientist's workbench. Bricks and chunks of marble shared tabletops with architectural drawings, newspaper clips, ink bottles, art history books, and the ledgers he used to track spending, manpower, and a vast array of supplies, including seventy-five thousand cubic feet of marble that made him especially proud. "I doubt whether so large a quantity of so beautiful a material has ever before been delivered at a public building in the same space of time," Meigs wrote in a report.

Some observers admired his stamina, saying he projected an almost "Atlas-like" aura. Not only did he inspect work sites, he drafted plans, managed payrolls, and signed requisitions for even minor purchases such as candles and sponges. On top of everything else, he decided to decorate the Capitol as he expanded it. What could an army engineer know about the nuances of art and decoration? To Meigs's mind, it was a simple matter of studying. He assumed he would absorb what he needed. He committed himself to ensuring that every space in the building inspired visitors with the promise of America.

Like Capitol builders before him, Meigs drew inspiration from the Pantheon in Rome. He also keyed his ambitions to the Parthenon in Athens, an indication of his engineering and aesthetic ambitions. Built five centuries BC, the Parthenon stood as a model of balanced architecture. Its proportion spoke of the universal. It had an added

appeal of being an engineering wonder. Over the centuries, the building had withstood earthquakes, fires, and relentless assaults by rain,
wind, and ice.

He began by working on the designs of the columns destined for
the expanded Capitol, spending an entire day drawing the tops, or capitals, of the columns of the eastern portico. That summer he turned
to the design of triangular pediments above the building's eastern en-
trances. To be complete, those spaces needed sculptures, so Meigs
reached out to Edward Everett for advice. Everett was a brilliant politician, diplomat, and orator from Massachusetts. While serving as a
congressman, he helped give shape to the Capitol's design and construction. He was well known for his taste and knowledge of culture
and the arts.

Everett recommended Hiram Powers and Thomas Crawford,
whom he considered among the best of American artists. Both living in Italy, Meigs wrote to them and spelled out his hopes. He said
he wanted images that would glorify the ideas at the center of the national narrative, including progress and freedom. "In our history of the
struggle between civilized man and the savage, between the cultivated
and the wild nature are certainly to be found themes worthy of the artist and capable of appealing to the feeling of all classes," Meigs wrote.
Powers demurred, while Crawford jumped at the chance, becoming
part of Meigs's expanding cadre of collaborators.

In addition to tackling the aesthetic problems, Meigs had the added
challenge of convincing lawmakers to go along with his scheme. Most
Americans took pride in their bland tastes. To them, stark interiors
and whitewashed walls reflected what Meigs called a "republican simplicity." In contrast, Meigs wanted to emulate the complex designs, vi-
brant colors, and richness that characterized much Renaissance art. In
a letter that August, Meigs assured Crawford that he and Davis would
have control over the art commissions for the Capitol. Meigs sent along
drawings of the Capitol's south wing and the pediment planned for the
eastern portico. "I do not see why a republic richer than the Athenian
should not rival the Parthenon in the front of its first public edifice,"

Meigs wrote. On October 31, Crawford sent designs for the pediment to Meigs. Called *Progress of Civilization*, it had fourteen figures, including European pioneers and a Native American family in distress. At the center was a symbolic figure representing America. Crawford had models of the figures photographed in Rome and included the photos in his dispatch. Meigs loved what he saw. With support from the president and Davis, he signed off on the commission.

————

At the end of October 1853, Meigs decided to break ground on the aqueduct. He had gathered workers, equipment, and supplies in the hills northwest of Washington. He rode with an assistant up the C&O Canal and found a ragtag bunch of laborers waiting for his arrival. If the construction site was chaotic and dirty, it represented a shining moment in Meigs's life. Here was his chance to erase his regret at sitting out the war in Mexico. With his workers looking on, he turned the earth. "[A]nd thus quietly and unostentatiously was commenced this great work—which is destined I trust for the next thousand years to pour its healthful waters in to the capital of our union," Meigs wrote in his journal that night. "May I live to complete it & thus connect my name imperishably with a work greater in its beneficial results than all the military glory of the Mexican War."

Aware of the political support he needed, Meigs organized a more formal ceremony on November 8. President Pierce, Secretary Davis, Senator Stephen Douglas of Illinois, local politicos, and dozens of others rode with him up the Potomac in a small steamboat. Meigs provided champagne and food. He made a few remarks, and then he wisely handed a spade to Pierce, making way for the president to break ground.

Proud as he was of these public milestones, Meigs was in private consumed by grief. Two of his boys had died just weeks before. Both succumbed to an ailment that Meigs called bilious fever, a combination of high temperature, severe headaches, and vomiting. Charles, eight, passed in early September, followed by Vincent, two, a month later. Meigs and his wife, Louisa, could not know the exact cause of their illnesses, given the limits of medical science then. The boys may have died from foul water, one of the chronic problems Meigs aimed to fix. Their deaths were sadly commonplace. The chances of dying, in fact, had increased in recent decades for a growing proportion of Americans who lived in urban areas. The bigger the city, the higher the death rate. The reasons seem obvious now: crowding, open sewers, contaminated water, and, thanks in part to the spread of railroads, the rapid movement of people. American cities "had become virtual charnel houses," one historian wrote.

Meigs continued to work, even though he and Louisa could hardly bear their losses. Like other parents of their day, they clutched at pieces of the boys' clothing, toys, and other mementos. They commissioned a daguerreotype of Vintie and a medallion bearing the likeness of Charlie. They visited the boys' graves often, and they carried fear through the days like a virus, quaking even at a cough or sniffle among their surviving children. Meigs reasoned that God was teaching him and Louisa lessons about the nature of true faith. He was bowed and confused and found that it was "hard to walk uprightly in a heavenly course." About his boys, he wrote: "They loved each other in life and in their deaths they were not long divided."

Meigs had to move forward with his life, and quickly. In December 1853 several members of Congress began questioning his management, as they had done with Walter. Critics took issue with the Army Corps of Engineers' role in public works. The attacks came in the form of questions cloaked in the spirit of good government. Representative Richard Stanton of Kentucky wanted to know why a junior army captain was in charge of the Capitol extension projects. Who gave him the authority to make such sweeping changes to plans that Congress had approved two years earlier? Stanton promised to launch an inquiry about the military's control of the projects.

Meigs wasn't the real target here. Stanton and other lawmakers wanted to make life hard for Davis, who had committed the sin of outwitting them. When Davis took control of the largest public works projects in town for the War Department, they were deprived of patronage and power. Stanton had helped push forward the Capitol extension plans a few years earlier and wanted to control the project. To thwart him, Davis had arranged to have him stripped of a committee chairmanship with oversight authority—or so it seemed to Meigs.

Meigs knew that the political game in the capital was rough, and he realized that the wrangling might put his career at risk. After the holiday lull, the attacks came quickly. On January 3, 1854, an ally of Stanton from Tennessee submitted a "resolution for consideration" launching an inquiry into changes to the Capitol extension plans, the authority behind them, and the costs. Filled with anxiety, Meigs decided to visit Senator Sam Houston, the firebrand Texan who had served as first president of the Republic of Texas. Houston had influence and Meigs wanted to be sure of his support during the upcoming battles. Houston stayed in an upper room at the Willard Hotel, a preserve of the rich and powerful just off Pennsylvania Avenue. When Meigs arrived, the living legend lay on the floor, a red blanket under him, his head on a pillow made of newspapers. Houston was unwell, but he remained feisty, pouring out invective, blasphemies, and gobs of tobacco spit. Meigs was relieved to hear that Houston did not harbor any personal grievance against him or his work. He came away feeling mildly reassured about his chances to survive the political fight with Stanton and his allies.

CHAPTER 6

America's Curse

Up on Capitol Hill, lawmakers were contemplating matters that would have far greater import than the building projects. As Meigs reached out to Houston, Senator Stephen Douglas of Illinois was urging Congress to endorse the construction of a rail line to the Pacific Ocean. Douglas was a little man with a big head and grand ambitions for himself and the country. He argued that it was in the government's interest to establish pathways to the West, where droves of gold miners and pioneers were seeking riches and new lives.

On the surface, Douglas's idea seemed just the thing for a young, sprawling country. He had watched the effects of a transportation revolution in Chicago, which now served as the locus for more than two thousand miles of new rail lines. He wanted to use iron rails to stitch together the continent. For his proposal to succeed, the government would need to provide land subsidies to the railroads. Douglas reasoned that the best route for the railroad would be windswept plains of the vast region known as Nebraska. Obviously, the government had to survey the land before it could be handed over to railroads. But before any official survey could be conducted, the land had to be organized as a territory. This posed a great problem. Powerful Southerners would not support new territories unless slavery was permitted.

Slavery was America's curse. Congress had twice limited its spread into the territories. The Compromise of 1820, also known as the Missouri Compromise, prohibited slavery west of the Mississippi and north of latitude 36 degrees, 30 minutes—land that had been acquired

through the great Louisiana Purchase of 1803. That angered Southerners. The Compromise of 1850 tried to maintain the balance of slave
states and Free States during the nation's westward expansions. It also
gave slave owners certain prerogatives. The Fugitive Slave Act, part of
the Compromise of 1850, allowed white Southerners to abduct run-
away slaves and take them back to the South. This complex deal infuriated abolitionists. Ironically, it depended on federal authority at a
time when the call for "states' rights" was a refrain across the South. In
its wake, the writer Harriet Beecher Stowe wrote *Uncle Tom's Cabin*,
an instant bestseller about the horrors of slavery. The book infuriated
readers in the North—as well as those in the South who objected to its
slant.

Douglas's legislation sought to create two territories, Nebraska and
Kansas, with a combined area that now encompasses Colorado, North
and South Dakota, Kansas, Montana, Nebraska, and Wyoming. Under
his proposal, the new territories would be situated west of Missouri,
a slave holding state. During the debate, Douglas, following the lead
of Southern senators, took the momentous step of including language
that would repeal the old geographic limits on slavery. Over the furious
opposition of abolitionist members of Congress, the Kansas-Nebraska
Act passed Congress in May 1854. Representative Abraham Lincoln
said, "Little by little, but steadily as a man's march to the grave, we
have been giving up the old for a new faith. Nearly eighty years ago, we
began by declaring that all men are created equal; but now from that
beginning we have run down to the other declaration, that for some
men to enslave others is a 'sacred right of self-government.' These principles cannot stand together."

Meigs had little faith in Douglas, whom he once described as having
a "perverted moral sense or none at all." But his reaction to Douglas's
proposal revealed the limits of his opposition to slavery. He privately
considered the legislation a "great wrong in the course of freedom," because it could allow slavery to flourish in new territories. At the same
time, he was cautious in expressing his views. Meigs wrote little about
it in his journals, and he was not inclined now to take a public stand.

Meigs clearly did not want to alienate Davis, the man who held sway
over his future.

––––

Now Meigs became even more focused on his own legacy. He was
"perfectly occupied with the desire to build the dome of the Capitol
and to make it more beautiful and graceful than any other." He often
paged through *Recueil et Parallele des Edifices de Tout Genre, Anciens
et Moderne*—a decades-old book that contained hundreds of drawings,
plans, and elevations of notable buildings in world history. Meigs loved
the prints of Raphael's decorations, details of Roman vases, drawings
of columns. Most of all, he treasured images of domes: the Pantheon in
Paris, St. Paul's Cathedral in London, and St. Peter's Basilica in Rome.
He saw them as a personal challenge.

The Capitol dome posed another problem that Congress had put
off for years. Made of wood and sheathed in copper, it rose 140 feet
above the ground. It formed an interior rotunda 96 feet high, giving it
more balanced proportions inside. The foremost issue was fire. The
blaze that consumed the old Library of Congress had come close to ig-
niting the dome. With the building expanding at a rapid clip, the dome
also represented an aesthetic problem. It was far too small to balance
with the larger building. Even philistines who cared nothing about design or architecture could see that it would look comically small on the
new structure, a little like a beanie on the head of a giant.

Meigs's obsession was fueled by an architectural rendering by Walter. Seven feet long, the drawing of an imagined Capitol included people, horses, and carriages moving about on the east plaza. Crowning the
building was a towering new dome topped off with a statue. Viewers
flocked to Walter's office for a look. When Meigs saw the drawing, he
realized the new dome would be one of the most recognizable pieces of
architecture in the country. He had to get credit for building it. He examined every detail of Walter's drawings. While he admired its grace,
he found shortcomings. Among them were columns at the base of the
dome. They looked appealing on paper, but in Walter's plan, they were

purely decorative. Meigs believed that every part of a building ought to serve a structural purpose. Working in private, Meigs allowed his ambition to take flight. He studied the engineering. He imagined the aesthetics. Then he drafted his own plans. Looking down on his work, his self-regard blossomed like a hothouse flower. "I have in the *Parallele des Edifices* most of the domes in the world of any celebrity," he wrote, "and I think mine is better than anyone of them."

———

The pace of work caught up to Meigs, who was beginning to look less like a soldier than an irritable, burly accountant whose battles were mostly with his ledgers and meddlesome politicians. At thirty-nine, he weighed about two hundred pounds. One day in October 1854, he decided to go hunting with John, his oldest boy, and exercise. For hours, they trooped through the ravines near Little Falls, and scanned the colorful trees and undergrowth for targets. Squirrels, bullfrogs, blackbirds, or rabbits—it didn't matter. Meigs loved shooting. After huffing along all day, he was so stiff that he could barely walk up the stairway at home. In his journal he vowed to exercise more often.

"For I am thus losing the strength which enabled me to go through with the fatigue of my survey when I came here, fresh and vigorous," he wrote. "It is not making the best out of my time or doing my duty to myself or to the country to give up the cultivation of health of body while using my brains for the service."

He continued handling the growing demands like a circus juggler who keeps mismatched objects aloft. No task was too small for his attention now. He managed even after Davis added still more to his portfolio by placing him in charge of the construction of Fort Madison, a battery in Annapolis, Maryland. His accounting at this time shows the remarkable scope of his work. In just one month, workers had put into place more than 200 blocks of marble. They had received delivery of 576,906 bricks and laid 543,774. He calculated the average time it took for contractors to make window jambs for the new wings: seventy days, at $2.50 per day for cutting and carving the marble. That didn't include the fine work, such as the carving of decorative foliage.

Meigs was becoming a better manager. Once while doing his tabulations, he realized that a contractor had unwittingly far underbid on its work. The mistake put the firm at risk financially. Meigs, rigid in his demand for honesty from contractors, nevertheless showed a pragmatic flexibility that was becoming a hallmark of his management style. Instead of enforcing the contract dogmatically, as he would if he thought contractors were trying to cheat, Meigs altered its terms to make it fair. He wanted to pay able contractors a fair price for good work. This fastidiousness went beyond the ledgers. He examined the friezes he had commissioned for the building's windows and demonstrated how craftsmen could use a "bolder style of modeling" for the decorative details in the gallery of the House of Representatives. Once, he whipped out his own pocketknife and carved minute changes to an artist's work.

There was not enough time in a normal workday for all of this. Meigs regularly stayed at his Capitol office until ten o'clock at night, trying to plow through paperwork, and fatigue sometimes overwhelmed him. One evening at home, he fell asleep in a chair while looking at a sketch of the Louvre in the *Illustrated London News*. Domestic troubles added to his load. That summer, he and Louisa had a baby girl. While trying to stay on top of her household, Louisa discovered that one of the family's servants had been stealing. She was vexed by the problem and distressed by Montgomery's chronic absence. One evening, she gathered the kids, trooped to the Capitol, and surprised him at his office. He had the sense to know when it was time to bow with good cheer to a greater force: the love he had for his family. After they "burst in upon me and took possession of me, I showed them the curiosities of the office and then came home with them."

———

Meigs often sought ways to become more efficient. This was not because he subscribed to Benjamin Franklin's famous adage "Time is money."

For Meigs, a more important idea was at stake. More time meant more work. It was the work that held out the chance of making something memorable. One of his guiding lights was the British educator Sir Isaac Pitman, an unorthodox Christian who believed in helping people improve their lives through efficiencies. "[T]ime is life," Pitman once said. Meigs reckoned he could squeeze extra minutes free from his days by learning to write more quickly. As it happened, Pitman had developed a kind of script aimed at enabling people to do just that. It's what we now know as shorthand.

Meigs started reading *Phonographic* magazine, which provided instruction for enthusiasts, and he studied a manual for specialists, pasting an index of shorthand symbols in his journal. Near the end of the year, he bought a gold pen designed specifically for shorthand writing. An inveterate tinkerer, he was thrilled when it arrived. "This is written with it, and I am much pleased," he wrote in his journal that night. He practiced shorthand whenever he had a spare moment and tried to sell others on the method, including his son John. Meigs was "seduced by the beauty of the forms and the ease with which the thoughts are put upon paper." He could be evangelical about it, and when one of his clerks rebuffed a suggestion to learn shorthand, Meigs refused to give him a raise.

Meigs's enthusiasm was a mixed blessing. His normal script was generally illegible, sometimes undecipherable. His shorthand script would prove to be nearly impossible to read, at least for all but a few specialists. He used the pen on Christmas morning and then again on the last day of December 1854, when he posed a question to himself: What have I done and learned this year? His answers say much about who he was becoming. Meigs believed he had worked hard and honestly and had much to show for it. Though the aqueduct work had slowed because funding from Congress ran low, the Capitol had progressed rapidly. The interior walls now rose to the level of the roof, which was being built of iron in a shop that Meigs had also designed.

He thought of all the men he had employed—more than five hundred directly under him—along with the blessings their jobs had brought to their families. He took pride in the legions of other men who benefited from the public works projects, men who worked "at the quarries; at the brickyards; at the forests from which the lumber, the firewood for the brick, comes; in the boats bringing sand; in the vessels bringing marble and other materials, in the factories, [with] the lime and cement; in the machine shops, making machines and cast iron in the foundry and rolling mills making the iron, a vast number of others who have in part, at least, derived their living from this work, and thus have, through my hands, obtained some good."

CHAPTER 7

The Saturday Club

One of Meigs's favorite activities involved a group called the Saturday Club. It was an informal collection of science-minded men who gathered each week to share ideas and make sense of a torrent of scientific and technological advancements in Europe and the United States. Its organizer was George Schaeffer, chemist and examiner at the Patent Office who specialized in the use of microscopes. Schaeffer had worked with Meigs at the aqueduct, helping assess the quality of water, and invited him to attend a meeting in January 1855.

They had much to consider. In the United States, the number of patents had soared from fewer than 500 a year on average in the 1840s to 1,892 in 1855. So many new tools and devices were being created that the Patent Office in Washington became a destination for tourists. At the same time, new building methods were transforming Europe and the United States. The British engineer Isambard Kingdom Brunel, for instance, revolutionized travel with iron railways, suspension bridges, and tunnels, all built with innovative methods and designs. The Crystal Palace, which housed the Great Exhibition in London several years before, had demonstrated a new way of using mass-produced cast-iron building components. The builder James Bogardus had recently made the first all-iron building facades in the United States. Along with new technology came revolutionary ideas. Charles Darwin proposed that all life on earth had common ancestors. James Maxwell, the Scottish theoretical physicist, delved into the notion that electricity, magnetism, and light shared common properties. Physician John Snow, a pioneer of modern epidemiology, had recently traced the origins of a cholera outbreak in London to a single public water pump. His innovations would help transform public health.

The Saturday Club in Washington had no rules, formal leaders, or organizational chart. The only requirement for entrance was technological or scientific achievement. Even that requirement was interpreted broadly. Members included engineers, explorers, naturalists, and painters. Most pursued their passions as amateurs while working in other careers. Joseph Henry, one of the group's unofficial leaders, was an exception. A professor at Princeton, he had conducted scientific research into electricity, magnetism, and solar spots. For nearly a decade, he had served as secretary of the Smithsonian Institution. A. D. Bache, the friend and collaborator of Henry and Meigs, was another science luminary. In the 1830s he had investigated the causes of steam-boiler explosions, a deadly problem that came with the advent of steam power. The federally funded investigation was the first time the government turned to scientists to inform public policy. Bache served on the board that selected Henry to lead the Smithsonian. He was also the head of the Coast Survey—the oldest scientific organization in the government—and president of the American Association for the Advancement of Science.

Another member was Titian Peale, son of the artist Charles Willson Peale. He was an artist and illustrator as well as a naturalist, collector, and explorer. A decade earlier, Peale had taken part in the US Exploring Expedition, a four-year scientific journey that named the continent of Antarctica. He now worked at the Patent Office. A passionate lepidopterist, he would create one of the great collections of butterflies in North America.

Each man presented his discoveries, experiments, and oddments in show-and-tell style, often with great enthusiasm. These included a gyroscope, a homemade air gun, microscopes, fossils, chromolithographs, an electromagnet, and the plaster cast of a rabbit's head. Meigs was happy the group had a great appetite for conversation, cold beef, and white wine. As one friend put it later, "The discussions were always able, and when, as was often the case, the views of the members were not in accord, they were warm and keen. No one spoke who had not some thing to say, and he fared badly who advanced theories he was unable to maintain."

In Meigs's first meeting, the group took time to assess a new kind of photograph made on glass plates through a process known as collodion. Some of the images, produced by John A. Whipple, depicted the Cambridge Club in Boston. Meigs displayed photo plates made by Thomas Crawford, showing sculptures destined for the Capitol pediments. As Meigs recalled it, everyone declared Crawford's to be "more skillful as photographs than Whipple's and were generally admired as works of art." Meigs liked the "pleasant intercourse with intelligent and scientific men" and assumed he would be able to turn to them for advice. In the coming years, the meetings would add pieces to the clockwork of his training, helping him to become one of the great innovators and managers of his day. The club would also help secure Meigs a place in the history of American science. Along with at least five other Saturday Club members, Meigs would years later become a part of a new organization called the National Academy of Sciences.

———

The range of Meigs's activities stands in contrast to our specialized world. One day, while managing hundreds of workers and millions in spending, while solving engineering problems and fending off political threats, Meigs took time to watch a painter spread plaster on the wall above his office door, mix colors into pots of lime, and then apply the mixture onto the wall. It was February 1855, and Meigs was witnessing the first fresco painting in the United States, a work that he had commissioned. Over the next several weeks, he would return to the room often to observe. The artist was Constantino Brumidi. Born in Rome in 1805, Brumidi had been trained at the prestigious Accademia di San Luca. When he was thirty-five, he joined a group of artists restoring frescos in the Vatican. He earned a certain fame, with one reviewer in Rome declaring that Brumidi's pictorial effects were second "only to the great masters of the High Renaissance."

While it is open to debate whether Brumidi's talent merited such hyperbole, there's no question that he was a skilled and insightful painter. Meigs liked him from the start. He recalled when he first met "the lively old man with a very red nose, either from Mexican suns or French brandies." When Brumidi offered to show what he could do, Meigs had pointed out the area above the room's doorway, a semicircular space known as a lunette. He told Brumidi to use the space to demonstrate his skills, and selected as a theme the famous account of Lucius Quinctius Cincinnatus being called from his plow to serve as dictator of ancient Rome. After painting an oil study, Brumidi began working in the unheated room. News of the fresco spread quickly. Before long, Meigs escorted President Pierce, Senator Douglas, Jeff Davis, and the art connoisseur William Corcoran through viewings. Brumidi became a sensation on Capitol Hill. With Meigs's support and direction, he devoted the rest of his life to decorating "the new cathedral of human freedom." Brumidi would document and celebrate several of the most important innovations and inventions of the day: Cyrus McCormick's mechanical reaper, steam engines, an ironclad ship, electrical generators, and the telegraph.

Those successes bolstered Meigs's desire to make the Capitol a palace of art. Meigs went on to commission oil paintings, elaborate ironwork, and columns adorned with carvings of native plants and vegetables. He secured permission from the Capitol gardener to gather sticks, leaves, and flowers as models for metal ornaments to decorate doors of the House chamber. In fulfilling the captain's artistic vision, a foundry at the Capitol also produced decorative cherubs, grapevines, lizards, beetles, and flies. When he learned that two Ojibwa leaders were in town to settle a treaty with the federal government, he called on a decorative stonecutter to make likenesses of them. The busts remain among the finest nineteenth-century depictions of Native Americans. Meigs eventually "dispensed federal funds in patronage of the fine arts on a scale rarely rivaled before the Twentieth Century," one historian wrote.

———

For all the pleasure he took from engineering and art, political strife on Capitol Hill now became Meigs's greatest preoccupation. Work on the aqueduct languished for lack of funding, and opponents on Capitol Hill held up proposals for new infusions of cash. Representative Stanton, Meigs's nemesis, began investigating the military's central role in public works projects. But in early 1855 Davis and Meigs pushed back. They pressed their allies for help, including a freshman congressman named Edward Dickinson. Meigs told Dickinson that Stanton's "inquiry was to me a great trouble, taking me from my duties and occupying my mind and attention, which had enough without any such distractions to keep them fully employed." He urged Dickinson to make clear to Congress that it would find nothing untoward. Dickinson, a lawyer from Massachusetts, had only a few weeks left in his term. His daughter Emily was something of a recluse whose short, idiosyncratic poems would later earn her renown as one of the literary geniuses of the nineteenth century. At her father's suggestion, she, her mother, and her sister had come to Washington. During their visit, on February 20, Representative Dickinson went on the counteroffensive when speaking on the House floor. He asked Stanton a series of tart questions about the investigation. Stanton declined to play along, saying it would take "more time to explain my opinions on that subject than it would be proper to take now."

Dickinson would not be put off. He said the investigation had found that the work on the Capitol and aqueduct "was progressing in the most skillful, the most scientific, and the best possible manner." He went further, edging up to insult, saying that most members involved in the investigation considered the allegations a "farce." As for Stanton, Dickinson said the "subject had become a perfect monomania with him." The attack was well timed. On March 3, 1855, the funding questions came to a head as the House voted on appropriations in the Civil and Diplomatic Bill. The aqueduct was only one part of the bill. For many, including those interested in Washington, DC, and politicos fascinated by the power struggle involving Meigs, the project provided the sort of political drama that many Washingtonians craved. The budget proposal had strong Senate support, but no one knew which way the House vote would go. The city bubbled with anticipation, and the House galleries, packed with onlookers, hummed. As the day wore on, lawmakers raised and tabled opportunities to vote on the aqueduct. Meigs remained on hand even as representatives left for dinner. No one knew what would happen because support seemed to be breaking down along unpredictable lines.

Representative William M. Tweed changed his mind to vote in favor of the aqueduct to spite an enemy who had declared his opposition to the project. (Tweed was tough and later came to be known as "Boss" Tweed while running New York's Tammany Hall political machine.) Laurence Keitt of South Carolina went home and to bed after concluding the vote would not take place. Someone in Meigs's camp went to rouse him in time to cast a vote in favor of the funding. Stanton, meanwhile, decided to back away from voting at all. He had abandoned his campaign under the pressure from Davis and fellow lawmakers. He slipped off the floor of the House and hid out in the House clerk's office. Stanton did not want to vote because he worried his constituents would not like it if he supported the aqueduct after having taken such a strident stand against the project.

A little after three in the morning, a vote was finally called and the project approved, 82 to 77. Congress appropriated $250,000. The crowd still in the House chamber cheered. Meigs went home, sat down at his desk, and recorded his thoughts. "God grant to me a grateful heart for the high privilege bestowed upon me in being a humble instrument in his hand for the outpouring of this great blessing. One that does not stop in the brief space of one mortal life but flowing on down the long stream of time for a thousand years . . . Making more healthful the dwelling of the poor, more grateful the heart of the humble as of the high."

CHAPTER 8

The Workload Grows

In the days after the vote, people approached Meigs on the street to offer congratulations, as though he personally had won a great political battle. Meigs thought that some of them were mostly happy that the value of their land would now soar as a result of all but certain access to water. New waves of work also came at Meigs, including an assignment to expand the Post Office Building. Engineers, managers, clerks, and draftsmen filed through his office looking for work. Among them was the son of Major G. W. Whistler, an army colleague of Meigs's. Whistler's son James was an unorthodox young man who had recently been kicked out of West Point. At the academy, he had been something of a fop. He was nicknamed "Curly" because he wore his hair longer than was allowed. He didn't impress Meigs, who had no interest in hiring the young man. "He is evidently smart and quick but self-conceited and vain," Meigs recalled. "I heartily tired of him, feeling no great disposition to bring him within my reach." It's probably just as well. James Whistler later moved to Paris, where he would paint, among many important works, his *Arrangement in Gray and Black No. 1*. It is better known now as *Whistler's Mother*.

Meigs had another interesting visitor, Representative Stanton, the enemy himself. Stanton came with Walter and Douglas to talk about architecture. Awkwardness thwarted matters until Meigs nodded at Walter to indicate that an introduction was warranted. Meigs and Stanton shook hands. Walter took Stanton to see Brumidi's fresco, and Stanton announced he was delighted by it. He made it clear he was happy now to support Meigs in his endeavors, or at least stay out of the way.

About this time, Meigs began pursuing dreams of creating a new kind of bridge to carry the water over Rock Creek in the capital. His plan would make double use of the cast-iron water pipes by employing them as the bridge's structural support.

Meigs was nearly always working, but he wasn't always grim. Occasionally, he indulged in a sort of off-kilter humor involving snakes. Meigs loved snakes. During hikes or while touring work sites, he chased them down and then showed them to colleagues or his children. In the spring of 1855, during a trip to Fort Madison, he caught two black snakes and took them back to his office. About five feet long, they slithered around or rested on shelves while Brumidi painted and visitors came and went.

Meigs pondered their movements, as though they were sculptures come to life. He noticed that one of them was rather benign, while the other tended to be cranky and excitable. He left it to his visitors to discern the difference, chuckling when the cranky one startled them by lashing out. He asked his favorite caster to make bronze likenesses of the snakes. The unusual bronzes were used as handles on doors leading into the expanded House chamber and can still be seen by visitors. Meigs also admired a plaster cast of a snake coiled on a table, made by one of the Capitol artists. Moved by the delicacy of the rendering, Meigs called it "this transcript from nature."

———

Throughout that year, Meigs focused much of his time on the Capitol dome, a project that he realized required a mix of hard work, ingenuity, and inspired logistics. First, an army of workers had to tear down the old dome, the wooden structure covered by copper. Then they had to install the many iron parts of a far larger dome that was proportioned properly for the expanded building. During the work, Congress had to be able to conduct its business below.

The iron dome, first suggested by Walter, offered remarkable advantages over stone, the material traditionally used in the world's great domes. Iron was far stronger and lighter than masonry. It would not crack if the building's foundation shifted, as happened to other domes. Cast-iron columns and other components would be far easier to produce than those carved from marble, saving months of labor and untold dollars on supplies. Once a single pattern was made, it would take only days to produce the lot. The "Great Dome," as Meigs referred to it, would be a semi-elliptical form that rose 228 feet, essentially like that Walter had envisioned. Topping it off would be Crawford's *Freedom* (also called *Freedom Triumphant in War and Peace* and, earlier, *Armed Liberty*), the 16-foot-6-inch-high statue of a classical female.

Meigs realized that something else was needed, a new kind of derrick to lift all the components into place. Derricks were nothing new. Construction projects, quarries, and railroads relied on them every day. At the Post Office, he connected four of them in a row, like masts on a ship, distributing the weight and concentrating forces so that workers could easily lift stones weighing up to seven tons and gently put them into place. But the construction demands posed by the dome were unprecedented. Almost nine million pounds of iron components had to be lifted one by one and bolted into place by men who had never worked at such heights. There was little room for error. Meigs devised a simple, ingenious wooden tower, 100 feet tall. On that would sit a derrick with a timber mast and a long boom. The entire machine would rest on an 18-foot base that distributed weight across the floor of the rotunda. When rotated, the boom above would sweep over the outer edge of the dome's base.

Two giant timbers for its superstructure arrived in late spring, giving the project momentum. Now one crucial challenge remained. How would the tower stay upright during the strain of lifting? For the answer, Meigs turned to the techniques of ship rigging. Stays like those used on the mast of a schooner would hold the derrick in place. But under the pressures exerted here, hemp ropes like those used on ships would shred. Meigs turned to John Augustus Roebling, a brilliant, innovative engineer from Prussia, who'd immigrated to western Pennsylvania two decades earlier. While working as an engineer for the Allegheny Canal system, Roebling imagined a new kind of wire rope that could withstand the strain of pulling canal boats through the mountains. Roebling moved to Trenton, New Jersey, and worked on a variation of the cable, made with strands of twisted iron wire, using a method adopted from the mines of his native Prussia. In the summer of 1855, he used the cable for a spectacular suspension bridge across the Niagara River gorge in western New York. The 825-foot span hung on four 10-inch cables.

Roebling traveled to Washington to meet with Meigs. The two struck a deal that would solve a crucial engineering problem, while also saving taxpayers money. With this tower and derrick, Meigs could eliminate the need for massive, expensive scaffolding. As for Roebling, his invention would later become a component of some of the technological and engineering triumphs in the coming century: deep mines, elevators, and suspension bridges, including the Brooklyn Bridge. The cable arrived in the fall, and Capitol workers attached it to the towering derrick. Meigs ordered a steam engine placed on the roof and the wood from the old dome used as its fuel. He described these developments in a long note to Davis on November 26. He laid out the design, engineering, and construction efforts, while deftly outlining his own claim as creator of the dome. He wrote that Walter's inspiring drawing was a mere sketch that conveyed the "general effects of the whole building as completed." He said his rival's drawing did not include any engineering detail and fell short from an aesthetic point of view.

Meigs described how the final dome would include a nine-foot vertical wall inside, a space he said would be used to create an enormous frieze to illustrate the nation's progression from "the depths of barbarism to the height of civilization." He underscored his belief that the dome would eventually serve as the symbolic center of the nation. On December 7 he climbed up ladders to watch as workmen removed the last piece of the old dome. A temporary roof and windows were installed, allowing in brilliant light that brought the old paintings below to life. Three days later, a workman tested the finished derrick against a stone weighing eleven thousand pounds. It worked well. A delighted Meigs called it "a beautiful machine."

CHAPTER 9

Rowdy Looking

By early 1856, Meigs was becoming frustrated. He focused endlessly on his projects, among the most ambitious in the country, aiming for work that would last. He used steam engines and modern construction methods to minimize the costs. But while admirers marveled, a handful of journalists and politicians criticized the expense and his management. Stories in the *New-York Daily Tribune* galled him because they appeared to have been planted by lawmakers who disliked Davis and the War Department's involvement. Meigs sought a meeting with the powerful *Tribune* editor Horace Greeley, one of the principal critics.

Greeley's influence went deep. As a backroom politico, he had helped William Seward win election as New York's governor and as US senator. As a reformer, he urged young ambitious men in the East to "Go West!" in search of their fortunes. Greeley was pale, with light hair, and he often wore scruffy coats. He struck friends and strangers alike as both intense and distracted. To some, he seemed to be a scatterbrained crank. ("Had God granted him a little practical sense, he would have been a great man," a fellow New Yorker once wrote.) In a few years, he would become one of the nation's fiercest abolitionists—and a thorn in the side of Abraham Lincoln.

Now, on April 4, 1856, Greeley grilled the engineer about the particulars of the public works project. Had Meigs made the original estimates for the Capitol extension's cost? How much over the estimates had the project run? What about the wages Meigs was paying—were they inflated? In each case, Meigs's answer surprised Greeley, or so

Meigs believed. Meigs was not impressed by Greeley, describing him as an odd duck who did not "look like a man of character or of strong personality and honesty of purpose."

A week later, Meigs turned his lobbying effort on Congress. Funding for the aqueduct appeared to be threatened again. To head off another budget crisis, he decided to show key lawmakers that the Treasury's money was being well spent. Meigs spent a lot of time on Capitol Hill and worked hard to maintain political support. He and his team arranged for a workboat called the *M.C. Meigs* to carry selected politicians up the Potomac. They put together a cold picnic lunch, including wine and liquor. About two dozen passengers showed up on April 12, 1856, a warm and windy Saturday. They were a surprisingly ecumenical bunch, given the mounting disputes over slavery, states' rights, and other matters. Representative John Wood, a Republican newspaper owner from Maine, was there. So were representatives Preston Brooks and Laurence Keitt, both of them Democrats and proslavery advocates from South Carolina.

The Potomac is beautiful in the springtime, with blossoms and tender leaves foreshadowing lush green. Only the "quiet, temperate men from the North" took note of the scene. The Southerners, those "rollicking, roistering sons of the South," as Meigs called them, focused on the stores of whiskey, brandy, champagne, and sherry. He didn't really care what they did, so long as the trip produced the political support he needed. Meigs and his team showed the men aqueduct brickwork, culverts, and tunnels. They explained how the water from the Potomac would flow downhill to the District, and all the benefits that would bring.

———

The threat of violence wafted through Washington these days. The country was losing patience with itself, as regional stereotypes and biases calcified into stony feelings. One Northern cliché held that Southerners would hang on to an agrarian way of life even if it doomed their economy. They would do almost anything to defend their system of slavery because they treasured their leisurely way of life. Southerners believed that Northerners welcomed the coldly efficient blessing of the industrial revolution, even if it meant losing their souls.

The tensions were reflected in the reaction to a new book by a progressive Northern writer named Frederick Law Olmsted, a social critic and journalist who later earned renown as a landscape architect. The book, *A Journey in the Seaboard Slave States,* provided a first-hand account of plantations and Southern society. Northern readers found it appalling and barbaric. Southerners denounced it as antislavery propaganda. About the same time, the country was troubled by news from the West, where the territories struggled toward statehood. Ever since the Kansas-Nebraska Act opened the possibility of slavery's expansion, trouble in the western territory seemed to presage a dark future for the country. The tensions reached a breaking point when a zealous outsider named John Brown began operating as kind of latter-day prophet, organizing Free State residents in Kansas for violent resistance. He said the North must "strike terror in the hearts of the proslavery people." As if to demonstrate his resolve, Brown, four sons, and three other men massacred five proslavery settlers, killing them with broadsword blows to the head. A large proslavery gang, meanwhile, broke into a federal arsenal in Liberty, Missouri, taking guns, swords, and cannons. The proslavery group was convinced that the Free State forces had created a secret army to attack Southerners. The antislavery town of Lawrence, Kansas, was besieged by eight hundred proslavery men. Leaders barely averted a crisis, but the relief was temporary.

In Washington, congressmen and others talked openly about the possibility of a fight between North and South. Militaristic rhetoric grew more extreme by the week. On May 8 the District was jolted when a Southern-born representative shot dead an Irish waiter at the Willard Hotel, an anchor of political and social life in the city. The shooting had no direct connection to slavery, but Northerners saw it as a symbol of Southern aggression and intolerance. Meigs was appalled, writing,

"This is one example of the evil of carrying weapons." Then violence seeped into the Capitol itself. This time the instigator was Representative Preston Brooks of South Carolina. He was angry at Massachusetts congressman Charles Sumner for a speech that Sumner called "The Crime Against Kansas." Sumner blasted the South and its ways, taking pains to deride Senator Andrew P. Butler of South Carolina, a relative of Brooks's, for supporting popular sovereignty about slavery in the western states. Sumner likened Butler and Senator Douglas, coauthors of the Kansas-Nebraska Act, to Don Quixote and his squire, Sancho Panza. For good measure, he claimed Butler had fallen in love with "the harlot, Slavery."

Sumner was a handsome man and something of a hero in New England, where he seemed to embody that region's flinty values. Yet he was not well liked in the Senate. His fiery abolitionist rhetoric alienated many of his colleagues. Most Southerners would not speak to him. On May 22 Brooks walked up to Sumner at his Senate desk, where he was preparing mail. "Mr. Sumner, I have read your speech carefully, and with as much calmness as I could be expected to read such a speech," he said. "You have libeled my state, and slandered my relation, who is aged and absent, and I feel it to be my duty to punish you for it."

Brooks began pounding Sumner with a gold-headed cane made of gutta-percha, a hard, rubbery substance. Brooks chose the cane because he thought it would deliver maximum pain without actually killing. The first blow stunned and blinded Sumner. Others came quickly. Sumner was helpless, trapped by his own small desk until he tore it up from the floor. Standing nearby was Representative Keitt, one of the "roistering sons of the South" who had enjoyed Meigs's whiskey on the excursion up the Potomac. A flamboyant proslavery radical, he called himself a "visionary and a theorist." He would come to be known as the "Swashbuckling Secessionist." When others in the Senate moved to help Sumner, Keitt held them off.

The attack stunned the nation. Northerners saw it as an effort to silence "an eloquent and erudite" spokesman for freedom. In the South, editorialists applauded the episode, with some deriding Sumner as "an inanimate lump of incarnate cowardice." Brooks was lauded as a hero and given canes to replace the one he had broken during the attack. Radicals in the South would do almost anything now to protect slavery, the institution that anchored their society. "If the northern men had stood up, the city would now float with blood," Keitt wrote to the woman he was courting. "Everybody here feels as if we are upon a volcano."

————

On the same day, May 22, illness took hold of Meigs and forced him into bed with fever and vomiting. Over the next six weeks, he lost thirty pounds. It was a hard blow for the bluff, kinetic man who was so often seen prowling around blocks of marble and statuary that he came to be known to some as "Meigs among the ruins of Carthage." He seemed so close to death that his parents rushed to Washington for a last visit.

But he recovered—and then he had to answer aggressive questions from lawmakers who could not believe he was properly managing so much work and money. A report he submitted to Congress carried a power that belied his illness. He documented with math and fine print the complexity of the three-year-old operations under his control. For starters, Meigs showed he had maintained the financial integrity of every job. He took on no debt because everything had been bought with cash, almost as soon as the bills came due. He catalogued the supplies involved, including hundreds of tons of cast iron for pipes, window sashes, and ceilings in the House and Senate; heaps of marble, shipped in from quarries in Vermont, Massachusetts, and Tennessee; scores of columns; and about eighteen million bricks. He named each vendor, the day of each purchase, and the cost of delivery, down to the penny.

The report also contained an analysis of the costs of hiring and feeding horses and oxen. It enumerated the wagons and other vehicles used in the course of his work, as well as all the workspaces, including smith shops, machine shops, sculptor sheds, sawmills, bronze shops, and marble shops. His list goes on and on, illustrating his growing prowess at organization. How much was Meigs getting paid to manage these operations? He mentioned that too: $1,800 a year, the standard salary of an officer of his rank.

Somehow Meigs remained focused on all these details while the presidential election of 1856 stirred passions in the city and raised profound questions about the country's future. Many across the political spectrum considered disunion a possibility. The election itself was a mess, in part because the character of the political parties had evolved rapidly in recent years. Democrats selected James Buchanan of Pennsylvania, a bland sixty-five-year-old bachelor. He had served so long and often as a lawmaker and diplomat that he was nicknamed Old Public Functionary. The fledgling Republican Party went with John Frémont, the politically connected but inexperienced "Pathfinder," who had earned renown for his exploration of the West. The American Party, which promoted nativism, chose former president Millard Fillmore of New York as a compromise candidate.

The South generally lined up behind Buchanan. In the North, it was not clear who the electorate would support. Many Northern regular voters were energized, even radicalized, by events in Kansas. Voters pored over newspaper accounts of the campaign and turned out everywhere for raucous political rallies, concerts, and picnics. They were treated to a remarkable array of stump speakers, including Greeley, Seward, and Ralph Waldo Emerson. Abraham Lincoln gave close to ninety speeches.

Meigs followed along like everyone else. But he seemed most concerned about the impact of the election on his work. Lawmakers had recently signaled a reluctance to reauthorize spending on the aqueduct until they knew who was going to occupy the White House. Nativist lawmakers, emboldened by the campaign's anti-immigrant rhetoric, were considering holding back funding because the ranks of Meigs's workers included Irish Catholics. When Buchanan won Pennsylvania and Indiana, and it became clear he would prevail, Meigs wrote, "This ends the long agony of the two parties and frees the South from its fears and threats of a dissolution of the Union." He could not know then how wrong he was.

CHAPTER 10

Energetic, Obliging, Firm

With change coming in the White House, Meigs acknowledged his debt to Jeff Davis for giving him immense authority and political cover. Just before Buchanan's inauguration, Meigs gave Davis rare photographs of the Capitol. In a note, Meigs told his friend that he thought the images "would be interesting as memorials of the connection [Davis] had with this, one of the great buildings of the world."

Davis, touched by the gesture, offered a warm response the next day.

Captain M. C. Meigs

Dear Sir:

Accept my thanks for the photographs that you sent me yesterday. You are not mistaken in supposing that they would be of interest to me. When hereafter I shall revert to my connection with the great building from which they are taken, I shall not fail to remember that whatever the pride and satisfaction I may feel in consequence of that connection will be mainly attributable to your having been put in charge of them immediately after they were placed under my general direction. I hope the country will appreciate your services as fully as I do and that your good reputation may outlast your durable structures.

Very truly yours,
Jefferson Davis

Davis was stepping down as secretary of war and resuming his post as Mississippi's senator in Congress. He would continue to support Meigs in the fights against critics and corruption. In one letter, Davis would describe Meigs as being full of "resources, above personal jealousy, calm, energetic, obliging, firm, discreet, just, patient to hear, and willing to instruct." He said Meigs's "scientific attainments, architectural knowledge, and mechanical skill" had been pivotal to the success at the Capitol and aqueduct.

Another influential man now offered himself to Meigs as a supporter. He was Senator William Seward of New York, one of the most powerful political forces of his day, whose abolitionist convictions and antislavery speeches helped to frame the Northern case against Davis's South. A gregarious, warm-hearted man, Seward liked Davis personally, and the two shared an appreciation of the Capitol architecture, new technology, and the talents of Montgomery Meigs. He had recently become a vocal supporter of the Capitol project, saying it served as a symbolic retort to "weak and foolish talk" of disunion.

One day not long after giving his gift to Davis, Meigs ran into Seward. The senator invited him to a party at his home that night in honor of a sculptor who was making a bust of Seward. It was a classic Washington affair (if better provisioned than most, with the claret and cigars that Seward enjoyed), filled with politicos, journalists, and other talkers. Meigs was sitting with a group in the corner of the library when Seward walked up. Seward directed the group's attention to a series of reference books. When he was New York's governor, Seward said, he had managed to get such a set into every school district. He was proud of the gesture, saying that the books contained "a whole range of human knowledge." Seward said he was seeking congressional support for another endeavor that he thought would help transform the world. It was a transatlantic telegraph cable linking North America and Europe. Meigs was captivated by the idea of a long-distance wire under the Atlantic Ocean. He told Seward that he thought the Washington Aqueduct was a "great thing which would live after me and do good."

On March 4, 1857, one of the most hapless men in American history was inaugurated president of the United States, declaring that events in Kansas were "a matter of but little practical importance." With him came the man who would make Meigs's life miserable.

President James Buchanan stood on the east front of the Capitol, against a backdrop of columns. More than twenty thousand people gathered around—the men dressed in long overcoats and wearing tall black hats, many of them standing on a platform that Meigs had built to hide the construction debris. Watching through a window in the Senate wing, he was as content as he could be. The House had that morning approved $1 million in spending on the aqueduct and Capitol projects. Across from his perch, Meigs had built a small stage for a photographer Meigs had hired the year before. His job was to photograph the swearing-in ceremony, something that had never been done before.

Photography was a new technology that captivated people across the Western world, Meigs among them. Recent improvements had made the process of taking a photograph easier, while driving down the cost of prints. Portrait studios had begun producing an unprecedented number of images. In Massachusetts alone, more than four hundred thousand daguerreotype portraits were taken in one year. Meigs embraced both the aesthetic and technical challenges of the technology. He often remarked in his journals about the beauty of the images he saw. He realized that photography could also be employed as a tool for builders. About the time he hired the Capitol photographer, John Wood, Meigs told Davis that he could save money by making photographic copies of building plans. Meigs promised to create a visual record of the projects for the Library of Congress and the War Department. Cheering him on was Titian Peale, his Saturday Club friend and also an experimental photographer. It was Peale who urged Meigs to hire Wood, the Capitol's first official photographer. The shot of the inauguration was a clean-cut success (with few smudges and little blurring), perhaps the last that Meigs would have in the Buchanan years.

Meigs's new boss, Secretary of War John B. Floyd, was a former governor of Virginia. He came into office with the apparent conviction that it was his right to provide patronage to his friends. He also thought that slave ownership was the natural right of Southerners, one that needed defending at all costs. To the degree that he was known around the country, it was for a proposed tax on products of Northern states that refused to return fugitive slaves to Virginia.

Meigs had his first pangs of doubt about Floyd after a brief meeting with him on March 12. He thought Floyd lacked a quality he could not pin down. It dawned on him that his professional life might be in jeopardy. "I hope that I may find him as much disposed to put confidence in me as I did Davis," he told himself after the meeting. "If not, my work will not be so pleasant as it has been heretofore."

Signs of trouble stacked up quickly. In April two men walked into Meigs's office and said that one of them was going to be appointed master blacksmith of the Capitol extension project. They were not seeking his support, they said, merely telling him as a courtesy. Meigs set them straight, making clear that he would oppose them. He fired off a letter to Floyd asking him not to make any changes until Meigs could explain his management system.

Then Meigs received an alarming letter from his friend Joseph Totten, still chief engineer of the army. Totten told him that Floyd had been asking about the huge sums of money flowing through Meigs's operation. He thought it was likely that someone had been whispering in the war secretary's ear about the possibilities of getting control of that money. Totten recommended that Meigs visit Floyd as soon as possible. A few days later, Meigs spoke with Floyd for about ten minutes during a walk to the White House. The meeting ended poorly when one of Floyd's clerks offhandedly suggested that Meigs had been deceptive about an appointment on the aqueduct. Meigs was taken aback. No one in the department had ever questioned his integrity before.

Totten further stoked Meigs's qualms with a story about a curious land deal in New York. It seems that a representative of the War Department had been dispatched to New York to buy 111 acres on the East River for a fort. The deal was set for about $125,000. At the last moment, Floyd claimed he needed to give it more attention. Other investors known to Floyd then got involved, and the war secretary privately approved paying $200,000. Totten was flabbergasted at what he thought was evidence of blatant corruption—Floyd overpaying for land apparently controlled by his friends. Meigs tried to remain hopeful, deciding that Floyd must have been deceived "in some way or other."

———

Washington was showing signs of becoming the national center that it presumed to be. It wasn't just the new gardens and monumental public works. It was the people. They streamed into town from everywhere. Officers in uniform, explorers from out west, the occasional Native American in traditional dress, and the social elite wearing fine suits and billowing dresses. The city's culture had long been dominated by Southerners. Because of its proximity to the rural Southern states, it held attractions for Southerners that eluded those in the North used to the more cosmopolitan charms of Boston, New York, and Philadelphia. The Buchanan administration was filled with Southerners, who jammed the parties and seemed at times to be celebrating their standing in the capital.

Floyd took advantage of the power that flowed from the South's dominance. Soon after taking control of the War Department, he began turning his authority on Meigs. In one move, he urged the captain to begin applying a political litmus test to his workforce. He wanted to purge followers of the Know-Nothing movement, who objected to Irish, Germans, and Catholic immigrants. More to the point, they also opposed slavery, which offended Floyd. Meigs and other sensible folk—including Abraham Lincoln, then a lawyer in private practice in Springfield, Illinois—thought the group's members were nearly unhinged. "Our progress in degeneracy appears to me to be pretty rapid," Lincoln wrote to a friend. "As a nation, we began by declaring that *'all men are created equal.'* We now practically read it 'all men are created equal, *except ne-groes.'* When the Know-Nothings get control, it will read 'all men are created equal, except negroes, and *foreigners, and Catholics.'* When it comes to this, I should prefer emigrating to some country where they make no pretense of loving liberty—to Russia, for instance, where despotism can be taken pure, and without the base alloy of hypocracy [*sic*]."

Floyd's obsession with the Know-Nothings verged on paranoia, and it would haunt Meigs in the coming months. More pressing now was another of Floyd's demands. He wanted Meigs to award every contract automatically to the lowest bidder. At first blush, this seemed reasonable. Competition helped keep prices low for taxpayers. But Meigs knew that something else was afoot. Experience taught him that certain companies engaged in a type of legal extortion. They lowballed their original bids and then, when the work was too far along to stop, demanded more money. These were the kind of outfits Floyd appeared to have in mind. Word among Meigs's allies was that contractors from Pennsylvania and New York had been whispering in Buchanan's ear about just such arrangements. The idea of it was almost unbearably distasteful to Meigs.

By June 1857, evidence of a web of corruption became compelling when an old friend of Meigs's father called on the doctor in Philadelphia, saying he represented business interests in New York and Pennsylvania that wanted to build the aqueduct. The man claimed Buchanan backed those interests. He said if Montgomery Meigs were to direct the work to the right people, everybody would benefit financially, including Meigs himself. They would also use their influence in Congress to "secure the prompt appropriation of money and finish the public work."

Dr. Meigs was outraged to be solicited in this way. He hid his anger and asked his friend to put the proposal in writing. He then sent the document along to his son, who shared it with Totten. They agreed the president needed to see it as well. Totten, a savvy insider, told Montgomery Meigs to take care. The original document had to be protected at all costs! Meigs, assuming Buchanan would take swift action, wrote a long letter to the president. He underscored the nature of the corruption and defended his tenure in Washington, saying he had never been tempted to cheat or steal. "I fear no investigation. Every action of my life during its four best years, devoted to the public service in an honorable employment, has been dictated by the desire to leave an unblemished fame as the only heritage my children can look forward to."

Buchanan brushed aside Meigs's evidence, saying he had no doubts about Floyd's integrity. Despair began crowding out Meigs's native optimism. He wondered whether he had enough support left in Congress to stand up to this new array of adversaries.

———

Floyd's games and machinations rarely ceased. He ordered Meigs to hand over detailed financial estimates for upcoming work, a task that took weeks to complete. The report showed that substantial sums were in play, $150,000 or more each month. Floyd insinuated to Meigs that he might not be trustworthy enough to handle so much money flowing through his coffers. Administration leaks suggesting that Meigs was about to be fired soon wafted through the capital, eventually becoming speculative newspaper stories.

Floyd then added to the pressure, ordering Meigs to provide advance notice of any impending purchases worth $2,000 or more. In late August Floyd redoubled his effort to purge the workforce of political undesirables. He suggested the removal of a watchman at the Capitol who was known for his Know-Nothing connections. Since no official order had come, Meigs took no action. Floyd also asked for a copy of Meigs's payroll. This time Floyd included an incentive for cooperation by promising to boost Meigs's pay. The idea was repulsive to Meigs, who declared his boss to be a "a two-pennies politician." He realized his job could end any day and reached out to Davis repeatedly for help, complaining about Floyd and expressing fears that Walter might be given control of the Capitol project. He resolved to "strive, in the cause of truth and justice, to endeavor to finish my great works."

A few bright moments helped dispel Meigs's gloom. The end of the year found him hustling throughout the Capitol with his old enthusiasm as he prepared to open the new House chamber. His workers connected the boilers of his innovative heating system, installed the last of the lawmakers' desks, and laid the carpeting. With only a few days to go, Meigs invited his Saturday Club friends Bache and Henry, along with Davis and Seward, to help him sound out the acoustics. The men spread out across the room and sampled the effects of their voices. Meigs quietly read a short statement he had written about the military's role in public works projects. He asked Davis if he was satisfied with the sound. "Perfectly. It is a great success, a solution of the problem," Davis responded. "We had no right to expect such perfect success." Meigs turned to Bache and asked him whether the application of their scientific principles had paid off. "Wonderful, wonderful!" the scientist responded from his spot on the other side of the chamber.

The next evening, Meigs went to the Capitol with Louisa to sign letters. In the waning winter light, she sang a few verses in the new room. Meigs was enchanted by the effect of his wife's voice. On another night, Meigs went to discuss the space with House members who had gathered there. He found them trying out desks, like students in a new schoolroom. Meigs explained a few technical details and then turned on the lights, attracting still others to the dazzling room. Opinions about the new chamber varied. Some praised the circulation system. Others grumbled that the temperature was too high or low. An article in the *Boston Post* said that the acoustics could not have been worse. One unsigned piece published in the *Philadelphia Inquirer* predicted that the hall "is, I fear, to prove an entire failure. I have not met the first man yet who speaks of it favorably."

Still others lambasted the ornamentation as garish or complained it did not have "a republican simplicity" they preferred. The wife of a sitting Supreme Court justice later reached out to Meigs to pass on her opinion, saying right-minded people in Washington considered the decoration "in very bad taste, that it was vulgar, tawdry, gaudy." Meigs thanked her and said he did not take her criticism to heart. After all, he said, the decoration was the result of much study. A Vermont senator thought that the room was "overburdened and disguised and thrown out of sight by the great variety of colors put in," and he publicly urged that Davis and Meigs include "a little more chastity" in the Senate chamber.

The *Washington Evening Star* provided an assessment that Meigs welcomed. It said the "new Hall is, by long odds, much the finest deliberative chamber in the United States in all its conveniences and appointments, and is destined very shortly to become universally popular with the House and country." The unnamed writer noted that the new space "affords no opportunities whatever for lobbying—an achievement in its construction of incalculable advantage to the future of the National Treasury."

CHAPTER 11

An Inscription for All Time

The acclaim Meigs received never seemed to sate his need for approval. Six years into his stint in the nation's capital, he wanted more than ever to be remembered. He simply had to leave his mark. Early in February 1858, Meigs had his legacy in mind as he walked through the aqueduct conduits. He focused on the ill-lit walls. Half of the tunnel was lined with masonry, the other half prepped for its new skin of bricks. He was proud of the work, and for good reason. This stretch had come within an inch of engineering projections at either end. And it was looking as though he might push water through the system, at least for the purposes of testing, by the end of the year as planned.

Meigs relished these weekly inspections. They got him away from Capitol Hill, where the harassment was becoming unbearable. He savored the smells and light along the Potomac. The tours also gave him ever-needed exercise. Meigs carried a pedometer to track how far he walked, and once recorded an outing of more than ten miles through underground conduits. The inspections also soothed his sense of obligation. Though he delegated work to talented subordinates, he felt compelled to stay on top of the details himself. It was as though Frontinus, the Roman engineer, was ever present on Meigs's shoulder and whispering, "Do it the right way!" His walk through the conduit that February day took him into a section of tunnel that was nearly finished, with wet stucco still exposed. Standing in the half-light, Meigs indulged in a timeless impulse, scratching his name into the soft surface: "M. C. Meigs, Capt. of Engrs., Chief Sup. of the Washington Aqueduct, 16th Feb. 1858."

For another man, the graffito might have been a lark. Not for Meigs. As he noted in his journals, he knew that similar markings had been found after centuries in the buried homes of Pompeii, as well as inside the Egyptian pyramids. He hoped his inscription would also endure and one day call attention to him. What lay behind such exalted thinking? The history of engineering is filled with the gestures of men anxious to be remembered for their work. Consider Frontinus and his lead pipes.

Whatever the reason behind it, the ad hoc memorial was only one of many steps Meigs took that year in the hope that his role in building up Washington was not forgotten. He had come to think of himself as a kind of engineer-artist, with his "poems written in marble, granite, brick and clay, lasting materials." In March he commissioned two dozen shiny copper plates etched with these words:

WASHINGTON AQUEDUCT

A.D. 1858

CAPT. M. C. MEIGS

CHIEF ENGINEER

One morning in late winter, intent on embedding the plates as soon as he could, Meigs guided his carriage toward the bridge at Cabin John, the span that would carry the aqueduct conduit across a creek that flowed down the rugged valley and into the Potomac. Meigs loved this bridge, which was several miles northwest of the city. Originally, he'd designed it with multiple arches. But he realized that he could construct something unique without adding to the cost of the project. Without seeking approval from Davis or Congress, he had changed the plans to include a single masonry arch, the longest in the world. Meigs delegated much of the design work to Alfred Rives, a brilliant young engineer from a distinguished Virginia family, who had trained in France. Meigs admired the young man and learned much about modern engineering techniques from him.

When the captain arrived on this morning, though, he became annoyed with Rives because the cornerstone had not been laid as planned. Meigs became surly when he noticed that the masonry work also lagged behind the progress of the arch. He ordered the foreman to gather the men and place the first block. Just before it was set permanently, Meigs put into place one of the small copper plates inscribed with his name. He applied mortar to the stone in a sort of ritual before declaring the beautiful structure "the greatest arch in the world." Then he traveled farther upriver to the aqueduct's rubble dam, where he learned with satisfaction that another cornerstone had been laid, also on top of one of the copper plates. He decided also to have a stone block, inscribed with his name and the date, to be placed just beneath the surface of the water. There's no telling how many memorials Meigs left behind, but there's no question that he obsessed over the matter. Once, when reading about the world's great architecture, Meigs considered the Roman bridge of Alcantara in Spain. In his journal he wrote that the markings on the bridge showed the name of the builder and the date it had been installed 1,755 years before. Meigs hoped his name would live at least that long in the nation's memory. He even wrote a note to himself about it: "Will my copper plate or the inscriptions I am putting upon the bridges and other structures of the aqueduct be legible after the lapse of 1800 years—that is, in the year 3658?"

To commemorate his work on the Post Office, he had created a time capsule out of a copper box. In it he put a list of government leaders, a report about work on the aqueduct, and transcripts of congressional debates about Meigs's management of the public works projects. He sealed the box and placed it in a hole under a four-ton pillar. He was sure the contents would prove him worthy. "If these are opened 10,000 years hence and read, they will give the readers some idea of the manner in which those who built this great edifice have been attacked and interfered with by interested persons," he wrote in his journal. "But this has been the fate of all builders of great works: Michelangelo at St. Peter's, [Sir Christopher] Wren at St. Paul's, and I. Doubt not that Phidias and Ictinus at the Parthenon were served just in the same way. Their works stand, and so will mine."

New disputes in Kansas threatened to tear apart the nation. At issue was a constitutional convention in Lecompton to decide whether a future state would allow slavery or remain free. The idea of a convention was sound. The reality was a sham. Slave-rights advocates used rigged elections to pack the meeting with sympathizers. Of the sixty delegates, forty-eight were from slave states. Many could barely read. Bellicose and drunk much of the time, the group blundered its way through meetings as federal troops stood by to keep order.

Buchanan folded under pressure from Southerners and endorsed Lecompton, another misstep of his mediocre administration. Leaders in his own party rebelled, Stephen Douglas among them, while the fledgling Republican Party, born just a few years earlier out of the old Whig party, gained confidence nationally. Kansas voters overwhelmingly rejected the constitution the following year.

In the midst of this tumult, Floyd ramped up his campaign against Meigs. The secretary of war directed the captain to use a particular contractor to speed along contracts for supplies, hardware, lumber, and groceries. What's more, Floyd lashed out in petty ways. In one instance, Meigs was forced to wait an entire day at the War Department for a meeting with Floyd—only to be told at the end that Floyd had gone home. Aware of the game, Meigs spent the day in a borrowed room, working on his correspondence.

To make matters worse, Floyd had begun to show sympathy for a group of American artists who were complaining about Meigs's use of foreign painters to decorate the Capitol. Among those signing a petition were Rembrandt Peale, Willson Peale's son; Albert Bierstadt; and George Inness. In June 1858 the artists convinced Congress to charter an arts commission to investigate. Meigs was disgusted by Floyd and his "dishonest, unfaithful ways." He began "to wish that I was relieved from all this labor and responsibility."

Meigs had an unexpected chance to distinguish himself on a steamy day in August 1858. He was riding up the C&O Canal on the deck of a small, fast steamboat when he heard a loud splash and looked over the side. A woman had fallen and was sinking under the surface of the water, looking like a "bundle of old clothes thrown overboard." Almost without thought, he jumped in, waded over to shore, and ran down the canal path, sloshing boots and all. He dove back into the water and, with another man, pulled the woman to safety. It was a noteworthy effort in part because she was "mulatto," as Meigs put it in his journal. Many people would not have thought of risking themselves to save her. Meigs seems to have regarded his effort a simple matter of obligation to another human being. "I was much exhausted," he wrote in his journal. "I had no idea it was so difficult a matter to manage a woman in the water."

As so often happened, just as he was losing hope in his future, the work steadied him and brightened his mood. The keystone had been installed in the Cabin John Bridge, and Rives personally delivered photographs of the arch. It looked like art, a circular segment 220 feet long and just over 57 feet above the creek, supported by a matrix of timbers. Meigs thought of it as his masterpiece. It was far enough along to be considered complete, and whatever humiliation Floyd delivered now could not diminish the achievement.

Meigs decided to celebrate the progress with a bit of engineering theater. By combining the operational parts of the aqueduct with temporary pipes, he could deliver water from the Potomac to the Capitol. He had a perfect day in mind for his unveiling, the January 4 opening of the new Senate chamber. He could get credit for both projects at the same time. Yet again he ramped up his busy schedule. He moved his desk into the new Senate chamber in order to oversee the work and he pressed members of the Committee on Public Buildings to pay for last-minute necessities. Near the deadline, he even provided personal preview tours for lawmakers. One night, he turned on the gaslights and showed them the room's color scheme in all its warm glory. He worked through New Year's Day, skipping the president's traditional celebration at the White House. He carried on through the night of January 2, after learning that two water pipes were misaligned. Then, on January 3, he stood by as a wave of muddy water coursed east, gaining speed as it dropped by gravity through conduits and pipes toward the Capitol. Meigs raced ahead of the water on horseback to a meeting on Capitol Hill. As he chatted with several senators, a messenger handed him a note. After reading it, he turned to Davis. "It is reported to me that the water which I left on its way down from the reservoir will be in the grounds in a few minutes," Meigs told his friend. "We can see it in the fountain from the western windows." They watched as a modest jet of water rose twenty feet above the fountain. It was insubstantial against the winter sky and the mammoth, unfinished Washington Monument. But it looked fine to them, silvery evidence of years of devotion to a vision of the city as a healthy, safe, thriving metropolis at the center of an expanding empire. Davis shook both of Meigs's hands with enthusiasm.

———

January 4, 1859, was a bittersweet day in the Capitol's history. The Senate was finally getting a fresh new home and the city, a vast, steady source of water. Yet there was no escaping the undertow that threatened to capsize the nation's government. Two months earlier, the Buchanan White House had suffered a humiliating setback in the midterm congressional elections. Democrats lost eighteen seats in the House, largely as a consequence of the administration's support for the Lecompton constitution in Kansas. Many in the North were elated by the outcome. They were certain that it represented a catastrophe for Buchanan Democrats and an opening for Republicans. But clear-eyed observers recognized that it would further destabilize the precarious relations between North and South. Among them was Vice President John C. Breckinridge, who stood to deliver the old chamber's valedictory address. Tall, erect, and handsome, he was the gifted scion of Kentucky politicos. He had served in Congress and, at thirty-five, was the youngest man to be elected vice president in the nation's history. With hundreds of lawmakers and visitors on hand, he gave a moving appeal for national unity and against secession. One newspaperman called it the best speech of Breckinridge's career.

The Kentuckian described the vulnerable state of the nation and appealed to his colleagues to draw together in its defense. He reminded them of how Congress had overcome sectional challenges in the past, including the question of where to locate the seat of the new government. He said the power of the American system prevailed in 1790 with the selection of the District. Breckinridge noted that Congress had been meeting in the same place for decades, despite the burning of the Capitol by the British. "We see around us on every side the proofs of stability and improvement," he said. "The Capitol is worthy of the Republic."

Breckinridge expanded his argument. He said the country was thriving—with twenty-eight million citizens and fast-expanding borders—thanks to a federal system that had distributed power among the government and states. In a half century, the Senate had doubled to sixty-four members. Now it was up to them, Breckinridge told his colleagues, to preserve what the giants of the past had created. He pointed to the seats where John C. Calhoun, Daniel Webster, and Henry Clay had sat and fought and compromised to secure the fate of the county. Their extraordinary deeds obligated lawmakers to create an equally promising future. "[To] all this we were born, and, like heirs upon whom has been cast a great inheritance, have only the high duty to preserve, to extend, and to adorn it."

Meigs was deeply moved, writing that "it was the most eloquent oration I have ever listened to." It's no wonder. It could have been his father speaking to his children about the familiar themes of honor, family, patriotism, and achievement. (Never mind the irony that we can see now: Breckinridge would soon turn his back on the Union, join the Confederacy, and eventually serve for a short time as its secretary of war.)

After speaking, Breckinridge led a procession of lawmakers to the new room. The galleries above were packed with dignitaries, press, and an unusual number of women. On the floor, the senators' desks were arrayed in crescents in front of the speaker's dais. Skylight illuminated the scene, the air was fresh, and the temperature a steady 70 degrees. The room was well received. One writer described it as light and airy and even more finely proportioned than the House chamber, with two grand stairways that looked gorgeous, even though unfinished. The writer took note of the imported, patterned ceramic floor tiles along with the elaborate decorative painting by Brumidi near the chamber's entrance.

The fountain outside did not perform quite as well as Meigs wanted. But after workers made some adjustments, the water spurted as much as a hundred feet into the cold winter air. Meigs exulted quietly, privately thanking God for his role in the work. "I wish you could see it, my jet d'eau in the Capitol Park," he wrote to his father later that day. "I look upon it with constant pleasure, for it seems to spring rejoicing in the air & proclaiming its arrival for free use of the sick & well, rich & poor, gentle & simple, old & young for generation after generation, which will have come to rise up & call me blessed."

Three months later, almost a decade after fire consumed the Library of Congress because of a lack of water, one of the chief aims of the aqueduct project became manifest. Residents of Georgetown tapped into a hydrant that Meigs had installed and sprayed Potomac water to fight a fire. The Meigs household rejoiced for more personal reasons. That's because he had connected a pipe from the aqueduct directly to their home, and they were able to take baths. Meigs was pleased that Louisa could now understand one goal he had been striving toward, "to place within the reach of every household in Washington and Georgetown forever the luxury she had this day enjoyed." (Many years later, the water system's capacity fell short of the needs of the growing city, and Meigs's recommendation of lead pipes to connect homes proved ill-advised.)

Finally, he was able to bring a happy focus on his family. Gone was the raw, consuming grief that he and Louisa experienced from the loss of their two boys six years earlier. They relished their youngest, little Loulie, who liked to dive into her father's arms when he returned from work. There was also Monty and Mary. Their hopes were most immediately invested in the oldest, John Rodgers Meigs. John like his mother was tall and upright, with a thick head of light brown hair and a hint of arrogance on his face. He was headstrong, like his father. Louisa once beat him with a whalebone and put him in a closet as punishment for misbehavior. Meigs once bound him to a wardrobe as punishment for bullying his little brother and then whipped him after he escaped.

Poised for college, John was showing a talent for science and math. In late 1857, he said he wanted to attend West Point, a choice that would help the family financially, since Meigs could not afford private school tuition on his captain's salary. John had submitted a superb application, including a letter of recommendation from Jefferson Davis that had been endorsed by an array of powerful lawmakers on both sides of the aisle: Stephen Douglas (Illinois), Robert M. T. Hunter (Virginia), Albert Gallatin Brown (Mississippi), Zachariah Chandler (Michigan), and the fiery John Slidell (Louisiana). The letter noted John's family lineage, his scientific talents, and the achievements of his father. Secretary of War Floyd let it languish.

In the spring of 1859, Meigs again lobbied unsuccessfully on John's behalf. He lost hope when the president's annual list of appointees appeared without John's name on it. But when word emerged that two new cadets had failed their entrance exams, Meigs rushed to the White House to appeal directly to the president. Buchanan expressed sympathy but made clear that Meigs's public fights with Floyd had hindered John's application. Buchanan said that while he wanted to support John, he'd had enough of the squabbling. If Meigs could make peace with the secretary of war, Buchanan said, he was confident the application would sail through. The stubborn Meigs got the message. A few days later, he handed a formal letter to Floyd, requesting the reconsideration of John's application. "I trust that while I have entered protests against action or want of action by this department which appears to me to injure me in my position or reputation, I have always confined myself within the just bounds of that official and personal respect which is due to your character and to your position." He even offered to read the letter aloud.

Floyd played the offended benefactor. Why had Meigs not come to him first? Why was the captain always so discourteous? Floyd said Meigs had completely misunderstood him. The captain assured his boss that was not the case and that they could work together effectively. After a long chat, Meigs secured the pledge of support he had been seeking, and before long, when one of the cadets again failed the entrance exam, Buchanan told Meigs John would be admitted. On the afternoon of September 5 Meigs and his son caught the three-thirty train to New York. Riding through the night, they arrived at four in the morning. After a few hours of sleep, they embarked on a hectic tour of the city, visiting Barnum's American Museum and the new Central Park, where they took photographs with a stereographic camera. Then they boarded a train for the last beautiful stretch up the Hudson River to West Point. For Meigs, it was a visit to the past. He met with old professors and savored the Hudson Valley views. For John, it was the beginning of his own remarkable career in the military. After turning in the best exam performance of any cadet in years, he submitted to upperclassmen who immediately began his initiation, sending him on drills and teasing him.

Just before his departure, Meigs handed John an envelope. It contained a personal note and a copy of a letter that Meigs would deliver to Floyd. "I trust that you will always bear in mind the fact however my differences with the Secretary may terminate that to him you are under lasting obligations," it said.

CHAPTER 12

"Everything into Confusion"

The country now confronted another crisis, making Meigs and many others uneasy and confused. On October 17, 1859, the afternoon papers reported there had been a "negro insurrection" in Harpers Ferry in western Virginia, a few hours west of Washington at the confluence of the Shenandoah and Potomac Rivers. For readers in the capital, the idea of an organized slave uprising so near was shocking.

Over the next few days, the news got worse. It wasn't slaves leading the attack. It was John Brown, the abolitionist notorious for his savagery in Kansas. At Harpers Ferry, his gang had taken a prosperous planter and a farmer hostage. They freed ten slaves and blocked the Baltimore and Ohio Railroad lines. They also took over a federal arsenal and its weapons, with the apparent hope that slaves and radical whites would rush in to help. In August, it was learned later, Brown had told his friend Frederick Douglass, the social reformer, abolitionist, and writer, "When I strike, the bees will begin to swarm." The reports from Harpers Ferry triggered jubilation among many in the North, furor and terror in the South, and panic in the White House. As militia moved into position on Washington's main thoroughfares, Buchanan convened a meeting with Floyd and Colonel Robert Lee. It was agreed that Lee would lead a company of marines to the scene. At his side would be another talented West Point graduate, Lieutenant James Ewell Brown Stuart, also known as Jeb.

The siege was not universally applauded in the North. Meigs and others like-minded were mystified by the events. He did not trust the newspaper accounts and speculated that "this strange riot" simply might be a labor dispute involving arsenal workers who had been dismissed. By the time Lee and Stuart arrived in Harpers Ferry, Brown's raiders had retreated to the arsenal's engine house, some of them with mortal wounds from shots by local farmers and townspeople. On Tuesday, October 18, Lee directed Stuart to deliver a note to Brown that demanded surrender and guaranteed the raiders' safety. He refused. In the melee that followed, Brown was knocked senseless and his small force captured or killed. Though the raid lasted less than two days, its impact as a symbol grew quickly. The brief speech he delivered calmly in court resonated long after Brown's death.

"Now, if it is deemed necessary that I should forfeit my life for the furtherance of the ends of justice, and mingle my blood further with the blood of my children and with the blood of millions in this slave country whose rights are disregarded by wicked, cruel, and unjust enactments, I say, let it be done." Evidence presented at the trial, along with the Northern reaction to the strange events, convinced Southerners of a conspiracy against them. Some began arming themselves in preparation for another attack. On the December day that Brown was hanged, Northern towns rang bells and fired cannons in his honor.

This was too much for Meigs. While he opposed slavery, he was no abolitionist. He was not ready to put the country at risk in a fight about it, certainly not with an apparent lunatic leading the way. The more Meigs learned about Harpers Ferry, the more he was repelled. The republic he loved suddenly appeared more fragile than he had imagined. For now, Meigs was so anxious about the repercussions of the raid that he wrote to his father, urging him to organize rallies against Brown and his methods. Meigs and others like him wanted to send a clear conciliatory signal to the South.

His views would change before long. His eyes and heart would open to the obvious impossibility of reconciling slavery with his Christian views about justice. His rhetoric would soon resemble the fiery language of Brown's favorite New Testament passage: "Without shedding blood, there is no remission of sin." But not yet. He was not ready.

The relative peace with Floyd that had led to John's appointment soon fell apart, as the secretary of war continued to make outrageous decisions. Meigs began criticizing him openly. One of their disputes focused on a contract for marble columns. Floyd wanted to replace the contractor, a firm called Rice, Baird and Heebner. Although the firm's work was uneven and it had sometimes annoyed Meigs, it was performing well just now and might have been the only firm that could deliver the columns. For months, Floyd disregarded Meigs's opinion and insisted on a change. Meigs and Floyd also tangled over a contractor at the Post Office. Floyd insisted that Meigs use a man named E. C. Robinson to build the heating system. Robinson, a dentist from Virginia, had no business getting involved in such a complex engineering challenge. His only purpose could be to sop up the fees. A journalist at the time described Robinson as a straw man for pass-through money.

Meigs again fought back, launching a long letter of his own. Floyd was away from Washington, recuperating from an illness. So Meigs wrote to Floyd's chief clerk and asked the question on many minds. Was Floyd's dentist friend involved merely to get at "a certain liberal portion of the public money?" Meigs's meaning was clear—that Floyd might be lining his own pockets—and the consequence of saying so hit him hard and fast.

On November 2, 1859, Meigs received formal orders relieving him as engineer in charge of work on the Capitol, its dome, and the Post Office. Floyd claimed he sacked Meigs for "flagrant insubordination," citing his refusal to give Walter, resident architect at the Capitol, all engineering and architectural drawings related to the Capitol projects. To Meigs and others, the real reason was the captain's refusal to bow to Floyd's many schemes. "I have for the last two years been so tormented by attacks of the secretary of war, pushed on by his own resentments and by intrigues of Walter, that I would long since have received orders relieving me honorably from my charge with pleasure," Meigs wrote in his journal.

It had been an extraordinary run. He had taken on more in his seven years in the capital than many engineers could manage in a career. The dome was not finished, but Meigs put all the pieces in play and, with aplomb and ingenuity, solved the significant engineering problems. He had managed more than $9 million of government spending without a blemish on his honor. Meigs gathered his foremen together in a room near the new Senate chamber. An aide read aloud a brief speech Meigs had prepared. "If in the press of business I may at any time have seemed to speak too quickly, believe it was from preoccupation, not from impatience of intent," the message said. "That we have worked faithfully the walls around us will bear witness." One of the workers offered a heartfelt response on behalf of the group. "Your genius and skill are indelibly impressed upon these walls, and the imperishable building which now surrounds us that stands as the monument thereof as long as our beloved country shall endure," the laborer said, noting "the yet nobler fact that Capt. M. C. Meigs is an honest man."

Meigs was indeed honest. He was also fierce and stubborn, as those who crossed him knew well. Meigs's sense of what was right ran deep to a self-righteous core. He was convinced he had been removed at the Capitol because he had stood by his principles and refused to bend to Floyd's corrupt wishes. Thankful that he still controlled the aqueduct, Meigs turned his energies to finishing its crowning achievement, Cabin John Bridge. But that work wasn't enough to absorb his attention because he couldn't let go of his anger about being cut out of the Capitol project. He kept a close eye on the work there and took grim satisfaction that his replacement, Captain William B. Franklin, a fellow West Pointer and Saturday Club member, found himself at odds with Floyd, describing him as "an exceedingly bold and unscrupulous man." Franklin also came to dislike Walter, the Capitol architect, calling him a "great sneak and liar."

For his part, Meigs wanted vindication. He also decided it was his duty to prevent abuses by the administration. Though work on the Capitol was at a standstill because of a lack of funding, he urged his allies in the Senate to take a closer look at Floyd and his relationships with contractors. It was plain from recent newspaper accounts alone that there was plenty of fodder for an inquiry, and Meigs's suggestion helped spur on lawmakers. The Senate demanded records from the War Department, and the House formed an investigative committee to examine corruption even more broadly in the administration. Leading the committee was Representative "Honest John" Covode, a big, tough coal company owner from Pennsylvania. Covode pressed his inquiry relentlessly throughout the spring of 1860. He followed a long paper trail and gathered testimony from witnesses, filling hundreds of pages. The findings implicated the Buchanan administration with evidence showing that many of the sordid rumors about corruption were true. The Lecompton, Kansas, constitutional convention had been manipulated through bribes. Buchanan had misused patronage for political gain. The committee also found evidence that government officials had been misusing printing contracts to generate illicit cash.

Floyd stood out among the damned. Though it remained unclear whether he benefited directly, evidence showed that he had abused his public post with impunity, helping political and personal friends in schemes that reeked of illegality. Although Floyd was disgraced, he was not removed. It was only a matter of time before he would seek revenge on the uppity captain who had made so much trouble for him and his friends.

CHAPTER 13

"Eternal Blot"

In January 1860 the widening rift between North and South became a family matter for Meigs. The occasion was a visit from his younger brother Henry, who had married a Southern woman and settled in Columbus, Georgia. Henry, owner of a prosperous mill, had taken on the outlook of a Southern gentleman. It was the second time in two years that Henry had gone to Washington. On the earlier visit, Meigs had proudly guided him on a tour of the Capitol's workshops, ventilation system, and Brumidi's decorated corridors. This time they spent hours talking about the growing sectional tensions. The brothers, born five years apart, realized they were at odds over slavery and states' rights.

Meigs had a hard time accepting that his younger brother tolerated slavery and considered secession a legitimate possibility. The Meigses generally considered slavery no less than an "eternal blot" that "defiles all." He decided that Henry had sold out, trading his family's veneration for the country for "the almighty dollars which he has invested in Columbus Mills." His brother's overt turn was the latest in a chain of events that was altering Meigs's outlook. First came Floyd's behavior. Then John Brown and the crazy attack at Harpers Ferry. Now this, his own kin edging close to treason. Meigs was being pushed to confront hard questions. Where did he stand? What was he going to do about it?

Meigs had some rare personal victories. One of them had to do with his self-styled role as art patron. His push to make the Capitol a national showcase of art and creativity had been unprecedented and lavish. In a backlash, the American artists demanded that Congress require Meigs to use American-born artists. Meigs remained defiant. He believed that the work of most American artists was not worthy of a county courthouse, never mind the nation's Capitol. He sought the best artists he could find, regardless of their origins. Some House lawmakers jumped on the dispute, expressing concern about the reliance on foreign artists. They formed an arts commission to investigate, a panel of artists that had a decidedly nationalistic bent.

In February 1860, the commission finally delivered its report, describing the decoration as "tawdry and exuberant ornament" executed by "an effete and decayed race which in no way represents us." It said that artists' "patriotic hearts should perform the work." The victory for Meigs? Nobody really cared about the findings. Soon after the report was issued, the commission was dissolved. The money it had called for from Congress was never appropriated. And Brumidi continued carrying out designs for murals that Meigs had approved.

Meigs took comfort from another pet project, aqueduct Bridge No. 6 at Rock Creek. Meigs originally intended to carry the water through pipes laid under the creek, which was deep enough for boat navigation. But then he reasoned that he could use the forty-eight-inch water mains to support a bridge, and he envisioned an innovative structure that melded form and function. Now his idea was becoming a reality with a design that included cast-iron cross braces and, at road level, two long iron girders. On the girders sat crossbeams made of timber. The timbers in turn supported a road for carriages, rails for trains, and a footpath. There was no other bridge quite like it in the country. It represented another advance in the education of Montgomery Meigs.

———

The last battle between Meigs and Floyd began in June. Perhaps inevitably, it had to do with money. Elevating the dispute this time were constitutional questions. Despite being weakened by the Covode committee findings, Floyd remained in his post, pushing his advice on the pliable, overwhelmed president. The captain would not be deterred. Sensing that Floyd was about to fire him, Meigs went outside the chain of command and again reached out to friends in Congress. Davis and other lawmakers—worried that Floyd would gain unfettered access to the project's funding—quickly intervened. They reasoned that as long as Meigs remained, Congress would at least have an honest broker.

The lawmakers proposed allocating $500,000 for the water system and then pushed it through the regular committee paths in the House and Senate. Then they took an added step, using a new bit of legerdemain that remains a congressional tactic to this day. To ensure that Meigs controlled the project, Senator Robert Toombs of the Finance Committee proposed language that the money be spent by "the Chief Engineer of the Washington Aqueduct who shall be as heretofore an officer of the corps of Engineers not below the rank of Captain and having experience in the design & construction of Bridges & aqueducts."

The move pleased Meigs. It also raised constitutional questions. Could Congress dictate how the president spent the money, and, in effect, tell the commander in chief how to manage the military? Buchanan sidestepped a direct fight, dismissing the provision as a mere recommendation. "I deemed it impossible that Congress could have intended to interfere with the clear right of the president to command the army," he said. The president added an oblique dig at Meigs, saying that he could not go along with Congress because it might encourage military men to seek help from lawmakers. "Officers might then be found, instead of performing their appropriate duties, besieging the halls of Congress for the purpose of obtaining special favors and choice places by legislative enactment."

Meigs paid the price for his temerity. Not long after the $500,000 was appropriated, Floyd ordered him to hand over control of the waterworks to another officer. Floyd named Meigs the financial director, a transparent effort to maintain a fiction that he was complying with Congress's wishes. Davis, consulting privately with Meigs, counseled restraint. He said Meigs should take only those steps that would "preserve your reputation and manifest your faith to public service." Meigs would not relent. He fired off a long letter to the president, claiming that Floyd's arrangement violated the law. He even lectured the president about the army's customs and urged him to honor the wishes of Congress. Buchanan wrote back, saying Meigs was close to insubordination. US Attorney General Jeremiah S. Black agreed. "I do not permit myself to doubt that Captain Meigs will obey his orders without being put under the 'strong pressure' of anything but his own sense of duty not as a 'reluctant and unwilling instrument' but with the cheerfulness and alacrity which becomes an officer of his grade and character," Black wrote.

When Meigs wrote the president again, Buchanan returned the note unopened. After many years, Meigs had lost his access to the White House. Still, he continued to resist. Acting in his capacity as financial director, Meigs declined to pay an inspector who he believed was not qualified. Meigs said the payment was not consistent with the mandate he had received from Congress. He told Buchanan that Floyd's orders regarding the aqueduct were no longer binding on him. That was it. When Meigs returned from a visit to the aqueduct on September 20, he found new orders waiting for him at home. Floyd relieved him of duty and ordered him to assume command of construction at Fort Jefferson in the Dry Tortugas, seventy nautical miles west of Key West, Florida. The *New York Times* wrote that "his unpardonable offence was his persistent efforts to guard the Treasury against the enterprises of Mr. Floyd's pet contractors."

The long fight was over. Meigs had been banished. By all appearances, his career as the capital city's builder had come to an end.

CHAPTER 14

Tall and Awkward Candidate

As Meigs prepared for his exile, the run for the White House entered its final stage. It appeared nearly certain in the North that Abraham Lincoln would win, an outcome that to many Southerners presented an existential challenge. Though Meigs could not know it, the election result would open the way for the greatest opportunity of his life.

It had been a colorful campaign with torchlight parades, barbecues, and incendiary rhetoric. The focus shifted inexorably to Lincoln. He had defined the terms of the contest during a brilliant speech before he was formally announced as a candidate. The pivotal event was staged in February 1860 at New York's Cooper Union for the Advancement of Science and Art. Lincoln had been invited to appear as a result of his eloquence during debates in Illinois, when he'd campaigned unsuccessfully for the Senate against Stephen Douglas two years earlier. People packed into the school's great hall, waiting to see what this little known westerner had to say. Savvy New Yorkers were initially unimpressed as Lincoln took center stage. They saw a "tall," "angular," "awkward," and "ungainly man." One man in the audience recalled being embarrassed on Lincoln's behalf. That impression changed the moment he began to speak, as Lincoln's "face lighted up with an inward fire."

The speech focused on the question of the federal government's authority to limit slavery in the territories. Lincoln had spent months researching the matter. He pounded home his points with the chop-chop-chop of logic rather than with rhetorical flourishes. He argued that Douglas, the most prominent Democratic candidate, and the

Supreme Court's Chief Justice Roger Brooke Taney, had been inconsistent and incorrect in their stances. Lincoln argued that the framers of the Constitution had no intention of limiting the federal government's role. He walked a narrow path through his logic. He conceded that slavery was a fact of American life, but he warned against passivity in the face of disunion. The partisan crowd cheered. Southerners who read the widely reported speech took it as confirmation of their worst fears about so-called Black Republicans—an epithet used to underscore their anger about the party's anti-slave agenda.

"Neither let us be slandered from our duty by false accusations against us, nor frightened from it by menaces of destruction to the government nor of dungeons to ourselves," Lincoln concluded. "Let us have faith that right makes might, and in that faith, let us, to the end, dare to do our duty as we understand it."

Lincoln's chief opponent for the Republican nomination was New York Senator William Seward. Though Seward thought the race was his to lose, his New York roots made him suspect to westerners, while a long history of opposition against slavery made him unacceptable to moderates. He had long ago lost any chance of Southern votes when he gave his "higher law" speech—arguing that certain moral laws transcended the Constitution—during the debate about the Compromise of 1850. At the Republican convention in May 1860, Seward initially led the voting, but support waned over fears that he could not take two key states, Indiana and Pennsylvania.

Lincoln advisors improved their candidate's chances by quietly promising that he would select Cabinet members from those two states. Lincoln won on the third ballot with a platform that opposed slavery in the territories, endorsed free labor, and rejected the tactics of John Brown.

The Democratic Party, meanwhile, was disintegrating. The party had met for its convention in Charleston, South Carolina, in April. Northern and Southern delegates engaged in a furious battle over a radical platform proposal that called for a federal slave code that would guarantee the expansion of slavery. Douglas supporters managed to block that plan, spurring Southern delegates to walk out. Douglas could not capture the two-thirds majority to secure the nomination. The party halted proceedings and opted to reconvene in June in Baltimore. In that session, Douglas edged out John C. Breckinridge for the nomination after Southerners again walked out and formed their own party. In a hastily organized meeting across town, the new organization, the Southern Democratic Party, named Breckinridge as its nominee. Yet another party formed as well. The new Constitutional Union Party was comprised of former Whigs and American Party members who felt the Republicans were too radical. They nominated John Bell, a former congressman from Tennessee, and Edward Everett, the diplomat, politician, and art connoisseur from Massachusetts.

Douglas was the only candidate who appeared as a stump speaker during the race. Lincoln and the others followed the accepted practice of laying low, meeting with delegates, and allowing proxies to do their work. Bell's campaign handed out bells to supporters. Lincoln's people, including thousands of young men, held stirring torchlight parades for the "Woodchopper of the West." Though Lincoln could not count on any electoral votes in the South, he dominated polls in the North.

Just before the election, on October 20, 1860, Meigs closed out his official accounts, paying the Treasury $93.56 to balance the books. Then he left his family and headed to Knoxville, Tennessee, his first stop south on the way to his new assignment. Louisa wanted to go along. Meigs declined, saying he thought Louisa's presence in the capital would serve as a reminder that he was in exile for his principles. He assumed Floyd and his friends would be swept out of Washington by the election and guessed he would be back in town before spring. He left Washington with a clear conscience. He didn't care that he had cemented his reputation among some Washingtonians as self-righteous. He found it amusing that otherwise sensible people thought he should have bent to the corruption to protect himself from Floyd. Meigs sent a note to the Army Corps of Engineers office. It was a final dart at the secretary of war, spelling out why he believed that the orders sending him south were il-legal. "I understand that the work of the Aqueduct and the expenditures thereon are going on in defiance of the law of Congress," he wrote.

For all the tumult in his life, Meigs seems to have looked forward to his trip to the Dry Tortugas as something of an adventure. He planned on sailing, studying, fishing, and hunting. He hoped to study the "rare & beautiful forms of life with which God had bedecked those tropic shores." He justified these diversions as ways to increase "my store of knowledge & make myself able to be of use to a people to whom Washington & Adams, Jefferson & Clay thought worthy of their highest efforts, their most unselfish devotion."

From Knoxville, Meigs went to Columbus, Georgia, and stayed with his brother. In the pocket diary he carried along, he noted only that he found Henry's family well. But it was a tense visit for Meigs, who saw many Southerners preparing openly for secession, behavior he considered treasonous. Henry's view of the nation's circumstances was nearly the opposite of his own. Like his white neighbors, Henry felt passionately that Southerners were being asked to bow "to the idea of a forced submission to the rule of the outrageous majority." Nothing would be resolved, Henry believed, "until the fields of this country are reddened with the blood of its people." Meigs passed through Montgomery, Alabama, and then caught a steamer in Pensacola, Florida, touching at Apalachicola, St. Mark's, Cedar Key, Tampa, and Key West before reaching Fort Jefferson on November 8. He took stock of the mood at every stop, as though he were a spy. He was chilled by what he was learning.

———

Election Day was anticlimactic, at least for many Northerners. Even the pugnacious Douglas had reconciled himself to a Lincoln victory. He had begun encouraging voters to actively support the president-elect against those who favored disunion. Lincoln swept the field with 180 electoral votes. He won every Northern state except New Jersey. Breckinridge came in second, with 72 votes. Douglas ran a distant fourth, behind Bell, with 12 votes. "We cannot tell yet what historical lessons the event of November 6, 1860, will teach," one New Yorker wrote in his journal, "but the lesson cannot fail to be weighty."

Meigs, a Democrat like his parents, would not know the outcome of the election until more than a week after the fact. His barren new home had no telegraph service, and the mail steamer arrived with newspapers only twice a month. He knew the consequences were likely grave. His trip had finally clarified for him what others had seen long before: the South would do almost anything to preserve slavery, the cornerstone of its culture and commerce. On November 10 Meigs wrote to General Winfield Scott, the aging commander of the army. The letter was an extraordinary deviation from the army's chain of command, but Meigs felt he had no choice because he no longer knew which of his superiors he could trust. The urgency of the situation demanded unusual action.

"Dear Sir: As the only Engineer present on duty upon the Fortifications in this vicinity, I feel compelled to address you on a subject of importance to the public service and yet one upon which I do not feel at liberty to write a formal official letter," Meigs wrote. "Pardon the liberty or the irregularity and make such use of the views which I present as your own opinion of their value and importance may require."

The enterprising captain told Scott that Southern Unionists had given up hope the country could survive. He said, "the temper of the South is excited, is dangerous. I do not think that any concerted plan is agreed upon, but Southern Senators are reported to intend resigning if Mr. Lincoln is elected." Meigs worried that rebellious Southerners might try to make a name for themselves by seizing Fort Pickens at Pensacola and other lightly manned fortifications, and he suggested that the army quietly add men and armaments immediately to serve as a deterrent to Southern adventurers. "At present both this place and Fort Taylor [at the tail end of the Florida Keys] are at the mercy of a party which could be transported in a fishing smack," Meigs wrote. "What a disgrace such an assault if successful would inflict upon our Government."

———

Fort Jefferson, Tortugas, Florida, November 25, 1860
Lat. 24 37 N Long 82 52 W

My Dear John:

I have not heard from home for two weeks or more, because the last steamer coming in from New Orleans brought me no mail, but tomorrow I shall send up the schooner to Key West to get the mail, which I expect the *Isabel* steamer to bring from Charleston.

I had no idea of the delightful climate which I find here at this season. The thermometer keeps between 75 and 80 . . .

The sea is white with wave crests which break over the harbor.

I went fishing today on *Two Sons*. We caught in the schooner some 12 or 13 fish which would make about 70 pounds all together. Fine fishing here. Some of the fish here are beautiful. The kingfish which we caught is the first of the season, a single fish about 31 inches in length, a fellow which can leap 20 feet and 6 feet in height from the water. Their jumps are like those of the deer . . .

Write to me and let me know how you get on with your studies. I am lonely and need letters from home, from those I love . . .

Ever your affectionate father, Meigs.

CHAPTER 15

Floyd Resigns

Events soon handed Meigs vindication, as a tide of truth turned against John Floyd. The change began with a report from a board of engineers that Floyd had formed to examine the aqueduct. It seems the war secretary assumed the board would find evidence that would indict Meigs's work and reputation. As it happened, the board's November 15 report could have been written by Meigs himself. It said the work was in good condition, had not cost more than necessary, and incorporated novel designs. Floyd's reputation slid further on news that he had resisted calls by General Scott and others to reinforce Fort Sumter and other federal garrisons in Charleston Harbor. When the commander at Charleston moved on his own to bolster defenses, Floyd replaced him. The new commander, Robert Anderson, was known to tolerate slavery. But he was an army veteran of the Black Hawk, Second Seminole, and Mexican Wars, and he would not lift a hand against the Union. Contrary to Floyd's wishes, Anderson immediately called for reinforcements to help keep the forts and harbor in Union hands.

On December 20 South Carolina electrified the nation with its decision to secede. In the following days, Anderson sensed with good reason that state militia intended to occupy the harbor's federal forts, including the one he occupied, Fort Moultrie. They were undermanned and could not fully use the guns they had in place. On December 26, under the cover of darkness, Anderson transferred his force to Fort Sumter, which offered a better defensive position than Fort Moultrie. When Floyd heard of the move, he was flabbergasted and accused Anderson of violating orders. In fact, Anderson's orders, which Floyd had endorsed, gave him latitude to make such a move. "It has made war inevitable!" Floyd declared.

In the midst of this crisis, new details about War Department corruption emerged from a House investigation. The findings were related to the so-called Mormon War in Utah, where Buchanan and Floyd sent troops in 1857 to enforce federal law and install a non-Mormon governor. Not only had the contractors supplying the army botched the job, the government fell behind on its bills. To avoid a lapse in funding, Floyd urged banks to advance money to the contractors. Then he endorsed the bills, which became known as the "Floyd Acceptances." Matters spiraled out of control when the time came for paying off the loans. No money had been appropriated for the expense. The contractor, facing ruin, persuaded a cousin of Floyd's at the Department of the Interior that scandal would erupt if the banks could not be paid. The House investigators found evidence that the contractor and Floyd's cousin eventually took close to $900,000 from a trust fund established on behalf of certain Indian tribes. The scheme surfaced when interest on the trust fund bonds came due.

Northerners became further inflamed when news emerged that Floyd had been shipping weapons and supplies to Southern armories. The shipments earlier in the year had included twenty-four thousand muskets from a national armory in the North to Charleston, South Carolina; Augusta, Georgia; and Baton Rouge, Louisiana. Some of the transfers were routine inventory management. They nevertheless suggested to secessionists that they had a friend in Floyd. The master armorer for the state of Virginia was open about this conviction in a treasonous note asking Floyd to ship weapons as soon as possible from the Northeast. "I desire to get all the assistance we can from the national armories before our much-honored and esteemed Secretary of War vacates his office, for I have no hopes of any assistance after a Black Republican takes possession of the War Department," the armorer wrote.

Near the end of the year, Floyd triggered outrage when he ordered 125 heavy cannons from Pittsburgh arsenals to garrisons in Mississippi and Texas, just as South Carolina seceded. Municipal and civic leaders in Pennsylvania were livid. They wrote to the president and recommended that he countermand the order. Buchanan did so on Christmas Day. Floyd resigned, attributing his departure to indignation at the administration's handling of the crisis in Charleston. Prosecutors in the District indicted him for "malversation"—a violation of the public trust—charges dropped later for lack of evidence. At the same time, Virginia embraced him as a hero, and he was soon made a brigadier general of the Confederate army. In early 1862 he was relieved of duty after fleeing a pivotal battle. Floyd's health soon failed. He died at his daughter's home in Abingdon, Virginia, in August 1863.

Years later, Ulysses S. Grant in his memoirs provided a damning coda to Floyd's life, a summation that must have pleased Meigs. Grant said that Floyd was never a soldier and probably was unsuited to be one. "He was further unfitted for command, for the reason that his conscience must have troubled him and made him afraid. As Secretary of War he had taken a solemn oath to maintain the Constitution of the United States and to uphold the same against all its enemies. He betrayed that trust."

———

Everywhere Meigs looked, there was something on his desolate island that caught his attention. Coral reefs were visible just below the surface of water that shifted constantly from sapphire to teal to green. There were varieties of crabs at every turn, pelicans gliding low just offshore, and scorpions in the sand. He marveled at the phosphorescent trail left behind the schooner *The Tortugas* that ferried him occasionally to Key West. He was transfixed as the "waves splash away in great maps of light." He thought that two local slaves (of the twenty-five who shared the island with him) were extraordinary, saying they looked as "black as the ace of spades." On one excursion, Meigs went to Havana. He was almost as dazzled by the culture and feel of Cuba as he was of the natural beauty on the Dry Tortugas.

He didn't have nearly as much time to study as he had hoped. At

Fort Jefferson, Meigs was the personification of the federal government, and the responsibility weighed on him. From what he had seen on his overland route south, he did not have a moment to lose in fulfilling his mission to fortify the island. After more than a decade of construction, it was far from finished. Also unfinished was Fort Taylor near Key West. Both installations took on strategic significance now because they commanded the route for ships sailing from key cities on the Gulf, including New Orleans and Mobile, Alabama.

Underscoring his fears was the formation of secessionist-leaning militia in Key West. They had already taken ammunition from a federal storehouse, and Meigs expected a call from Southerners to surrender any day. There were no guns or ammunition on the island, and he had no way to mount a defense. He hustled to use what little resources he had to prepare for a fight as he waited to hear back from Scott. He urged a unit of federal artillerymen based in Key West to set up quarters in Fort Taylor. Meigs and the artillery commander engaged in a public ruse that the men were merely practicing at the fort.

Meigs also convinced two navy steamers in the region to anchor nearby. After the navy recalled one of the ships, Meigs fulminated in his diary. He thought that "the President ought to be impeached & convicted of treasonable weakness." Day by day, he became angrier about the secessionists and more concerned about the country's core values. "Is slavery stronger than freedom?" he wondered. "My heart grows sick as I think of this prospect, & yet I believe that even in the greatest political trouble there is peace & happiness for those & those only who each hour & minute endeavor to do their duty & I hope to be able to do mine."

Finally, Washington showed interest in the Gulf fortifications. Joseph Holt, the new War Department secretary, and General Scott agreed to send reinforcements to the region. In January a steamship called the *Joseph Whitney* arrived at Fort Jefferson. Among those onboard was a new commander, who found the place ready for action. In addition to everything else Meigs had created a bombproof magazine for the small force's ammunition, reinforcing it with brick arches four and a half feet thick. At Fort Taylor, meanwhile, Meigs had fortified a wall facing a moat and pulled up bridges that provided easy access. Meigs was grateful for the new companionship, and he comfortably assumed a secondary role on the island as chief engineer. He shared his view that with enough supplies, ammunition, and men, the fort would enable the North to harass the Gulf ports. He was right. With the benefit of his foresight, the federal government kept the fort in Union hands throughout the coming war.

On February 13, 1861, his banishment ended abruptly. At ten in the morning, new orders arrived on *The Tortugas* directing Meigs to return immediately to the nation's capital, where he was to resume control of the aqueduct project. Two hours later, he headed home.

CHAPTER 16

He Plucked a Laurel

When Meigs returned to Washington at six o'clock in the evening on February 20, he had been gone almost four months. His family rejoiced to have their gruff, loving husband and father back. Many in the political world took comfort that he had prevailed so definitively over Floyd. "Meigs has been summoned back in good season," one newspaper declared. He has been "fighting for six years past a strong battle with the army of great thieves," and he "made it his business to see that the Government got the worth of their money." Francis Preston Blair, the politician and journalist, said his adversaries "sent Meigs to gather a thistle, but thank God, he has plucked a laurel."

Meigs reached out to his friend and mentor, army chief engineer General Joseph G. Totten, and together they went to see Secretary Holt. Meigs learned that Holt and his aides had been delighted by his rousing letters from Florida. Holt recounted with glee how Floyd had tried to thwart efforts to reinforce the forts by telling Buchanan "it was perfectly ridiculous that [Meigs] wanted men and guns to defend the Tortugas and some heap of rocks, perfectly indefensible." Holt's advisors had assured the new secretary of war that Meigs was smart, tough, and determined, and would fight off any attackers—by hand if necessary.

The atmosphere in Washington was electric. In Montgomery, Alabama, delegates from Alabama, Florida, Georgia, Louisiana, Mississippi, and South Carolina had adopted a Provisional Constitution of the Confederate States. They selected Jefferson Davis to be president of the new government, a development that fueled Meigs's bitterness about the rebellion. Lincoln, meanwhile, was on the way from Illinois to Washington for his inauguration. Despite all this, Meigs couldn't wait to get back to work on the aqueduct. He walked with Louisa to Cabin John Creek, and they looked with satisfaction at his unfinished masterpiece, now called Union Bridge. It was regarded almost universally, even in the South, as an engineering triumph. (Jeff Davis's name would be removed from the granite memorial honoring those responsible for the bridge's construction. And engineer Alfred Rives, who also went south, did not receive the recognition he was due for his role in its design.) On their walk through Washington, the couple was impressed by the city's martial air. Batteries occupied key points on bridges and crossroads. Soldiers seemed to be everywhere, and the sound of bugles filled the air. Rumors of plots to assassinate Abraham Lincoln shot back and forth across Washington. The president-elect was set to arrive in the capital by special train the next day. General Scott insisted on vigorous efforts to defend the city and the new chief executive. Though he was seventy-three and infirm, he was not going to let anything happen to Lincoln on his watch.

Meigs reunited with his friends in the Saturday Club. When talk turned to his banishment, he was asked about his intentions at the Capitol. Would he try to resume control? At least one member suggested it might be a good time for Meigs to show generosity and allow his replacement, Captain Franklin, to remain. Even though Meigs got along with Franklin, he was rigid about his goal. He wanted a complete restoration of every post that had been stripped from him the year before. Meigs hoped that Franklin would contact him with an offer to resign. He waited for two days before writing to Franklin and spelling out his wish that he step aside. Meigs cast it as a matter of honor, saying "no man has reputation enough to be able to throw away any" of it. "I have always held a firm conviction that with or without effort on my part if God spared my life I should place the Statue of American Freedom upon the Dome of the Capitol," he wrote. "To this end, I invite your cooperation."

Franklin declined, and for good reasons. He needed the assignment and worried about his own reputation. If he followed Meigs's lead, people might think he had been a willing pawn to dishonest leaders. That was something Meigs could understand, so he set about helping to arrange another post for Franklin at the Treasury Building. Holt agreed to the arrangements and put them into effect. The secretary of war also eliminated regulations established by Floyd that diminished Meigs's previous authority. Congress, meanwhile, appropriated $250,000 for the next round of work.

Meigs thought he ought to visit President Buchanan one last time, and found him a broken man. He wondered about how Lincoln would fare. He had heard wildly varying reports about him. Judging from the prints he had seen, Meigs thought Lincoln looked peculiar. "He certainly does not seem to come much to the level of the great mission," he wrote the day before the inauguration. That night, Meigs visited the Senate. He chatted with old friends, watching lawmakers work under the gas lamps on end-of-administration business. It was a strange atmosphere, thrilling and ominous. No one knew what lay ahead. Everybody assumed it would be something momentous. "Exciting times, these," Meigs wrote in his journal that night. "The country trembles in the throes of death."

———

The inaugural procession began at the Willard Hotel and worked its way slowly east along Pennsylvania Avenue. Lincoln was escorted by so many horsemen and guards that it was difficult for onlookers to see him. The carriage took him to the Senate chamber, where Lincoln greeted a waiting crowd. He led them to the Capitol's east front, where as many as twenty-five thousand restive people had gathered, some of them anxious about whether an attempt would be made on Lincoln's life. He took his place on a platform near a desk that held the Bible. Above him was the massive unfinished dome. Rising above that was Meigs's distinctive wood derrick. Lincoln stood above all those around him, looking both calm and sad. Nearby was Stephen Douglas, the Little Giant; the worn-out Buchanan; and Horace Greeley, the nettlesome editor of the *New-York Daily Tribune*.

Meigs squeezed in near the platform and watched as Lincoln put on his reading glasses, and listened as he began to speak. The sixteenth president said he would occupy forts still in possession of the United States. He would not attack anywhere, but he would resist attacks by anyone. He promised to be patient at the same time he urged citizens to do their duty. The speech left Meigs more devoted than ever to defending the Union. "No time was wasted in generalities or platitudes but he grappled at once with his subject & no one could doubt that he meant what he said," Meigs wrote later that day. "Each sentence fell like a sledgehammer driving in the nails which maintain states."

Meigs quickly resumed working in the capital. He awarded contracts and put 450 men and 150 horses to work on the bridge at Cabin John, Bridge No. 6 at Rock Creek, and related projects, but he was soon called away to serve his country in far more important ways.

PART 2

---★---

CHAPTER 17

A Secret Mission

Meigs returned home from work on the aqueduct one afternoon to find a letter from the new secretary of state, William Seward, who wanted him to come to a meeting at the White House. Seward had taken on the self-appointed role as dictator of defense. It was widely assumed that he, not Lincoln, was the "premier" who held the reins of power. When Meigs arrived, Seward told him that the president wanted to talk to a soldier about certain military operations. Though Lincoln had Scott and Totten to advise him, Seward said, "No one would think of putting either of those old men on horseback." The president needed someone who could be sent into the field. Seward escorted the captain to the White House and introduced him to the president, who spoke openly about his concerns.

Lincoln said he wanted to keep control of federal fortifications in Charleston Harbor and the Gulf of Mexico. He did not know whether the small standing army had enough men, and he did not want to provoke South Carolina into an open fight. Lincoln and Seward both feared that President Jefferson Davis would respond to any move on Fort Sumter with an attack on Washington. The president asked Meigs whether Fort Pickens could be held. Meigs was blunt, something Lincoln appreciated. "Certainly," Meigs told him, "if the navy would do its duty and had not lost it already." Lincoln asked if Meigs would be willing to lead a secret mission to make it so. Meigs said he was only a captain and could not command more senior officers who would be involved in such an endeavor. He said the president would need to select someone of higher rank. Seward jumped in.

"Well, I understand how that is, Captain Meigs. You have got to be promoted." Meigs would not grant the point, a matter of honor, even to the president. "That cannot be done. I am a captain, and there is no vacancy." Seward suggested that as the nation's commander in chief, Lincoln could make it happen without too much fuss. Leaving the question open, Meigs promised he would provide cost estimates as soon as possible. Lincoln then told a story about British Prime Minister William Pitt's decision to take Quebec, Canada, during its Seven Years' War (also known as the French and Indian War) with France in the mid-eighteenth century. Pitt did not send an old general, the president said, but instead called on a young man to take on the job. The comparison resonated with Meigs as he walked home with Seward.

On Easter Sunday, Meigs was about to go to church when an army colleague appeared at his front door. It was Lieutenant Colonel Erasmus Keyes, the military secretary to General Scott. He told Meigs that Seward wanted to see him immediately. Meigs learned that General Scott was more pessimistic than ever about keeping the forts in Union hands. Scott's mood that morning was due to Keyes, who had earlier explained at length the apparent impossibility of moving heavy guns and ammunition onto the beaches of Santa Rosa Island, where Fort Pickens stood. General Scott felt that Keyes had put into words all his fears about such an excursion. He had handed Keyes a rolled-up map of Pensacola and ordered him to go to Seward's home and repeat everything he had said.

Keyes did as he was told. Seward offered a terse response. "I don't care about the difficulties," the secretary of state said. "Where's Captain Meigs?" Seward ordered Keyes to retrieve Meigs and return immediately.

When the officers arrived, Seward told them to make a plan for reinforcing Fort Pickens, brief General Scott, and then deliver the plans to the White House at three o'clock. Keyes and Meigs went directly to an army office. They made lists of supplies, calculated the weight and size of weapons, mapped out sailing directions, and drafted requisitions. They arrived at the Executive Mansion with no time to spare. They found Lincoln sprawled out, one leg resting on a tabletop, the other on a chair. His hands were clasped behind his head. During the meeting, Lincoln shifted his position constantly. Keyes thought that he had never seen "a man who could scatter his limbs more than he." When the president asked if they were ready to report, Keyes hesitated. They had not had time to consult with General Scott, and Keyes was worried about operating outside the chain of command. Meigs had no qualms. "I'm not General Scott's military secretary, and I am ready to report," he said. He focused on the engineering logistics. Then Keyes joined in after all, describing the gunnery. Lincoln suggested no changes before telling them to see General Scott and launch the effort without delay. "I depend on you gentlemen to push this thing through."

———

The next week was filled with precedent, improvisation, and intrigue. Whenever possible, orders were given verbally to avoid disclosure to secret turncoats still employed by the government. The two officers spent hours at Scott's office and at the White House, refining their plans. There was much discussion about who should command the expedition. Scott confirmed that Meigs was right about his own status as an officer. He could not leap up in rank. Scott commiserated with Meigs, saying it was unfair he should have to leave the prominent projects at the Capitol and aqueduct for such a risky assignment, all on a captain's pay. Seward, who understood Meigs better than most, told the captain that "fame would come from Pickens as well as from the Capitol, and the Capitol might stop; there was no use in a Capitol unless we had a country." Meigs assured Seward that he was "ready for any duty, in any place, in any capacity, at any pay, so long as it was in my country's service."

He and Keyes decided that Meigs would serve as chief engineer. They selected Colonel Harvey Brown as leader. A veteran of the Mexican and Seminole Wars, Brown was known for his bravery and his administrative skills. Meigs began working closely with the new president. He drafted orders for Lincoln's signature, including one directing Navy Lieutenant David D. Porter to go to the Brooklyn Navy Yard and take any vessel suitable for the mission. Lincoln signed something of a carte blanche that said: "All officers of the Army and Navy, to whom this order may be exhibited, will aid by every means in their power the expedition under the command of Col. Harvey Brown, supplying him with men and material and co-operating with him as he may desire."

Over the next several days, they prepared secretly for what one historian called "that astonishing affair." Organizers gathered nearly five hundred men and tons of material at the Navy Yard. They chartered several fast vessels, including the steamships *Atlantic, Illinois,* and *Philadelphia.* And in Washington, Meigs finalized the administrative details, including obtaining the cash for the mission, which had to be extracted from the federal bureaucracy discreetly. There was no secret service budget in the army or navy. So Lincoln directed Seward to give Meigs $10,000 from his department funds. The effort to maintain secrecy created problems when one of the navy's most formidable warships, the USS *Powhatan,* was called for on two separate missions, one to Fort Pickens, the other to Fort Sumter. The commander of the Navy Yard in New York, meanwhile, was ordered not to tell his superiors about Porter's plan to take command of the *Powhatan.* Because even Secretary of the Navy Gideon Welles had been kept in the dark, he ordered *Powhatan* to join three other steamers in an effort to resupply Fort Sumter. Armed with Lincoln's orders, Meigs convinced authorities in the harbor to ignore Welles, and the ship left port at noon on April 6. That led to fireworks in Washington. After Seward told Welles about the scheme, Welles went to the president. Lincoln, sitting at his desk, looked up and said, "What have I been doing wrong?" When Secretary of War Simon Cameron caught wind of the mission, he claimed that Meigs was absent without leave and threatened to have him arrested and court-martialed.

Meigs sailed before dawn the next day aboard the *Atlantic.* He was joined by almost four hundred others, including companies of sappers, and light artillery. They took seventy-three horses with them. Following the *Atlantic* was the *Illinois,* carrying extra supplies. Meigs's enthu-

siasm bubbled over now. During the voyage, he drafted a dispatch to
Seward that suggested a purge of aging leaders of the army and navy.
They were excellent and patriotic men, he said, but they clogged up
the chain of command. And he exhorted Seward to rise to the demands
of the war, reminding him that it took England six months to mobi-
lize for its two-and-a-half-month war in Crimea against Russia, and
four months for the United States to get to Monterrey during the war in
Mexico. "Let us be supported," Meigs told Seward.

———

The trip south was an adventure in itself. The *Atlantic* ran into a violent gale at Cape Hatteras. With waves pounding the steamer, the crew
struggled to keep the men and horses from being washed overboard.
Meigs thought he had "never seen so magnificent a sight as this roaring, raging sea." The ship was forced to slow its engines and veer nearly
one hundred miles off course. Meigs was impressed with his ship and
already thinking ahead to the logistics and costs of the coming war. He
told Seward the federal government should buy it and the other leased
steamers as soon as possible. The expedition had chartered the *Atlantic* for a month at $2,000 a day. The government would do much better,
he said, to pay the $750,000 value of the ship outright. He was almost
giddy about the stealth of the mission and the confusion he believed it
would cause secessionists. "The dispatch and the secrecy with which
this expedition has been fitted out will strike terror into the ranks of
rebellion," he wrote Seward. "All New York saw, all the United States
knew, that the *Atlantic* was filling with stores and troops. But now this
nameless vessel, her name is painted out, speeds out of that track of
commerce to an unknown destination. Mysterious, unseen, where will
the powerful bolt fall?"

The enthusiasm of the men on the mission also moved him. No one
was sad or complaining, despite the fact that none had been told where
they were going or exactly what they were to do. "This loyalty and devotion is beautiful," he wrote. "At this time, the republic has need of all
her sons, of all their knowledge, zeal, and courage."

On April 16 the expedition anchored off Pensacola, near Fort Pickens. The trip had taken it to the Florida Keys and the Dry Tortugas, where the *Atlantic* picked up more howitzers, ammunition, and twenty black mechanics—some of them slaves said to be owned by former Florida senator Stephen R. Mallory, now secretary of the Confederate navy. The friends Meigs had made during his stint on the island had given him three cheers for returning. Meigs launched the operation just before midnight. A small fleet of boats went in a line to the beaches, and he directed them where to deploy. Meeting no resistance, they managed to get scores of men into the fort that morning. Over the next two days men, weapons, and horses poured into the fort. Then the other ships arrived, bringing to almost 3,200 the number of men occupying Fort Pickens. The Union would maintain control of the fort through the end of the war.

Meigs heard about the siege and loss of Fort Sumter only after the fact. Robert Anderson had surrendered a week earlier after enduring a thirty-four-hour bombardment from secessionist forces. The president issued a call for seventy-five thousand volunteers to serve for three months. It was official: the Civil War had begun. As he sailed home, Meigs worried. Would Washington be in Southern hands by the time he got there? He was confident, however, that the country would survive. He wrote in his journal: "I see a bright future in which this great land under a strong and united government will at length again be free and happy, when traitors will have received due punishment for their crimes, and the sin of slavery wiped out by the hands of an avenging God."

CHAPTER 18

A Soul on Fire

Meigs arrived back at New York on May 1, proud of the mission's success. He and his colleagues had received little news on the voyage back. All they knew for sure was that communications with Washington had been cut and that federal troops en route to the capital had been blocked from passing though Baltimore by secessionists. At the boat landing, he gathered up newspapers and learned that thousands of men had made it to the capital, many of them traveling by steamboat to Annapolis and then by rail to the city. He followed that route and reunited with Louisa at home on May 2, the couple's twentieth wedding anniversary. The next day was his forty-fifth birthday.

Washington was already a different place. Troops marched on the streets. Several thousand camped in the Capitol's House and Senate chambers, and around the derrick's base under the dome. It was a chaotic arrangement that included all the hijinks expected from green soldiers. The stench of human waste became unbearable. A long-serving doorkeeper was beside himself. "[It] almost broke my heart to see the soldiers bring armfuls of bacon and hams and throw them down upon the floor of the marble room. Almost with tears in my eyes, I begged them not to grease up the walls and the furniture."

Enemy forces also had collected nearby, and their sentries could be seen patrolling in Virginia at the ends of the three Potomac bridges. Panic had spread after Scott warned of an imminent attack on the capital several days earlier. That fear had given way to jubilation on the arrival of soldiers. Meigs went to the State Department and met with Seward, who sent him to Lincoln. The president was in a meeting with his Cabinet, and they invited Meigs to brief them about his adventure. Though he was cordially received, Welles and Cameron were still smarting at their exclusion from the mission's planning. Welles thought the assignment put the government at risk. "The extraordinary powers and authority with which Captain Meigs and Lieutenant Porter were invested in the spring of 1861 would have alarmed the country and weakened the public confidence in the administrative capacity of the Executive had the facts been known," Welles recorded in his diary.

Meigs had dinner later with Seward and learned more about the government's plans to raise an army. The secretary assured Meigs he would play a prominent yet undetermined role. He pined for promotion even as he worried about the corrosive effects of his ambition. He believed he should not pursue it too boldly. He told Montgomery Blair, the new postmaster general (and older brother of Francis Preston Blair Jr.), "I prefer in time of peace the place of Captain of Engineers, to any other on earth. But I am always at the service of the US in any place or position be they ordered."

The next few weeks were a blur for Meigs—and for almost everyone in official Washington. He attended to administrative matters, including paying back the Treasury the remainder of the secret service funds Seward had given him for the Fort Pickens mission. He accounted for it down to the penny, returning $6,229.55, with the rest having been spent on supplies, weapons, and informants. At Seward's request, he wrote memos regarding Florida and the wisdom of an offensive in Virginia. In them, he counseled a firm hand in Florida and urged caution about rushing on the offensive. He said the new army would need seasoning before confronting Southern troops. Seward gave the reports to Lincoln, who agreed with Meigs's assessment.

All seemed on track for Meigs until he learned that the Cabinet had decided to commission him a colonel, not a general. This was a blow after all he had been told about his chances. Apart from vanity, he felt that he could not serve the country very well as an infantry colonel. Better to remain a captain and serve as chief engineer of "any forward movement." Meigs thought his highest good might be to take on the job of quartermaster general, a post that opened when Joseph E. Johnston followed his native Virginia into the Confederacy.

As quartermaster general, Meigs thought, he would be able to apply his experience as a manager. He also could continue to be a scourge to the corruption that flourished in the military's vulnerable procurement system. He thought the post would be the second most important behind the commanding general, or at least that's what he wrote to his father that spring. He could barely stand the wait to learn what might come his way. Senator John Sherman of Ohio and his allies had been pressing to secure the appointment for his brother, William Tecumseh Sherman, then working as president of a streetcar company in St. Louis. For his part, W. T. Sherman did not think himself qualified to lead the department. "The only possible reason that would induce me to accept my position would be to prevent its falling into incompetent hands," he wrote his brother. "The magnitude of interest at issue now, will admit of no experiments."

It was all too much for Meigs. He decided to decline the Cabinet's appointment as colonel. Blair, his friend and admirer, said he understood. Blair was disgusted about how the promotion had been handled and had begun lobbying his Cabinet colleagues to award a more suitable post. He confided in Meigs there was still a chance he would be named quartermaster general. If it were offered, Blair told him, take it. On May 15 Meigs was on horseback, supervising the filling of a new reservoir, when he received a summons from Seward. It told him to go to the State Department immediately. Filled with pent-up excitement, Meigs turned his horse toward the city and let him run with abandon. Seward told him that Lincoln was troubled at the Cabinet's offer. The president apparently thought that it demeaned Meigs. Seward persuaded Meigs to accept the colonelcy as a step toward something greater. In the coming weeks, the new colonel of the Eleventh Infantry confronted a familiar hurdle: trouble from a slippery secretary of war.

A drizzle was falling on Washington when a note arrived from the White House. Despite the weather, it said, Lincoln wanted to follow through on plans to ride with Meigs to Great Falls and see the aqueduct. The president needed to get away from his burdens and enjoy a relaxing excursion in the woods. Meigs and Lincoln, joined by Seward, rode at an easy pace along the Potomac, chatting about the war, engineering, and diplomacy. Seward asked Meigs's opinion about a dispatch he had drafted for Charles Francis Adams, the lawmaker whom Lincoln had appointed foreign minister in London. The document urged Adams to cut off communication with Britain if its diplomats engaged in talks with the Confederates.

Meigs may have been pleased to be included in such lofty circles, but he burned to become more actively engaged in war preparations. He also yearned to punish those who had betrayed the federal government. Louisa wrote to her mother that she knew of no one who "seems inspired by the same ardor" to protect and avenge the Union. Meigs wanted the rebellion snuffed out and its leaders hanged. "His soul seems on fire with indignation at the treason of those wicked men who have laid the deep plot to overthrow our government and destroy the most noble fabric of freedom the world has ever seen," Louisa wrote.

"I tell him that the old Puritan spirit shines out in him," she continued. "I tell him he looks so dreadfully stern when he talks of the rebellion that I do not like to look at him—but he does not look more stern and relentless than he feels."

One of the "wicked men," of course, was Robert Lee. He also rued the coming of war, and with a more melancholy spirit than Meigs. In a letter to a young Northern girl who had asked for a signed photograph, Lee wrote, "It is painful to think how many friends will be separated and estranged by our unhappy disunion. May God reunite our severed bonds of friendship, and turn our hearts to peace." Lee went on: "Whatever may be the result of the contest, I foresee that the country will have to pass through a terrible ordeal, a necessary expiation, perhaps, of our national sins."

In late May Lincoln resolved to make Meigs quartermaster general, a move that was opposed by Simon Cameron, the secretary of war. Cameron was a shifty and wealthy lawmaker from Pennsylvania, a former Know-Nothing adherent who followed a loose set of ethical principles. He had not been Lincoln's first choice. He landed the War Department post as a result of Republican Party horse trading during the nominating convention. It was well known that Cameron often arranged patronage for friends, some of them thoroughly corrupt. Lincoln once asked Representative Thaddeus Stevens of Pennsylvania his opinion about Cameron's honesty. Stevens, one of the Radical Republicans who wanted no compromise in the fight against slavery, joked that he was confident that Cameron's *dishonesty* had its limits. As the story goes, he told Lincoln, "Well, I do not think he would steal a red hot stove." Cameron wanted nothing to do with Meigs, who was well known for being both hotheaded and honest. He made it clear he would block the newly minted colonel from becoming quartermaster general, despite the president's wishes. Lincoln was insistent, pressuring his team to persuade the war secretary, offering evidence of his uncanny talent for managing his unruly Cabinet, a group that historian Doris Kearns Goodwin refers to as Lincoln's "team of rivals." On June 5 he turned to General Scott, writing:

> *My dear Sir,*
>
> *Doubtless you begin to understand how disagreeable it is to me to do a thing arbitrarily, when it is unsatisfactory to others associated with me.*
>
> *I very much wish to appoint Col. Meigs Quartermaster General, and yet Sec. Cameron does not quite consent. I have come to know Col. Meigs quite well for a short acquaintance, and so far as I am capable of judging, I do not know one who combines the qualities of masculine intellect, learning, and experience of the right sort, and physical power of labor and endurance so well as he.*
>
> *I know he has great confidence in you, always sustaining so far as I have observed, your opinions against any differing ones.*

> *You will lay me under one more obligation, if you can and will use your influence to remove Sec. Cameron's objection. I scarcely need tell you I have nothing personal in this, having never seen or heard of Col. Meigs until about the end of last March.*
>
> *Your Obt. Servt,*
> *A. Lincoln*

Scott said he would be happy to comply, noting that Meigs had a "high genius" for science, engineering, and administration. The next day, newspapers carried stories predicting that Meigs would be appointed. Still, Cameron continued to delay. Finally, the president wrote a terse note on June 10 to the secretary of war: "Please let Col. Montgomery C. Meigs be appointed Quarter-Master-General."

Meigs soon received word that Cameron wanted a meeting. The secretary said he had resolved the difficulties in the way of Meigs's appointment as brigadier general and quartermaster general of the Union army. Cameron asked Meigs to remain quiet about the post until he could mollify others in the War Department who thought they deserved the job. After the meeting, Meigs prayed that "God will give me strength and wisdom for its duties so that I may discharge them with credit to myself and profit to my country."

CHAPTER 19

Building an Army

There might have been no man in the country better prepared than Meigs to be quartermaster general. Yet all his training as a soldier, builder, and manager fell short of the demands he faced in the spring and summer of 1861. The army's rapid growth was unprecedented. Only two months before, when Lincoln first appealed for volunteers, the standing force had been, by some estimates, as few as fourteen thousand men. Now more than three hundred thousand men occupied camps across the North. This outpouring triggered amazement and joy in the North that spring, "surpassing in unanimity and spirit the most sanguine expectation," as Lincoln put it. It also swamped the tiny government.

The pressure to use this force grew by the day. Many in the North demanded a swift attack, confident that the war could be won quickly. "On, to Richmond!" Horace Greeley's influential *New-York Daily Tribune* shouted. Mountains of practical problems lay in the way, such as how to feed and shelter the force. Patriotic Northerners and state governments had donated some $10 million in cash and goods, buying Meigs a little time. But those outlays had been lavish and uncoordinated and could not be sustained. The army quickly faced shortages. The new force needed a logistical machine that could feed and clothe and arm and move an unprecedented number of men for an unknown amount of time. To create that system, Meigs had to engage in what one historian has called the "art of defining and extending the possible" to provide "three big M's of warfare—materiel, movement, and maintenance." That would require improvisation, bold schemes, and perhaps most of all, imagination.

Meigs was occupied by the most basic questions. What clothing did the army have? What about boots, blankets, and tents? How would he acquire the horses and wagons needed to carry the food, guns, and ammunition? How to reconcile the need for speedy decisions against the obligation to prevent fraud and contracting abuses? And as he contemplated the army's strategic aims, Meigs thought about technology that might help win the fight, including a new kind of gunboat that could be used on the rivers in the West.

Secretary Cameron did not help much in all of this. He did not have the right experience, and Meigs did not trust him, in part because the war secretary seemed to calculate how his decisions could benefit him politically or his friends financially. Cameron was disorganized, often forgot details, became flustered, and gave too much room to untrustworthy associates, who would soon face accusations of corruption and profiteering. Meigs asserted himself and convinced Cameron to call on factories to produce rifle-muskets and 300 cast-iron cannons, 200 of them rifled. The government alone could not provide these essentials. Meigs told Cameron that, for now, speedy production was more important than quality, "the second best being good enough for practical purposes."

Like all the leading soldiers of his generation, Meigs's views on war had been shaped by Baron Henri de Jomini, a Swiss-born military thinker who served under Napoleon in France and Alexander I in Russia. He defined logistics as "the practical art of moving armies" and keeping them supplied. Meigs knew that wagons would win the war—along with trains, boats, and other means of transporting men and supplies swiftly over long stretches of difficult terrain. That meant that Meigs had to find horses, mules, and oxen. He sent telegrams around the country to order what the army needed, only to discover that defectors had absconded with most of the army's stock of animals.

———

Near the end of June 1861, Meigs began participating in the White House's war council. Lincoln wanted to decide whether the army could begin campaigning and, if so, when. Meigs joined the president, his Cabinet, Scott, and Brigadier General Joseph Mansfield, commander of forces in Washington. Scott outlined the circumstances facing them. Federal forces included perhaps fifty thousand men on either side of the Potomac in the vicinity of Washington and up to sixteen thousand more upriver, closer to the Shenandoah Valley. Confederate general Pierre G. T. Beauregard, who had unleashed the cannon attacks on Fort Sumter, commanded about twenty-four thousand men and two thousand cavalry spread across Northern Virginia in Manassas Junction, Centreville, and Fairfax. Scott said the federal recruits had better equipment than the Southerners, who faced shortages of food, money, and clothing. He said the rebel army had more experienced and disciplined soldiers, and warned that the Union's untested recruits would be susceptible to panic. They could be turned into heroes, he said, but for now, they ought to hold back.

The rest of the Cabinet disagreed. Scott asked Meigs how many men it would take to drive Beauregard out of Northern Virginia. The quartermaster put the figure at about thirty thousand, if they had a full supply of artillery. Scott asked what a full supply would be. Meigs suggested that more than usual would be better, say, three pieces for every thousand men, about ninety in all. Scott responded that was significantly too high and that fifty pieces manned by well-drilled soldiers would be enough. When the meeting broke up, Cameron asked Meigs to walk with him. Meigs praised the secretary for following through on an earlier suggestion to order new cannons. When Cameron acknowledged that he had not acquired the carriages to move the weapons, Meigs lectured him "that it was a time when someone must take the risk of being blamed, must act, and get guns, materials of war." Cameron claimed he would do whatever Meigs advised. Despite the initial resistance from Cameron, the men had found they could work well together.

The war council reconvened at the White House a few days later. This time it included Brigadier General Irvin McDowell, who had been named to lead the fight against Beauregard. The meeting did not

go well at first, at least in Meigs's view. Scott rehashed the general circumstances, adding little to their understanding, and then renewed his
case that the army should remain inert for now. Scott wanted to give
his so-called Anaconda Plan—to squeeze the South by blockading her
harbors and commerce on the Mississippi River—time to take effect.
But the rotund old general appeared overwhelmed. He confessed that
he no longer trusted his insights. He certainly did not want to bear responsibility for the direction of the war. The council rejected his caution. McDowell, Mansfield, and Seward called for action. They asked
Meigs what he thought. In his journal, the quartermaster general
spelled out his position:

> I did not think that we would ever end this war without beating
> the rebels, that they had come near us. We were, according to
> General Scott's information . . . stronger than they, better pre-
> pared, our troops better contented, better clothed, better fed,
> better paid, better armed. That here we had the most violent of
> the rebels near us; it was better to fight them here than to go far
> into an unhealthy country to fight them, and to fight them far
> from our supplies, to spend our money among enemies instead
> of our friends. To make the fight in Virginia was cheaper and
> better as the case now stood. Let them come here to be beaten.

The council decided the army would move as soon as it could. The
group asked Meigs when he could arrange sufficient transportation.
He said he would secure enough horses and wagons to support a move
to Manassas on July 8, a brash prediction that he would soon regret.

———

As the army prepared for its move, Meigs learned how deceptive appearances could be. At first, everything in his world seemed well. His
son John had returned home on furlough from West Point with the welcome news that he was at the top of his class in math and third overall
in general merit. The president and Seward favored Meigs with a visit

one morning to discuss several recent skirmishes between Federals and rebels. The capital hummed with excitement, as visitors filled the hotels and supplies arrived at the rail yards and wharves. The din of wagons, carriages, and marching troops resonated from the cobblestones. New technology added to the sense of novelty. Telegraph wires now connected various government departments in a new communication network. Overhead, a balloon aeronaut in an experimental craft could be seen taking practice flights to observe the enemy.

On Independence Day 1861, thousands of New York troops marched crisply by the White House as Lincoln and his Cabinet looked on. Meigs saw promise in the force, saying it was "a striking exhibition of the zeal of the people." That same day, the president went before Congress to make his case for all-out war. Lincoln said secessionists had forced the Federals' hand by attacking Fort Sumter without provocation. In "this act, discarding all else, they have forced upon the country the distinct issue, 'Immediate dissolution or blood.'" Lincoln called on the North to "go forward without fear and with manly hearts." He asked Congress to appropriate $400 million and give the government at least four hundred thousand fighting men. Lawmakers responded with enthusiasm, voting to give the president enough money for an army of a half million men.

In the following days, Meigs discovered that he had been too optimistic about his ability to muster animals to support the offensive. He had ordered six thousand horses and mules, but they could not get to Washington. Railcars filled with supplies jammed the depots in Washington. The quartermaster also discovered an acute shortage of wagons. Some nine thousand soldiers heading to the Shenandoah Valley could not go beyond Hagerstown, Maryland, because the army did not have enough wagons to move their supplies from a train depot into the mountains.

Meigs worked nearly nonstop, spending so much time in his office that he often slept on a cot he had installed there. McDowell's Army of Northeastern Virginia finally began moving from Washington on July 16, heading toward the rolling hills about thirty miles southwest of Washington. Everything seemed to go well enough at first. General McDowell reported the army had occupied Fairfax Court House and driven the enemy toward Centreville and Manassas. Though his men did not pursue the fleeing rebels, they captured flour, fresh beef, hospital equipment, and baggage. In truth, poor planning for the Federal's advance left the army vulnerable at almost every turn. The men had left their encampments around Washington with no wagons. Soldiers carried three days' worth of rations in their haversacks. Many of them demonstrated their lack of discipline, eating provisions with abandon and thus leaving themselves nothing for after the fighting. What's more, a number of troops let it be known they would leave the army at the moment their three-month enlistments ended.

Meigs and his son John both yearned to be in the field. John, still home on furlough from West Point, volunteered as an aide and messenger. Before John left, his father helped him buckle on his sword and pistol. Meigs had to stay at his desk in Washington for a few more days, arranging supplies and equipment for the army. He decided to "go up to the scene of action" on Sunday, July 21, when he expected the first great battle of the war to commence. Meigs arranged for his horse and carriage to be at his house at six o'clock that morning. He overslept and did not get on the road until after breakfast, about the time that much of Washington was going to church. He traveled south through Alexandria and then west toward Manassas. Along the way, he encountered ambulances carrying wounded men from a skirmish at Blackburn's Ford, Virginia. He also ran into a ragtag bunch of soldiers from Pennsylvania who had followed through on promises to go home at the end of their enlistment. While their disorderliness disgusted Meigs, he did not try to stop them. He reached Centreville in the afternoon and joined a group of senators, House members, and other spectators perched on a high, round hill that overlooked the creek known as Bull Run. Cannons thumped constantly, and clouds of smoke drifted over the verdant battlefields. Rumors circulated among the crowd that the rebels had the upper hand.

Meigs got out of his carriage and told a servant to turn it toward

Washington for an easy escape. He mounted a small bay horse that he had brought along. He rode to a wooded area, where he ran into some officers he knew and a group of soldiers they commanded. They had taken part in a flanking maneuver earlier that morning, when the army had seemed to make headway against the enemy. As Meigs prepared to move closer still to the shooting, an officer warned him that the enemy appeared to be closing in. So he stood pat. By now, Beauregard's forces had been reinforced by ten thousand troops under Johnston, Meigs's predecessor as quartermaster, who had been transferred from the Shenandoah Valley on the Manassas Gap Railroad. An officer asked Meigs to use his binoculars to examine the activity on a hill about a half mile away. He dismounted, steadied himself and watched a group of skirmishers. As he stood there, he listened to the sound of hostile shells for the first time in his career. Someone remarked that one cannon shot had recently decapitated two Union soldiers. Meigs thought the flying shells were like "someone was tossing paving stones at me."

Men around him seemed stunned by the fighting. Brigadier General Robert Schenck, a political appointee, struggled to get his brigade into line of battle. Meigs, without authority, urged a colonel to take control. Troops from forward units began falling back through their line, warning that the enemy was close behind. An officer told Meigs that he had a choice: stay put and lose his life, or follow a group of men out of the woods. "If you will lead," Meigs said decisively, "I will follow." They left the woods and joined a mass of Union soldiers streaming back to Washington. Meigs saw evidence the Union had been routed. Guns, cartridges, and demolished cannons littered the way. The stuff was so thick on the ground that he worried his horse might misstep and injure itself. Fear spurred the men to behave more like a mob than an army now. One officer, obviously drunk, infuriated Meigs with his incompetence. The quartermaster general tried to rally the frightened troops, but in the frenzy of retreat, and because he was there as a staff officer, no one listened.

He eventually found his carriage, offering it to lawmakers for the ride back to the District. Astride his horse, Meigs arrived in Washington at three o'clock in the morning. He went directly to the White House, where he had a long talk with the president. Meigs described what he had witnessed, and Lincoln told him what he had learned from the telegraph. The next day in Washington was sad and rainy. Meigs assumed that a new army would have to be re-created almost from scratch. One bright moment came when he learned that John had performed well in battle. A colonel commanding the Fourth Brigade who allowed John to serve as a volunteer aide during the fight reported that "a braver and more gallant young man was never to be in any service."

On July 23 Meigs ordered his quartermaster men back to camps occupied by Union troops before the battle. Ever frugal and practical, he wanted them to collect tents and other equipment before the rebels could get it. They returned with 175 four-horse wagonloads.

CHAPTER 20

Shoddy

The contractors came from everywhere that spring and summer of 1861, angling to sell an unprepared army everything the soldiers needed. There were contractors for bread, contractors for clothing, contractors for shoes. They provided horses, mules, forage, rail transport, steamers, coal, and construction equipment. They supplied the bullets for killing, surgical equipment to cut off mangled limbs, and ambulance wagons to take the wounded and corpses away. The men of the fast-growing army needed it all, and they needed it now, making the government an easy mark for chiselers. Many contractors operated with the cunning of butchers intent on peddling every piece of the hog. They sold sand in place of sugar, lame horses as wagon ready, and rusty muskets that the army had previously rejected as worthless. A single cattle broker made $32,000 (about $818,000 today) on one order simply by signing a contract and passing it on to a subcontractor. Shipping brokers arranged short-term leases worth more than the vessels themselves.

One product embodied the fraud and corruption accompanying the army's mobilization: *shoddy*, a fabric made of cuttings and other waste retrieved from the floors of clothing makers. Combined with glue, pounded and rolled, it had the appearance of sturdy cloth. Its lack of integrity became apparent only in the field, under a hot sun and exposed to drenching showers. It literally fell off the backs of soldiers. A muckraking reporter called it a "villainous compound" that was "no more like the genuine article than the shadow is to the substance." The material was "hastily got up at the smallest expense, and supplied to the Government at the greatest." *Shoddy* became a catchword for a national embarrassment.

A satirical song that summer captured the sentiment:

> *Close the record. O my country!*
> *Could it be you did intend,*
> *Wretches draped in shameful shoddy,*
> *To the battle-field to send?*
> *Shocking ripping, shoddy bursting*
> *Shoddy rotting in a day.*

Government employees enabled the profiteering. Horse inspectors in Washington endorsed the purchase of lame animals in exchange for cash bribes. A clothing inspector at the Schuylkill Arsenal in Pennsylvania approved vast piles of rotten stuff that later had to be condemned. A friend of Cameron's, appointed by the secretary to quickly procure goods for the army, bought useless straw hats and linen pantaloons at exorbitant prices from yet another friend.

In St. Louis, a fountain of corruption sprang forth from the army's new Western Department headquarters. In some ways, the department epitomized the blockheadedness, waste, and abuses of those early months in the war. The department was led by Major General John Frémont, the flamboyant former presidential candidate sometimes known as the Pathfinder. The Blair family had pushed Frémont on Lincoln as its particular friend. He undoubtedly had many qualities that recommended him, but strict honesty and administrative skills were not among them. Frémont leased a lavish mansion for his headquarters and surrounded himself with bodyguards—or sentinels, as he called them—in the manner of a prairie potentate. Major Justus McKinstry, a West Point graduate, served as Frémont's quartermaster. McKinstry hired others like himself: cronies of Frémont's who played loose with the government's money. Meigs permitted McKinstry to buy as he saw fit and, in an emergency, even to set the prices. Though he was energetic in arranging contracts, he cut corners. Meigs told

McKinstry and Frémont to follow proper contracting procedures whenever possible and to send proposals and bids to Washington for review. The men ignored his orders, and Frémont became brazen. In the summer of 1861, he went over Meigs's head and complained to Representative Francis P. "Frank" Blair Jr. of Missouri that he was not getting enough support from Washington. Meigs caught wind of the complaints after Blair spelled them out in a note to Postmaster General Montgomery Blair, his brother, who showed the letter to Meigs.

The allegations irritated Meigs, who had passed on every request for funding to the Treasury with alacrity. He wrote Frank Blair that he had purposefully given McKinstry room to pay whatever he thought was necessary to acquire needed goods under the pressures of mobilization. He shared a guiding principle for the Quartermaster General Department at the time: "the most rapid possible concentration of overwhelming force" by the United States. "Tell General Frémont that no man more than myself desires to sustain him; no one is more ready to take a responsibility to assist him," Meigs wrote. "The general is charged with *saving the country*. The country will be very careful to approve his measures, and will judge his mistakes, if any, very tenderly if successful."

Despite Frémont, Meigs's reputation for competence spread widely that summer. George Templeton Strong, a member of the new United States Sanitary Commission, a volunteer relief organization, thought he was the ablest man he had met in the capital. "He is an exceptional and refreshing specimen of sense and promptitude, unlike most of our high military officials. There's not a fibre of red tape in his constitution." The quartermaster worked hard not to be dogmatic about bidding, and he accepted a certain amount of extravagance during a crisis. But he would not tolerate fraud or theft—evidence of which came his way after Frémont granted a group of Chicago citizens the authority to help outfit new regiments. While making their arrangements, the volunteers discovered irregularities in the purchase of horses by Frémont's quartermaster agents. It seems that the agents were paying $75 and charging the government up to $110 for the animals. They took their concerns to Meigs, who launched one of several government reviews of the western operations.

Those reviews provided cautionary tales of what could go wrong. Contractors had double billed for forage on deals awarded without competition. Frémont had ordered his men to accept a load of rotten cast-off blankets for sick and dying men. He personally arranged construction of lavish brick barracks, at unknown expense. He and his subordinates also made more than two hundred irregular appointments to his bodyguard ranks. Among them was a "director of music"—an engineer with the rank of captain. By August, only a few months into the war, the Western Department was millions of dollars in debt.

All the spending seemed to do little to help where it mattered most, the fight against the rebels. Frémont was blamed for failing to give adequate support to General Nathaniel Lyon who, on a mission to clear Missouri of secessionist soldiers, was defeated at the Battle of Wilson's Creek. More than twelve hundred Federals were killed, wounded, or missing in furious fighting on August 10. Lyon was the first Union general killed in action.

The problems in St. Louis moved beyond procurement. At the end of August, Frémont declared martial law, confiscated the property of secessionists, and freed their slaves. Lincoln did not want this now, not at all. The president had worked hard to keep Missouri and other border states in the Union, and Frémont's declaration outraged the state's conservative Unionist Party members. The White House resolved to investigate matters in St. Louis and, on September 10, dispatched Montgomery Blair and Meigs to take stock. The men found an odd scene. Sycophants milled about Frémont's headquarters. McKinstry, recently jumped three ranks to brigadier general, spoke with them at a rapid clip and seemed untrustworthy. The citizens they spoke to described Frémont as more intent on launching a dramatic mission on the Mississippi than on protecting Missouri. They said he tolerated no dissent or criticism.

Montgomery Blair sent an urgent telegram to the president, imploring him to consider giving power in the state to Meigs. "Things are deplorable, and action must be decisive and prompt to save the state," the note said. Lincoln held off taking such a move. The day before their return to Washington, Frémont ordered the arrest of Rep. Frank Blair, a volunteer colonel, after discovering that he had criticized him in letters to Washington. Meigs and Montgomery Blair returned to Washington and went to the White House, where Blair fulminated about his brother's arrest. Meigs described Frémont as "prodigal of money, unscrupulous, surrounded by villains, inaccessible to the people, and ambitious."

Frémont knew trouble was coming his way. He fired McKinstry, making him a scapegoat. That did not deceive anyone. Major Robert A. Allen, a veteran quartermaster officer who replaced McKinstry, dove into the books. He found orders worth hundreds of thousands of dollars that were "informal, irregular, and not authorized by regulations or law." Allen called on Meigs to take strong steps. "If the reckless expenditures in this department are not arrested by a stronger arm than mine," Allen wrote, "the Quartermaster's Department will be wrecked in Missouri alone." Frémont lost his post that fall. More punishment was in store for McKinstry.

———

Congressional overseers, along with an investigative panel appointed by Lincoln, began to follow evidence of corruption. The most public of these reviews came from a select committee formed that summer at the request of Representative Charles H. Van Wyck, an anticorruption activist from New York. Van Wyck was a brawler disguised as an intellectual. The year before, he had accused Southerners of being cowards who burned slaves at the stake. When called out to fight by a representative from Mississippi, he proclaimed: "I travel anywhere without fear of anyone." In February 1861 three men attacked him as he walked on the north side of the Capitol. His life was saved when a notebook and a folded copy of the *Congressional Globe*—the record of debates in Congress—stopped a knife from plunging into his chest. Van Wyck punched one of the attackers and then shot another.

His committee's mandate included any contracts for provisions, supplies, transportation, and services. Congress authorized them to determine if the contracts had been properly advertised and bid, and whether anyone received inflated profits. The committee had authority to call witnesses and subpoena records. Its five members indulged in the usual aggression and hyperbole that transformed every oversight effort on Capitol Hill into a political fight. They focused much of their attention on St. Louis during Frémont's tenure and the activity of McKinstry and his aides. The men also drew on the work of the Lincoln commission, which was examining the debts of the Frémont operations. They collected two thousand pages of documents and testimony that showed wrongdoing across the country, involving people in every political corner. The abuses they exposed went far beyond anything that even the skeptical Meigs had suspected.

In the rush to war, McKinstry arranged to pay inflated prices to a single St. Louis firm, Child, Pratt & Fox. In one case, he paid 35 cents for thousands of mess pans that cost the firm 29½ cents. He paid 65 cents for camp kettles costing 42½ cents. The list of items bought from Child, Pratt & Fox at exorbitant rates went on and on: picket pins (for tethering horses), overcoats, pants, blue blouses, cavalry equipment. More than $800,000 went to the firm, at up to 40 percent profit. The army eventually charged McKinstry with corrupt practices as a public official. After much deliberation, a court-martial found him guilty of twenty-six transgressions. Lincoln himself dismissed McKinstry from the service.

The contracting committee then bore down on Meigs. It claimed to find evidence that he had tolerated Frémont's practice of paying railroads whatever they asked, much to the detriment of the Treasury and the public interest. It focused on one transaction involving a thousand horses. The horses had been transported by rail at substantial cost from Pittsburgh to Springfield, Illinois. The lawmakers expressed dismay. Why would the quartermaster pay to ship horses west on the railroad when they could have been just as easily purchased at less cost in the Midwest? The committee called the episode a disgrace. They got it wrong, though, according to a plausible account from Meigs. The army had sent the horses to Washington to move artillery before the cannons arrived. Meigs then shipped them west to avoid the great cost of forage. The committee eventually backed off and acknowledged the remarkable efforts of Meigs and his department.

Van Wyck gave voice to popular resentment about the corruption in general, saying that "harpies" and "vultures" had descended on the Treasury at the war's outset. "The mania for stealing seems to have run through all the relations of Government—almost from the general to the drummer boy," he said. Lincoln was among the angry. With his encouragement, Congress enacted the False Claims Act of 1863, a landmark law that gave whistle-blowers a reward for bringing forward evidence of contracting abuses. Sometimes called "Lincoln's Law," it remains one of the government's key enforcement tools against fraud today.

CHAPTER 21

"Hard Work and Cold Calculation"

The challenges facing the Quartermaster Department took on astonishing dimensions. Amid the confusion, corruption, and fear, Meigs and his men had to create a supply system that would satisfy the highest generals and the lowliest of volunteers, along with newspaper columnists and lawmakers ready to pounce on any sign of wrongdoing. They encountered an endless flow of obstacles with too few men spread across a rugged continent, always under tactical, strategic, and political deadlines. They had to succeed for the simple reason that the Union would lose the war without them.

Much has been written about the tactics and glory of battles. But as Napoleon said, an army marches on its stomach. Before a commander can even hope to attack, destroy, or simply wear down an enemy, he must first be able to deliver 3,000 calories a day to each soldier. He must keep them warm and healthy. Then he has to be able to move them from point A to point B in a reasonable amount of time. There is no glamour in this, only "hard work and cold calculation." Meigs embraced all of this as his lot. "The great part of a General's labor history does not record," Meigs wrote to his son John in November 1861. "The fighting, the direction, even the planning of the battles occupies in the whole seconds only to the hours of labor involved in the preparation & execution of marches."

Regulations mandated that the Quartermaster Department provide transportation for all men, food, weapons, and materiel, a list that grew as the war expanded. It supplied horses to haul artillery, cavalry, and wagon trains, as well as the forage to feed them. It built barracks and hospitals. It furnished uniforms, socks, shoes, needles, thread, pots, canteens, and other goods to the men. The department's men also constructed and repaired roads, bridges, railroads, and military telegraph lines. They chartered ships and steamers, providing the coal to fuel them and the docks and wharves to unload them. They paid all expenses relating to military operations, except those assigned specifically to other departments.

The department had changed little for many years before the war. Until Joseph Johnston's brief ten-month stint, the department had had only one quartermaster general in four decades. With secession, the authorized staff of thirty-seven officers and seven military storekeepers lost eight defectors to the Confederacy, Johnston included. A third of the remaining men had been in their jobs for more than two decades. New recruits learned on the job. Meigs often complained that he did not have enough people to handle the ocean of paperwork behind the logistics. This was not mere griping. More than two-thirds of the handbook of army regulations at the time focused on supply forms and procedures. Those rules, applied with discipline, served as grease that lubricated the enormous, powerful war machine just then sputtering to life. Congress saw that something had to be done. So it authorized quartermaster captains for every brigade, while also increasing the permanent force in Washington with two dozen additional officers. The department got a new colonel, two lieutenants, and four majors. It was not enough but it was something.

The Union retained experienced men who understood the nuances of supply systems—so far as they could be known in the midst of such rapid change. A dozen of the most important quartermaster officers came to their posts after training at West Point. They knew their business better than their boss, at least at first, and provided service as vital to military operations as harnesses are to a four-horse wagon. Without their determined efforts, the war machine would go haywire, pulling in a thousand directions. The supply system relied heavily on depots, and Meigs gave his depot officers room to run them and their field operations as they wanted, so long as they followed his rules and principles. He shouldered responsibility for ensuring that they had enough supplies.

From the first, he sheltered his men from political interference. He warned Cameron away from a plan to replace clerks with the war secretary's handpicked people. He even pushed back on job recommendations from the president and the first lady. The department had enough to worry about without political meddling. The surge in spending and acquisition had no precedent. In the first year of the war, spending shot up eighteenfold to $174 million annually. It kept rising in each of the next four years. By contrast, expenditures by the Quartermaster Department in the war with Mexico had jumped only eightfold to $21 million.

The outlays by the department now far exceeded any other category of spending in the *entire* federal government. Those were huge sums at a time when skilled artisans such as carpenters earned less than $2 a day.

Quartermaster employees needed to be entrepreneurial, dogged, and diplomatic. In every theater of war, at every supply depot and in the cramped offices they occupied in Washington, they engaged in a complex dance with clothing makers, weapons factories, railroads, providers of forage, and many others. They made up many of the steps as they went along. Among the best of Meigs's subordinates was Rufus Ingalls, who became a force of his own during the war. He wrote later: "It must be borne in mind that war on a scale inaugurated by this rebellion was decidedly new to us, if not the civilized world . . . It required the united abilities and exertions of our whole department, aided by the loyal producers and manufacturers of the country to meet the public wants; and, if there were temporary failures, the department should stand excused, for its labors have been unparalleled and gigantic."

To be sure, Federals had more to draw on than their Southern counterparts did. During the long boom after the Mexican War, the North's economic growth far surpassed that of the Southern states. Cotton textile manufacturing in particular soared, with production more than doubling since 1850. Yet the North's industrial economy, like American society in general, was still in a "gangling, adolescent state" and had far to go before it reached maturity. For all its growth, it remained diffuse and largely uncoordinated. Production lagged far behind what the growing army needed to stay alive and moving.

New technology helped Meigs overcome certain challenges. Consider Isaac M. Singer's sewing machine, which eventually helped the Union surmount the limitations of an industry in which seamstresses stitched most clothing by hand, or Gordon McKay's machine for stitching soles onto boots and shoes. Before the war, few people understood or valued the power of these innovations. Meigs's embrace of them—to produce forage caps, shoes, and cavalry boots in bulk—opened the way for their adoption almost universally. Sensitive to untapped possibilities of such technology, Meigs took time early in the war to personally inspect McKay's shoes. He overruled subordinates who dismissed machine-made boots as a passing fad. Northern factories went on to produce nearly a half million pairs. The army found that they typically lasted eight times longer than handmade shoes. Gordon McKay went on to become a shoemaking tycoon.

The quartermaster system hurtled into existence like a railroad engine being built on the run. It would soon dwarf all other industrial enterprises in the nation, including as many as 130,000 civilian participants. In superintending this colossal endeavor, Meigs provided momentum to the nation's economy for years to come. As historian James McPherson wrote, "In these and many other ways, Meigs and his Bureau left a permanent mark on American society."

For now, in the summer of 1861, Meigs still had to ensure that Union troops received guns to shoot and pants to wear and food to eat. And that was far from a sure thing.

———

In late July, Meigs learned that federal officials in charge of buying weapons asked Congress for only $2.5 million, a small fraction of the spending needed to arm the fastest-growing army in the world. Blame for the inadequate request lay with the dysfunctional Ordnance Bureau, which epitomized the organizational chaos during the war's first few months. The bureau's chief soon lost his job. His replacement, Lieutenant Colonel James W. Ripley, earned the nickname Ripley Van Winkle for his apparent inability to rise to the demands. Congress had the sense to appropriate $10 million. Though Meigs's portfolio did not include buying weapons, he took it upon himself to dispatch an agent to Europe to acquire a hundred thousand muskets, twenty thousand sabers, and ten thousand revolvers and carbines. At the same time, the quartermaster scrambled to address a shortage of clothing for the burgeoning army, which had already distributed everything it had. This was not merely a matter of keeping the men warm. Union troops died by friendly fire because of soldiers' inability to identify friend or enemy. Meigs ordered the irregular clothing replaced as soon as possible with blue uniforms made under exact specifications. (His demand for uniformity and efficiency left the nation with a novel legacy that has come down to this day: small, medium, and large sizes.)

"The nation is in extremity. Troops, thousands, wait for clothes to take the field. Regiments have been ordered here without clothes. Men go to guard in drawers for want of pantaloons. The necessity is far greater than I imagined," Meigs wrote. "I had no idea of the destitution, this want of preparation by this Department when I took charge of it. It has been forced upon me by gradual proof . . . We must bear the clamor of fools who would pick flaws in a pin while the country hangs in the balance."

Waste compounded Meigs's challenge. Infantry soldiers often abandoned heavy clothing on warm days. He wrote with frustration about a large, new regiment that cast aside eight hundred coats on a single march, only to find themselves freezing days later in a cold rain. The improvidence vexed the quartermaster, but he attributed it to inexperience. He adopted the pragmatic view that winning trumped his own ingrained sense of frugality. In a report to War Department leaders, Meigs wrote: "That an army is wasteful is certain, but it is more wasteful to allow a soldier to sicken and die for want of the blanket or knapsack, which he has thoughtlessly thrown away in the heat of the march or the fight than to again supply him on the first opportunity with these articles indispensable to health and efficiency."

Adjusting his view did not initially change circumstances in the textile mills, which simply could not keep up with the army's extraordinary needs. That was due in part to the nature of the garment industry. Seamstresses, who comprised one of the largest workforces in the nation, sewed by hand at home or in small workshops, generally earning about $4 a week. They fought against the adoption of the sewing machine, which they feared would drive down their already meager pay. Finding enough blankets posed an even harder challenge than providing clothing. Army regulations called for each soldier to receive two blankets every five years. Gray, wool, and warm, they were substantial affairs that weighed about five pounds each. The problem was that no one manufactured enough of them. Meigs reached out again to foreign suppliers, buying two hundred thousand blankets from brokers in England. In something of an experiment, he also turned to French contractors for entire sets of clothing and camp gear for ten thousand men—uniforms, belts, knapsacks, blankets, tents, cooking utensils, and more. He paid the same prices as the French army, about $800,000 in all. Meigs thought the sturdy equipage might serve as a model for the US Army.

Though undeniably creative, these efforts triggered political grief. Just as he had been criticized for hiring foreign painters at the Capitol, the America-first crowd now blasted him for spending tax dollars abroad. The Board of Trade in Boston reached out to Cameron and predicted dire consequences, including widespread unemployment and nothing less than the ruin of the American economy. The newspapers injected energy into the dispute by reporting incorrectly that the deal was worth up to $60 million. A younger Meigs surely would have overreacted to the criticism and drafted one of the long defensive screeds that had become a hallmark of his management style. Now he wrote a relatively temperate note to Cameron, explaining that he had no choice. He did include a dig at the disgruntled merchants. "Should the Board of Trade be right in its opinion, and the domestic manufactories be able to supply regulation cloth enough before cloth can be imported from Europe, it will be gladly purchased at any reasonable price and made up into clothing," he wrote.

The complaints from the industry eventually had an effect. Congress prohibited most foreign purchases for the rest of the war. Congress got involved with procurement in other ways, too. In an effort to crack down on fraud and waste, lawmakers mandated that supply officers create a paper record of every verbal agreement, appear before a magistrate, and swear to the authenticity of each deal. Though the measures seemed in accord with Meigs's devotion to good government, he recoiled at them. He thought it folly to even try to eliminate all corruption. Meigs wrote to the chairman of the Senate Military Affairs Committee, saying that such a law would have the unintended effect of choking off the sprawling supply apparatus he was trying to bring to life. To defeat the rebels, the federal government needed less bureaucracy and more unrestrained fighting. He used his note as a chance to lecture.

"[If] the conditions in regard to contracts imposed by this bill become law, the country may as well at once yield to the Southern rebels all they ask. They are directed by one mind, prompt, strong, determined, bold. They are not distracted by divided counsel; are not restrained by rules, regulations, laws, customs, precedents, all the paraphernalia which the good sense of the people has designated as red tape."

The Quartermaster's Department made headway throughout the fall of 1861, and by the end of the year, the army supply system had virtually supplanted the state and volunteer organizations. Meigs standardized contracting practices and imposed rules for army buying that generally required advertisements in advance, sealed bids, and the award of work to the lowest bidders. The results showed. The Union army now fed, sheltered, and outfitted nearly seven hundred thousand men. It had acquired tens of thousands of horses and mules, along with harnesses, wagons, and mountains of feed. Meigs even found money to fund the creation of an experimental balloon corps for military surveillance.

The nation's cottage industries, meanwhile, started working more closely with the military. "There never was an army in the world that began to be supplied as well as ours is," General McDowell told Congress in December. Despite the successes, new problems emerged. The rush to war spurred a triple threat to the North's economy, including a mountain of debt, rising prices, and a diminished Treasury. Even as Meigs surmounted the supply challenges, he prepared to tell Congress that the army was running out of money. That meant the army might soon be unable to pay for new expeditions, or even provide ample forage to the cavalry, artillery, or baggage trains. Civilian teamsters might desert the service unless they were paid, and then the army could be paralyzed at the moment when the Union needed it most to move and fight.

CHAPTER 22

"The War Cannot Be Long"

Major General George B. McClellan, the North's greatest hope in the early days of the war, soared into prominence after a string of small but encouraging victories in western Virginia. In the summer of 1861, he had been brought to Washington by Lincoln, who wanted a leader capable of giving direction to the Federal force. Lincoln named him commander of the new Army of the Potomac and then, after Scott retired in the fall, general-in-chief of all Union forces.

McClellan came from a wealthy family in Philadelphia. He attended West Point, joined the Army Corps of Engineers, served with distinction in Mexico, and then worked as a railroad executive. At thirty-four, he had a thick mop of hair and a lavish mustache. Because he was a compact man, some called him Little Mac, not always in a flattering way. He burned with ambition and spoke cavalierly about conflict. "The war cannot be long," he told admirers at a dinner in Philadelphia, adding: "It may be desperate." McClellan had one especially outstanding quality. He relished the work of whipping his two hundred thousand green soldiers into a fighting force. Week after week, he put the men in blue through their drills. In turn, they loved their leader's style, his direct demeanor, and his abundant energy.

In those first few months, Meigs shared the foot soldiers' enthusiasm for McClellan. But his confidence wavered as the year ended with no movement by the army. Meigs could not understand the commander's apparent unwillingness, in the face of the public clamor, to launch the giant force against Richmond, Virginia. He did not like McClellan's apparent arrogance or his disregard for the nation's leaders. McClellan showed no inkling that he understood or cared about the financial impact of his delay. Meigs estimated that the Army of the Potomac cost the Treasury $1,000 a year per man to sustain—$200 million in all— whether they were drilling or fighting. At the same time, no one outside McClellan's inner circle seemed to know what he intended to do, not even Lincoln. The president once was turned away by a McClellan aide who claimed his boss was sleeping. After the New Year, word seeped out that McClellan lay in bed, ill with typhoid, and yet he refused to cede control to subordinates.

Meigs was feeling surly about all of this when he received an unexpected visitor at his office. It was the president, and he was distressed. Lincoln lowered himself into a chair near the fireplace. It was January 10, 1862, one of the lowest moments of the war for Lincoln, Meigs, and the Union itself. "General, what shall I do? The people are impatient," Lincoln said. "[Secretary of Treasury] Chase has no money, and he tells me he can raise no more; the General of the Army has typhoid fever. The bottom is out of the tub. What shall I do?" Meigs counseled change. He told Lincoln that if McClellan had typhoid fever, it would take him six weeks to recover. Rebel forces could attack any day. Meigs said the president had to consider replacing McClellan and getting on with the war. He urged Lincoln to gather his generals. "Send for them to meet you soon and consult with them," Meigs said. "Perhaps you may select the responsible commander for such an event."

Lincoln agreed and moved quickly. He called for an emergency war council and asked Meigs to arrange for McDowell and Franklin, both division commanders under McClellan, to meet him at the White House. They convened that night and listened as the president repeated what he had told Meigs earlier. The president told the men that "he would like to borrow" the army if McClellan did not want to use it. Meigs, McDowell, and Franklin followed up with another meeting at Meigs's home to discuss the possible movement of thirty thousand men to the York River in Virginia. They concluded it could be done, but it would take up to six weeks to arrange enough boats to move the men and their supplies. When they returned to the White House for yet another war council, Lincoln said he had heard from McClellan. He had caught wind of the discussions to replace him and suddenly felt better. Lincoln said McClellan would attend a planning session the next day.

This gathering was dispiriting. McClellan took a seat near Meigs and Blair, chatting with them quietly as Lincoln and Secretary Chase shared a whispered conversation. Lincoln pointed to a map and asked McDowell to describe the idea for a campaign that he and Franklin had discussed with Meigs. McClellan was sullen and curt.

"You are entitled to have any opinion you please!" he said.

Chase, with his eyes on McClellan, said the group wanted to learn what the major general had in mind for the federal forces. Everybody turned toward McClellan, who remained silent, his head hanging down. After a long pause, the general spoke up. He said he had no idea what Chase was talking about, and, in any case, he did not recognize him as his boss. He lapsed again into silence.

Meigs moved his chair close to McClellan's and whispered, "The President evidently expects you to speak. Can you not promise some movement towards Manassas? You are strong."

"I cannot move on them with as great a force as they have," McClellan replied.

"Why? You have near two hundred thousand men; how many have they?"

"Not less than a hundred seventy-five thousand, according to my advices," McClellan said.

"Do you think so?" Meigs asked. "The president expects something from you."

"If I tell him my plans, they will be in the *New York Herald* tomorrow morning. He can't keep a secret; he will tell them to [Lincoln's son Tad]."

"That is a pity, but he is the president, the commander in chief," Meigs said. "He has a right to know. It is not respectful to sit mute when he so clearly requires you to speak. He is superior to all."

McClellan finally shared a few details, sketching in the outlines of his operations. Lincoln pressed for more. Getting nothing, he called the war council to a close. On the way out, McClellan approached Lincoln. He urged the president to trust him, saying that if he "would leave military affairs to me, I would be responsible, that I would bring matters to a successful issue and free him from all his troubles."

―――――

As the Cabinet struggled with McClellan, it also had to address the incompetence of Secretary of War Simon Cameron. Lincoln and his advisors worried about the corruption that had flourished among War Department contractors. They arranged to get him out of the way, sending him to Saint Petersburg as minister to Russia. Meigs knew the change was necessary. He saw Cameron's limitations as a manager up close. He nevertheless offered his thanks before Cameron left town. Meigs appreciated the latitude the war secretary had given him and the fact that Cameron supported him now—quite a shift given his professed dislike of Meigs just months before.

The quartermaster general also appreciated Cameron's outspoken support for using freed slaves to fight the rebels. At the risk of upsetting the president, Cameron told a regiment of soldiers in Illinois that he supported putting guns in the hands of former slaves and letting them do God's work. In a draft of his annual report, the war secretary went even further. "It is clearly a right of the Government to arm slaves when it may become necessary as it is to take gunpowder from the enemy," he wrote in a document shared with the press. Meigs admired Cameron for taking a principled stand on the matter at a time when Lincoln, Seward, and others aimed to put off questions about the slaves as too politically charged. He understood Cameron's passion now, in a way that had escaped him only a few years before, when his self-absorption blinded him to the true significance of slavery to the nation's future.

The war had given Meigs a new perspective, and he now considered the liberation of slaves part of a "great social revolution." As black refugees flocked to the capital, his men built housing, schools, and hospitals for them. The quartermaster general saw former slaves distinguish themselves as laborers, teamsters, and soldiers. It occurred to him finally that they too might want to contribute to the Union cause. As a practical matter, Meigs concluded there was no choice. In the first year of the war, in a more discreet way than Cameron, Meigs had begun advocating for the military's embrace of escaped slaves. In one report, Meigs wrote: "In this work the loyal inhabitants of the country, white or black, must be compelled to assist, and it is impossible to cast aside the millions of recruits who will offer themselves for the work, accustomed to the climate, inured to the labor, acquainted with the country, and animated by the strong desire not merely for political but for personal liberty."

Cameron's replacement was Edwin M. Stanton, a lawyer who had served as attorney general under President Buchanan. Stanton was a large man with a salt-and-pepper beard and unkempt, thinning hair. He had an insolent demeanor and held savage opinions about the nation's leaders, privately denouncing the Lincoln administration after Bull Run. He once described Lincoln as "the original gorilla." The press and public knew little of such remarks. Northerners honored Stanton for his performance during the secession crisis, when he worked tirelessly to hold the government together. Newspapers hailed his appointment as a wise move by Lincoln. "The army will move on now, even if it goes to the devil."

At first, Meigs chafed at the change. He knew Stanton as a Union Democrat and thought the war secretary capable of talking out of both sides of his mouth. Stanton could be harsh, even to those he liked. Meigs's disapproval soon turned to admiration, as the tectonic pressures the men faced together produced a warm relationship. Stanton generally gave Meigs room to confront problems as he wished. Stanton blessed Meigs's willingness, for instance, to coerce and counsel army leaders. As a consequence, the quartermaster imposed his will far into the field. During a meeting with Meigs in early 1862, Stanton collapsed. He had maintained an untenable schedule. Meigs told him to go home. Stanton said he did not have the strength to move. A physician was called, and for the next three hours, Meigs stayed at his side, keeping watch. The two men came to rely heavily on each other. A War Department clerk once told a story that offers insights about why Stanton valued Meigs. It seems a prominent senator went to Stanton in a full fury about something the quartermaster had done.

"Stanton!" he roared out. "I wonder how a lawyer, as you are, can keep that Meigs where he is! Why, he pays no regard to either law or justice."

Mr. Stanton looked at his excited visitor and replied dryly, "Now, don't you say a word against Meigs. He is the most useful man I have about me. True, he isn't a lawyer, and therefore he does many things that I wouldn't dare to do."

"Then why in the name of heaven do you let him do them?" demanded the senator.

"Somebody has to do them," the secretary answered quietly.

———

Meigs applauded the reforms that came with Stanton, including new rules governing War Department practices. Unlike Cameron, Stanton prohibited visitors to his home and curbed the access of lobbyists and lawmakers in the department, who previously had wandered through the offices at will. He also limited Congress's access to him to just one day a week. Contractors and other visitors also had a single day for lobbying and other business. Stanton reserved the rest of the week to run the war. Stanton also pushed to snuff out corruption. He told Meigs to order quartermaster officers to report any signs of fraud. And he brought a sharp focus on McClellan, urging him to reopen all Baltimore and Ohio Railroad lines and to clear the lower Potomac of Confederate batteries that were harassing Union ships.

To ensure that Stanton's directives to McClellan took effect, Lincoln himself issued Special War Order No. 1, on January 31, 1862, calling for the movement of army and naval forces against the rebels, to commence on February 22. He followed up with another order that called on the Army of the Potomac to seize the railroad at Manassas

Junction in Virginia. In response, McClellan asked for more time, telling the president he had a plan to attack Richmond by way of the lower Chesapeake Bay. Lincoln asked his general to provide a convincing argument that he had a better plan. McClellan pressed his case, and Lincoln yielded. And so began preparations for one of the most ambitious movements in the war: the Peninsula Campaign. For any chance of success, Meigs and his Quartermaster Department would have to pull off logistical feats on a scale the world had never seen.

Montgomery C. Meigs of the Army Corps of Engineers and Louisa Rodgers Meigs, the daughter of Commodore John Rodgers, had been married nearly two decades when they posed for these portraits. M. C. Meigs was called on by Abraham Lincoln to help build and sustain the Union force during the Civil War.

Children of then-Lieutenant Montgomery Meigs and Louisa Meigs on a donkey cart in Detroit. The children probably are Mary, Charles, Montgomery, and John.

An Army engineer, Montgomery Meigs also drew and painted with a sure hand. This is a view of a neighborhood in northwest Washington, DC, painted in 1850.

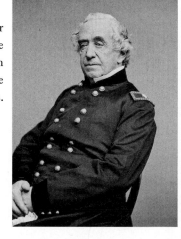

Joseph G. Totten was a soldier, scientist, and engineer who became chief of the Army Corps of Engineers. He saw promise in Montgomery Meigs and assigned him to conduct a water survey for the nation's capital. The two men became close allies and friends.

Jefferson Davis served as the secretary of war in the 1850s, a time when he showed great faith in Montgomery Meigs and his vision for the Capitol extension, its great dome, and the Washington Aqueduct. Davis boosted Meigs's career, and the two remained close friends until the Civil War. Then Meigs wanted Davis punished for leaving the Union.

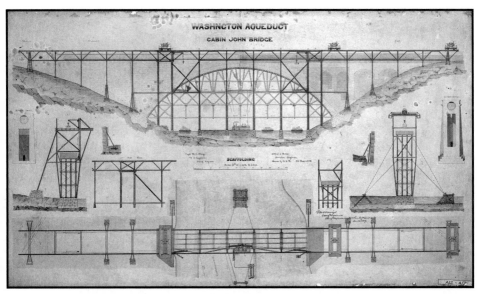

This gorgeous depiction shows the remarkable aqueduct bridge over Cabin John Creek—with the longest masonry arch in the world at the time. It was drawn by Alfred Rives, a talented engineer who helped design the bridge under Meigs's supervision, and who joined the rebels during the Civil War.
(WASHINGTON AQUEDUCT, US ARMY CORPS OF ENGINEERS)

In the mid-nineteenth century, Washington was striving to become a true metropolis. The most important and symbolic construction project in the 1850s and early 1860s was the Capitol extension and its great dome. Montgomery Meigs contributed to the designs and supervised the work; he fought with Capitol architect Thomas Ustick Walter over credit for the work and designs.
(UNITED STATES COMMISSION ON ART)

This bridge illustrates Meigs's quest to innovate. The bridge relies on aqueduct water pipes to serve as structural support.

John B. Floyd followed Jefferson Davis as secretary of war. A proponent of slavery and former governor of Virginia, Floyd was unscrupulous and untrustworthy. He eventually banished Meigs from Washington, not long before joining the Confederacy. Floyd died in disgrace after fleeing the fight at Fort Donelson.

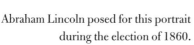
Abraham Lincoln posed for this portrait during the election of 1860.

Wagons were a key component to the Union logistical machine.
Here a wagon train crosses the Rappahannock River, near Fredericksburg.

Care was mixed for both Union and
Confederate soldiers. This is a field
hospital for Union soldiers who fought
at Savage's Station in 1862, during the
Peninsula Campaign.

John Meigs, the oldest child of Louisa and Montgomery Meigs, got into West Point with help from his
father. He could not wait to go to war and volunteer
to fight at Bull Run during a break from school.

President Lincoln and General George McClellan confer in a tent on the battlefield of Antietam. Lincoln wanted more aggression from McClellan, who sometimes blamed the Quartermaster Department for failing to deliver enough supplies.

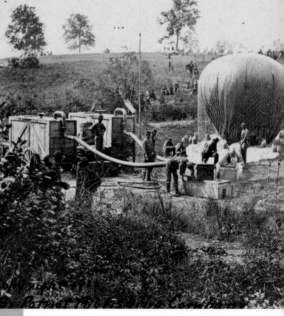

Gas-filled balloons manned by specially trained aeronauts were used during the Civil War for aerial reconnaissance of enemy movements. Montgomery Meigs helped arrange funding for the Union army's balloon corps.

Edwin Stanton replaced Simon Cameron as secretary of war in early 1862. He was a harsh, driven man who quickly improved the operation of the War Department. He showed great faith in Meigs, who in turn came to admire Stanton.

Quartermaster General Montgomery Meigs sat for this photo during the war. On July 5, 1864, he received a brevet promotion to major general.

Secretary of State William Seward, a charming and warmhearted former governor of New York, became a strong supporter of then Captain Montgomery Meigs before the Civil War. Seward introduced Meigs to President Lincoln, urging the president make use of him.

The Union war machine relied heavily on its expanding network of railroads, which proved a decisive logistical weapon. Crucial to the success of the railroads was the military railroad construction corps. Corps workers rebuilt this bridge over Potomac Creek in Virginia in just days.

Carrying food to soldiers was one of the many tasks of the Quartermaster Department. Keeping them fed was essential to victory. This photograph shows Union soldiers of the Sixth New York Artillery in front of a log kitchen cabin at Brandy Station, Virginia, in April 1864.

Montgomery Meigs and his Quartermaster Department struggled for much of the war to keep up with the demand for horses. Part of the challenge was providing enough forage. Some officers wore out the horses through mistreatment. In some cases, as shown in this photograph at Gettysburg, the horses became casualties of the fighting.

When Montgomery Meigs returned to Washington, DC, in January 1864 after an assignment in Chattanooga, he visited the Capitol to see how work on the dome was progressing. He saw this scene, captured by photo shortly after the statue *Freedom* was installed.

General Robert E. Lee was a West Point graduate and US Army Corps of Engineers officer. After entering the Corps of Engineers himself, Meigs worked with Lee in 1837 to find ways to improve navigation on the Mississippi River near St. Louis. They remained friendly until the Civil War, when Lee joined the Confederacy. Meigs started Arlington National Cemetery on the land previously owned by Lee's family.

Ulysses S. Grant became lieutenant general of Union forces in 1864. Grant's Overland Campaign that year relied on the Quartermaster Department. He later wrote: "There never was a corps better organized than was the quartermaster's corps with the Army of the Potomac in 1864."

These wagons, parked near Brandy Station, Virginia, suggest the enormity of the Union logistical effort in the Eastern theater during the war.

The Overland Campaign in May and June 1864 resulted in appalling numbers of casualties. These men are preparing to bury Union soldiers in Fredericksburg, Virginia.

The landing at Belle Plain, Virginia, was incredibly busy during the last year of the war. It managed incoming supplies and shipped out the wounded to Washington, DC.

Pontoon bridges greatly increased the Union army's mobility. The pontoons were pulled on wheels until they were needed and then were placed in the river, anchored and covered with timbers. This bridge was on the James River, near Jones' Landing, Virginia.

This is a commissary depot and supply wagon train at Cedar Level, Virginia, during the siege of Petersburg, Virginia.

Montgomery Meigs was a forceful advocate of employing freed slaves in the fight against the South. These men are working at the Quartermaster's wharf in Alexandria, Virginia.

Montgomery Meigs respected General William T. Sherman, depicted here, who had great confidence in the quartermaster. It was said that upon receiving one dispatch from Meigs—scratched out in his wretched script—Sherman endorsed it with these words: "The handwriting of this report is that of General Meigs, and I therefore approve of it, but I cannot read it."

Union soldiers tear up railroad track before leaving Atlanta, Georgia, on Sherman's great march to the sea.

As bodies stacked up in the spring of 1864, it fell to Montgomery Meigs and the Quartermaster Department to bury them. Meigs led the way in the creation of a national cemetery on the Arlington, Virginia, property of his former colleague, Robert E. Lee.

The troops of William T. Sherman remove ammunition from Fort McAllister near the end of the March to the Sea. Montgomery Meigs considered the Quartermaster refit of the army a short time later at Savannah, Georgia, one of the department's greatest achievements.

By February 1865, when this portrait was taken, the stresses of the war had taken their toll on President Lincoln.

This print illustrates the surrender of General Robert E. Lee and his army to Lieutenant General Ulysses S. Grant on April 9, 1865. Lee's forces, with limited resources to draw on and no room to maneuver, had few alternatives.

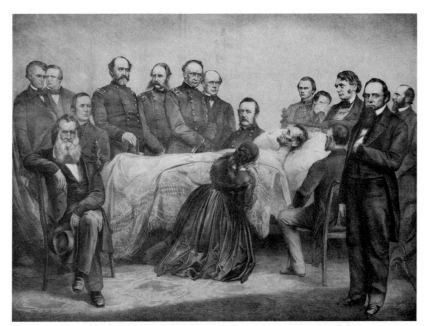

On April 14, 1865, Montgomery Meigs wrote in his journal that the nation's capital could not be happier about the ending of the war. "The country is drunk with joy." That night, an assassin shot Lincoln at Ford's Theatre. The president died the next morning, as Meigs and others looked on.

Montgomery Meigs suggested the army mount a grand review to mark the end of the war. Northerners flooded into Washington to witness the spectacle.

The National Cemetery at Andersonville, Georgia, where thousands of Union prisoners lost their lives.

After the Civil War, Montgomery Meigs designed and built several important structures. Among the most interesting is the building he created to house the growing federal Pension Bureau. Meigs's design drew on the Farnese and Cancelleria palaces in Rome. It was the world's largest brick building when it opened. It is now the National Building Museum.

CHAPTER 23

Gunboats

The Union's first important blow to the rebels came in the west, on February 6, 1862, during a short, spectacular battle at Fort Henry on the Tennessee River. The story of that victory began months earlier, in Meigs's office on his first day as quartermaster. As he sorted through the chaos of mobilization, Meigs was asked to assess plans for gunboats that could pummel rebel forts, protect river traffic, and support infantry movements. The idea for the boats came from the recognition that the Union had to control the western rivers to prevail. The rivers ran deep into the South and offered promising alternatives to the rutted tracks that often passed for roads there. The Mississippi bisected the Confederacy and served as a highway of commerce. The Tennessee offered a direct route to the rear of the enemy.

Meigs saw promise in the plans, which included using a skin of heavy timbers to protect the boats. He also realized that even the stoutest wooden boats would turn into splinters under attack by modern rifled cannons. He sought advice from navy commander John Rodgers, his brother-in-law, who had recently been assigned to develop navy armaments for the Mississippi and Ohio Rivers. They agreed that at least some of the boats ought to be shielded by iron plating, and Meigs began a search for the money to make the ironclads possible. They had no time to lose. Commerce stood at a near standstill on the Mississippi south of Cairo, Illinois. Lincoln did not need economic chaos in the West on top of the other troubles he faced. The Union also desperately needed a victory to encourage Northerners after the debacle at Bull Run.

Meigs put out a solicitation to boat builders even before the plans were complete. He received eight responses, the lowest of which came from an engineer in St. Louis named James Eads, forty-one, who specialized in salvage operations on the Mississippi. A small man with a high forehead and penetrating eyes, he came from a struggling family. He earned a fortune through brilliance and hard work. He had invented new machines and improved on existing technology. His work, including the creation of a diving bell and special small craft, improved dramatically the recovery of sunken riverboats. Eads later built the largest bridge of its time across the Mississippi, a pioneering steel structure that included the longest arch of any kind in the world.

After the fall of Fort Sumter, Eads examined his maps and understood instantly the importance of aggressive action on the rivers. He sold the idea of a gunboat flotilla to Edward Bates, a fellow Missourian and Lincoln's attorney general, who had invited Eads to explain his conception for the president and Cabinet members. On August 7, Eads and Meigs signed off on a deal for seven virtually identical boats at $89,000 each, to be delivered by October 10. Meigs loved the project. He craved novelty and saw the boats as experimental technology. They would be slow, clumsy, and odd looking, but they represented a leap in warship construction. The specifications called for a frame of thick white oak timbers, bolted throughout. The deck would be 175 feet long and 50 feet wide at its broadest point. To lower the risk of sinking, designers divided the craft with watertight compartments. Each boat would be clad in tons of iron plating and loaded with thirteen guns. A steam boiler provided power to a paddlewheel in the rear.

Work began almost immediately at a boatyard about ten miles south of St. Louis, in the small village of Carondelet. In September, Commander Andrew Foote arrived in St. Louis to take over control from Rodgers. At the time, the flotilla consisted of just thirty-eight fortified flatboats to hold mortars, nine incomplete ironclads, and three freight-and-passenger steamboats that had been modified into war boats. It took Foote and Meigs months to cobble together the gunboat fighting force and to find the money to support it. They worked through a hybrid chain of command that mixed navy and volunteer army forces, all under the control of the Quartermaster Department. Their struggles showed the primacy of paperwork during the war— even as the Union's fate hung in the balance. The challenges included resolving the differences in accounting methods used by the army and navy. Under navy custom, sailors' pay included clothing and "small stores." The army system did not account for such transactions. They had to sort out these details because neither man wanted to raise doubt about their integrity.

Meigs had to contend with delays and cost overruns. Eads had been overly optimistic about the time and funding the project would need. Though these wrinkles irritated Meigs, he understood the stakes and managed to find an additional $227,000. Foote, Eads, and their construction crews worked relentlessly. With improvisation under impossible deadlines, they drafted and revised designs, invented machinery to make new parts, and built boatyards and docks from scratch. Meigs pulled on the levers of the War Department in Washington to enable it all. The first boat emerged from the dockyards in mid-October and steamed to the staging area at Cairo, Illinois, commanded by a little-known brigadier general named Ulysses S. Grant. As the boats received their guns and supplies, Foote proposed taking four of them and six thousand of Grant's men up the north-flowing Tennessee to attack Fort Henry. Grant wanted to target Fort Donelson, on the Cumberland River, but he agreed to Foote's plan.

The black-painted boats went into service at the end of January, mounted with 32-, 42-, and 64-pound guns, some of them rifled. Each had a distinctive band painted on the smokestack for identification. The fighting men called them turtles for their humped shape and low waterline. At noon on February 6, four ironclads, the *Cincinnati, St. Louis, Essex,* and *Carondelet,* along with three all-wood boats, steamed up the Tennessee. They went by Painter Creek Island and then directly to Fort Henry through a storm of rebel shot and shell. Grant's foot soldiers missed the battle because they were stuck on nearly impassible muddy roads. The *Essex* soon drifted away after a shot exploded a boiler, scalding and killing several crew members. The other boats held firm as shells deflected off their iron angles. After just over an hour, the Confederate forces struck their colors. When word of the victory spread, the North rejoiced.

A week later, the Union force moved on Fort Donelson. The boats pummeled Confederate forces before being disabled and hauled off for repairs. This time Grant's men stepped into the fray, forcing the rebel garrison to capitulate. The commander, Brig. Gen. John Floyd, fled. It was a decisive victory that put federal forces on the path into the South. By the end of the month, Nashville and much of Tennessee were in Union hands. The ironclads served as a fearsome weapon for the rest of the war in battles on the Mississippi and its tributaries. The effectiveness of the boats—and the bravery and resolve of Foote, who was wounded during the Battle of Fort Donelson—delighted Meigs. "Whenever you need authority or advice, write, and your dispatch will have prompt attention," he wrote to Foote. "At other times, stick as you have done to the work of crushing out this Rebellion. I wish we had the same single mindedness and energy in some other places."

Meigs took great pride in the Quartermaster Department's role in the victories. He crowed that an enterprising subordinate had, in the midst of chaos, found a way to save money. Because so many riverboats had been idled by the rebels' blockade of the Mississippi, a quartermaster officer in St. Louis was able to negotiate steamboat leases for troop transport at a fraction of the normal cost. Meigs told Stanton they had "been obtained at rates probably below those of any similar movement ever made." In spite of his grueling workload, Meigs continued studying how to improve the gunboats. He shared his thoughts with Lincoln in an eight-page letter, recommending changes that would modify the vessels for use along Southern coasts. He included a diagram to illustrate his innovations. "I have thought much lately upon the result of our experimental Gun Boats on the Western Rivers," Meigs told Lincoln. "They have done even better than I had hoped, and it appears to me that the experience thus far gained may be made available for important operations."

——————

The daring shown by Foote and Grant contrasted starkly with McClellan's caution in the East. Under pressure from Radical Republicans, Lincoln relieved McClellan of overall command of the army, assuming the role for himself and Stanton. He continued to back McClellan as leader of the Army of the Potomac, and stood by his plan for the advance on Richmond. Lincoln issued general orders that it commence on March 18. With preparations under way, Washington received unsettling news: the CSS *Virginia* had appeared on March 8 near Fortress Monroe, a Virginia staging area for McClellan's impending campaign. Known to Northerners by its former name, the USS *Merrimack*, it was an ungainly seagoing ironclad vessel that some thought looked like a submerged house with its roof just above water. Rebel officers soon put to rest any doubts about its lethality. They steamed directly at two Union frigates at the mouth of the James River, ramming and sinking one and helping to capture and burn the other. At least 240 Union men died, the navy's worst day in its eighty-six-year history.

The attack set off panic. The president, Stanton, and others feared that the *Merrimack* might steam up the Potomac and target a nearly defenseless Washington. Lincoln asked a navy admiral for advice. When the officer had nothing to offer, the president sought Meigs's opinion. The quartermaster general urged extreme caution. Meigs shared the fear that the vessel might go on a rampage and attack the capital. On March 9 he ordered troops in Annapolis to prepare to ambush the vessel. Caught up in the drama of the moment, he recommended sending "a number of swift steamships full of men, who should board her by a sudden rush, fire down through her hatches or grated deck, and throw cartridges, grenades, or shells down her smokepipes; sacrifice the steamers in order to take the *Merrimack*."

Meigs added: "Promotion, ample reward, awaits whoever takes or destroys her."

He also put into motion a plan to tow canal boats into the Potomac channel and sink them to form a massive blockade. Both measures turned out to be unnecessary. The USS *Monitor*, another new Union ironclad, was coincidentally on its way to the Virginia coast when the *Merrimack* attacked. On March 9 the two ships squared off in an unprecedented battle that resulted in a bloody draw.

That battle was a sideshow to McClellan's offensive, which finally got under way. Day after day, the army departed from Alexandria aboard side-wheel steamers, schooners, brigs, and barks leased by the quartermaster department. Hundreds of vessels transported more than a hundred thousand men over several weeks' time. Meigs worked closely with Assistant Secretary of War John Tucker, a former shipbuilding executive whom Stanton had assigned to the initiative. The flotilla formed the core of a huge fleet that the Quartermaster Department would maintain for ocean transport during the war. Department officers under Meigs eventually leased 753 steamers, almost 1,100 sailing vessels, and more than 800 barges. They bought or commissioned construction of about 300 additional vessels. Drawing on contracting lessons learned from his public works projects, Meigs inserted a clause in every boat charter that allowed the government to take ownership if it proved financially beneficial to taxpayers.

In addition to moving men, the Peninsula fleet transported more than 14,000 animals, 3,600 wagons, 700 ambulances, mountains of feed for the horses and rations for the men, pontoon bridges, telegraph gear, and vast amounts of other equipment. Even veteran officers had never seen anything like it. One supply officer wrote, "The magnitude of the movement can scarcely be understood except by those who participated in it." After the force left Alexandria, Meigs's involvement with the Army of the Potomac became less direct. He stood by his commitment and the practical need to allow his capable subordinates to solve the endless problems of supply they encountered. Among them was McClellan's chief quartermaster, Brigadier General Stewart Van Vliet, who had learned the craft of logistics during the Mormon War several years earlier.

Van Vliet and his men eased the massive army onto the coastal terrain, and by the end of April, it was stretched across the peninsula,
from Yorktown to the James River. Moving those supplies to the mobile troops posed a far greater test than expected. While planning the
offensive, McClellan told Stanton that the roads were passable in every
season. As it happened, the flat, sandy pathways became quagmires
in heavy rain that spring. Even lightly loaded wagons sunk down to
their beds. Only mules could get them through. The department officers quickly adapted to the conditions, and Van Vliet reported that
the army was well supplied. Even so, McClellan complained endlessly.
And he soon blamed delays in his movements on a shortage of horses
and wagons, claims later dismissed as exaggeration. McClellan might
have been looking for excuses. He and his senior officers also insisted
that his force was not large enough to take on entrenched Confederate
forces. One of his senior aides called the rebel front line "one of the
strongest in the world."

Meigs and others in Washington seethed as the army tarried. In
June the president implored McClellan to move. "I beg to assure you
that I have never written you or spoken to you in greater kindness of
feeling than now, nor with a fuller purpose to sustain you, so far as, in
my most anxious judgment, I consistently can," Lincoln told his general. "But you must act."

CHAPTER 24

"His Best Name Is Honesty"

The quartermaster general met with Stanton and Lincoln every day now—sometimes several times a day—to discuss the army, its movements, and its leadership. Though Meigs lacked battlefield experience, he offered them loyalty, brilliance, and an understanding of military culture. Neither Lincoln nor Stanton had much military experience. They did not know many of the basics of army life, such as framing orders properly and putting them into effect. They did not feel free to turn to McClellan and some other field generals, who seemed reluctant to work closely with the White House. Lincoln secretary William Stoddard illuminated Meigs's role in a cornpone vignette about open visiting hours at the White House. In the story, a restive crowd waits for a chance to see the president. Suddenly three men barge through and go into Lincoln's office. Two onlookers discuss the situation:

"Who's that there tall feller that doesn't have to wait? And the short feller with him, that's mostly beard and spectacles? Three of 'em, and more beard, who are they, pushin' straight in?"

"One of them is War, and one of them is Honesty, and one of them is Ocean."

"Was that there Stanton? Well, now, if he wasn't mad about somethin' he looked it. I'd ought to ha' known old Welles from his picture, but you didn't call the other feller."

"Yes, I did. His best name is Honesty, but his other name is Meigs. He buys things for the army. He is quartermaster-general, and when he gets clean through, there won't be a stain on him, nor the smell of fire on his garments. Could you spend four or five thousands of millions of dollars and not steal some of it?"

"I guess I could. I wouldn't steal a cent, but some of it might stick, somewhere, or sift out into the backyard somehow, while there was such an awful heap bein' carted."

"There won't any stick to old Honesty, nor sift into his backyard. He and a few men like him are the main reasons why we're going to win this fight."

Meigs became Stanton's "political ally, professional colleague, and personal friend," as one historian has written, and Stanton often sought Meigs's advice. When Lincoln demoted McClellan from general-in-chief, Stanton asked Meigs what he thought. Meigs was blunt and reassuring, saying that no general operating so far from military headquarters, with two hundred thousand men under his immediate direction, could manage such a post. "Gen. McClellan ought not to have such responsibility & I should think be glad to be relieved of it," Meigs wrote.

Stanton turned to Meigs again when he discovered that McClellan left behind inexperienced men to guard the capital, contrary to Lincoln's orders. Out of pique and concern, Stanton initially refused to honor a request from McClellan for more men. When he finally agreed, Stanton asked Meigs to draft an order, on May 17, dispatching General McDowell to join the right wing of McClellan's force with nearly forty thousand men, with an emphasis on protecting Washington from a rebel attack. Meigs did so after consulting with Lincoln, General Totten, and at least two others. Meigs edited those same orders after Lincoln added language he thought would encourage McDowell to make decisions on the fly. Lincoln offered these words: "You will retain the separate command of the forces taken with you; but while co-operating with General McClellan you will obey his orders, except that you are to judge, and are not to allow your force to be disposed otherwise than so as to give the greatest protection to this capital which may be possible from that distance."

Meigs convinced the president that such guidance ran contrary to army custom. He told Lincoln it "is dangerous to direct a subordinate not to obey the orders of his superior in any case." Meigs counseled him to make the suggestion to McClellan and then give a copy of the orders to McDowell. The president went along. The quartermaster also got directly involved with movements in the field. On May 23, while working in Washington, he took on a commanding role briefly after Confederate General Thomas "Stonewall" Jackson overwhelmed the Union garrison at Front Royal, Virginia, dangerously close to the Potomac. Early in the afternoon, General John W. Geary, commanding a small force near Rectortown, Virginia, fired off inaccurate telegrams warning about an enemy buildup east of the Blue Ridge Mountains. He expressed concerns about the possibility of a move against the railroad at Thoroughfare Gap. At eleven at night, Major General Nathaniel P. Banks sent a telegram addressed to Stanton from Strasburg, saying the Union force had withdrawn in the face of superior numbers and was seeking reinforcements. The anxiety of army leaders was palpable. Lincoln and Stanton were away, steaming back to the city after meetings with McDowell at Fredericksburg, Virginia. An assistant secretary of war reached out to Meigs. "The secretary will be here in the morning. Have you any suggestions to make?" Meigs didn't hesitate. He issued orders over the signature of the absent Stanton, commanding a regiment of troops to prepare for movement.

Meigs played an important role in helping to formulate a response to Jackson's presence in the Shenandoah Valley. On May 24 Lincoln and Stanton suspended the order directing McDowell to McClellan. In an order drafted by Meigs, Lincoln told McDowell instead to go to the valley in pursuit of Jackson. Meigs expressed "hope it will result yet in capturing a part of Jackson's force." It was a fateful decision, though, one that diverted reinforcements away from McClellan. "This is a crushing blow to us," McDowell wrote Stanton at the time. There is no way to know whether the presence of McDowell's corps at McClellan's side would have spurred a successful drive on Richmond. But "the lack of it made McClellan more cautious than ever and gave the Confederate army defending the capital much-needed breathing space," according to historian Peter Cozzens.

———

The campaign on the peninsula lasted more than two months and yielded little of strategic value. McClellan's caution taxed an already struggling supply system. He lay siege to Yorktown and then, when the rebels retreated, slogged up the peninsula over the bad roads. The logistical demands were unprecedented. The army consumed six hundred thousand tons or more of supplies every day, nearly all of which had to be shipped in at great expense. McClellan made matters still more challenging by prohibiting troops from foraging in enemy fields unless they paid for whatever they took or issued receipts guaranteeing government payment later. He thought this benign approach would win over Southerners and shorten the war—a notion that Meigs condemned as silliness, or worse. Meigs had come to believe that to win, the Union had to turn away from this "tenderness for the rights of property" in enemy territory. In his judgment, the Union had to use every means to support its soldiers and exhaust the rebels' will to fight. This included using enemy land to feed the army's great herds of horses and mules.

The provision of forage presented one of the great challenges of the war to Meigs's department. Every horse needed to eat fourteen pounds of hay and twelve pounds of corn, barley, and oats, while each soldier required just three pounds of food. All together, the animals of the Army of the Potomac needed more than four hundred tons of forage each day. Without that fuel, the army could not move. Buying that feed and moving it to the right place, in a timely way, without bankrupting the government, was a stupendous logistical problem.

At the beginning of the war, Meigs had left it to quartermaster officers at each depot and with each army to buy feed as needed. Those officers soon began competing with one another for supplies, driving up prices and further depleting a nearly empty Treasury. To contain the costs, a senior quartermaster officer launched a plan to cut corners by feeding the animals a less expensive mix of corn and oats. Contractors soon grasped that they could jack up profits by secretly bulking up the feed mix with less costly and less nutritious grains. Meigs investigated those scams, studied the market, and imposed price controls. To minimize manipulation of the market, he gave a single quartermaster officer in New York authority to negotiate giant forage contracts for the armies in the east. After those initiatives took hold, delays due to winter storms, railway disruptions, and simple chaos sometimes put the animals perilously close to starvation. But the department eventually got a grip on the problem, accumulating enough grain and hay to feed sixty-five thousand animals for forty days straight.

———

To keep the army moving on the peninsula, the quartermaster men solved many problems. At a supply depot along the Pamunkey River, for instance, they constructed temporary piers. To fashion the piers, they pulled boats and barges onto shore at high tide, covered them with planks, and then linked them together. They herded cattle over land, maintaining them in corrals and butchering them as needed. To minimize chaos, Van Vliet ordered that supplies remain aboard ships until needed. His men constructed a steam-hoist to speed the movement of food, ammunition, and other supplies onto wagons. The systems worked, but available food often could not be moved quickly enough over narrow, crowded, and mucky roads. Inevitably, many soldiers could never get enough to eat, and became churlish when their coffee failed to appear. They suffered from the shortage of vegetables, and as the campaign dragged on into summer 1862, sickness spread among the troops. They naturally blamed the quartermasters. "The means of transportation are still incomplete," one observer wrote. "And the quartermasters [are] incompetent."

Still, the quartermaster officers did their part, and the army eventually moved so close to Richmond that soldiers could hear church bells ringing. Then a momentous change in rebel leadership altered the war's complexion. Robert Lee assumed command of the Confederate army after General Joseph Johnston was wounded. Lee brought a new aggression and intelligence to the rebel war effort. On June 25 the brutal fighting now known as the Seven Days Battles began. The next day, Lee launched an attack aimed at forcing McClellan to defend his supply lines and engage in battle away from Richmond. Lee was intent on preventing a siege of Richmond. Federal soldiers suffered thousands of casualties before McClellan decided to retreat to Harrison's Landing on the James River, about twenty-four miles southeast of Richmond.

In the rush back, the trains of wagons supporting each brigade were permitted to make their own way. Instead of one well-organized line, there were as many as nine, all of them vying for position. Competition to get to the head was fierce because the roads were inevitably ruined for those lagging behind. Confusion often resulted. The Quartermaster Department bore responsibility. "A struggle for the lead would naturally set in, each division wanting it and fighting for it. Profanity, threats, and the flourishing of revolvers were sure to be prominent in the settling of the question," wrote John D. Billings, a soldier with the Army of the Potomac.

McClellan considered his retreat a success. He sent off notes to Washington that expressed his excitement. To Meigs and others, though, the campaign was a failure. The capture of Richmond had for a brief moment seemed only a matter of will—something that McClellan seemed to lack.

Meigs's view of the war shifted now, as hopes for a swift resolution disappeared. He realized the South would resist even if it became apparent that it could not win. The rebels would have to suffer before they would capitulate. Like a growing number of Northerners, he thought the Union needed a different kind of general, someone who would fight a different kind of war—an encompassing war sustained by industrial power and righteous resolve. "In the mean time the north must hold this wolf by the ears until it is exhausted by starvation or destroyed by the kicks & cuffs which it may yet receive," Meigs wrote at the time. "Death or victory is the . . . necessity of our case, & I do not

the less doubt the ultimate victory that God for our sins leads us to it
through seas of blood."

––––––

In the summer of 1862, the White House faced another strategic
question: Should McClellan and his army stay at Harrison's Landing
or evacuate? McClellan maintained that the force opposing him was
200,000 strong. A growing number of doubters questioned his estimates. It seemed no one could know for sure. To clarify matters, Meigs
studied Southern newspapers and the reports about recent battles.
He identified the divisions, brigades, and batteries involved in each,
and then pieced together an estimate of the size of the rebel force at
about 105,000 men. If his sleuthing showed a clever turn of mind, it
did not make much of a difference. McClellan sent so many mixed messages to Washington that fear of sudden annihilation at the hands of a
quick-moving rebel army lingered among those in the White House.
Though McClellan claimed he wanted to try for Richmond again, he
also suggested that Lee might try to pin him on the peninsula with
some of his men and make a move on Washington with the rest. Meigs,
Seward, and others quaked at this prospect.

Meigs's anxiety peaked one night in July after reading gloomy
dispatches from McClellan and his staff. He rushed up to Lincoln's
summer retreat, at the Old Soldiers' Home in the District, woke
the president, and urged him to ship the men off Harrison's Landing. Meigs recommended killing the horses that could not be taken.
It was a strange, overheated moment. Even the tolerant Lincoln
thought it was odd. "I who am not a specially brave man have had to
sustain the sinking courage of these professional fighters in critical
times," he told an aide. If nothing else, it showed that Lincoln was
not easily pushed to do something against his judgment, even by a
trusted advisor. For his part, Meigs thought the president misjudged
the threat. "President thinks I tried to stampede him," Meigs wrote
in a pocket diary he kept during the war. "How long before he comes
to my opinion to withdraw the army from a dangerous and useless

position, and use it to defend the free states and as a nucleus for new armies?'"

Lincoln decided to go to Harrison's Landing and take stock for himself. He was relieved by what he found. All was not about to be lost. Meigs was not mollified. He thought McClellan might be disloyal and maybe even capable of a coup. After all, McClellan had made clear he did not have faith in Lincoln. His troops revered him, even after the recent setbacks. Lieutenant Colonel Rufus Ingalls had replaced Van Vliet as McClellan's chief quartermaster after Van Vliet requested reassignment to New York. Ingalls told Meigs in late July that the army was in magnificent shape, and its leader the "pride and boast" of the men. Their faith in McClellan unsettled Meigs. "They cling to him with love and confidence even through these fatal delays & these terrible retreating combats," Meigs wrote Louisa. "It would perhaps be dangerous to our state to have a great leader with this power."

In July Major General Henry Halleck arrived in Washington as the army's new general-in-chief. Halleck asked Meigs to accompany him to Harrison's landing on the 24th. Unknown to McClellan, the new commander had the authority to decide what next to do with McClellan and his Army of the Potomac. Meigs worried about insurrection again one night while Halleck conferred with McClellan. Sitting at a campfire at twilight, he listened as officers vented their frustration about Lincoln, Stanton, and others in the capital. One officer said he'd like to "march on Washington to clear out those fellows." When another general questioned the tone of their chatter, the men scattered into the dark. Halleck decided the army would withdraw from the peninsula and occupy Aquia Creek, bringing the unfortunate campaign to an end.

Historians have debated the many reasons for McClellan's failure in the peninsula, but no one can blame the quartermaster men. McClellan asked them to do what had not been achieved before. And in dismal weather, on bad roads, and in the face of endless demands, they performed well. For them, it was an unqualified victory. "The success of these movements gives striking evidence of the greatness of the military resources of the nation," Meigs wrote in his annual report. To the end of his life, Meigs defended his suggestion to Stanton and Lincoln that McDowell confront Jackson in the valley instead of joining McClellan as planned. Meigs claimed later that the country was "shocked by telegrams" about Jackson's defeat of Banks in the Shenandoah Valley, saying the setback spread "terror in Maryland, and doubts in Washington." He acknowledged responsibility for supplying McClellan's offensive, even though he thought it ill-advised and assumed it would end in defeat. But he held McClellan and his strategy almost entirely accountable for the failure on the peninsula.

CHAPTER 25

"Vast in Quantity"

Events now offered conflicting evidence about which side was winning. Confederate armies dominated battle after battle through grit, sacrifice, superior leadership, and daring. The brash cavalry officer Jeb Stuart became so confident about the superiority of his men that he personally taunted Meigs after capturing a telegraph station. "To Quarter Master Gen. Meigs, Washington—In future you will please furnish better mules," he wrote in a telegram. "Those you have furnished recently are very inferior."

Clearheaded leaders on both sides knew that day by day, even as the accounts of their victories were being written, the Confederacy was losing ground in the logistical war. Stoddard, one of Lincoln's secretaries, later described this dynamic: "As [rebel] resources are to be rightly counted, every battle he fights brings him near his final defeat." Lee's strategy reflected this reality. He had to balance the need for battlefield victories against the search for new supplies, while also keeping an eye on political developments that might turn the tide. Lee understood the success of the Confederacy depended not primarily on waning supplies or battlefield victories, but "on his army's influence on the minds of civilians," one historian wrote. At the ebb of the Peninsula Campaign, he moved north and west. His scouts and informants learned that McClellan was finally leaving Harrison's Landing. The Union general aimed to join forces with Major General John Pope, whom Lincoln had named head of the new Army of Virginia.

Lee wanted to get at Pope before that combination could occur. He moved swiftly and secretly toward Virginia's Piedmont region, and then worked in concert with Jackson's forces. They skirmished with Pope at the Rapidan River and thereafter as Union forces retreated across the Rappahannock. On August 24, Jeb Stuart's cavalry mounted a daring night attack at Catlett's Station. The horsemen not only captured Union soldiers but also found Pope's baggage and a dispatch book. Lee then made a series of audacious decisions that created new threats to the North. He divided his army of fifty-four thousand in two and ordered Jackson to take twenty thousand men on a rapid forced march into Pope's rear. Lee told Jackson to cut the rail line to Alexandria and disrupt Union communications.

Jackson's three hardened divisions had grown used to his extraordinary demands. Now he told them to leave behind their haversacks in order to speed their march. They hustled all night long, going some thirty miles to Manassas Junction. On their arrival, they saw evidence of what the fight against the North really entailed. Packed warehouses, overloaded railcars, and long lines of barrels held one of the great stores of supplies brought into the field during the war. Fifty thousand pounds of bacon, a thousand barrels of salt pork, hills of flour; jellies, coffee, and tea; piles of uniforms, new boots, and rifled muskets; toothbrushes and candles. "The hungry, threadbare rebels swooped down on the mountain of supplies at Manassas like a plague of grasshoppers," one historian of the war wrote.

As they frolicked, the men must have sensed the underlying reality, that the enormous stockpile of supplies represented a deep, complex enterprise working to destroy them. Jackson's report to Richmond distilled the idea well. "It was vast in quantity and of great value," he wrote. After stuffing themselves and putting on needed clothing, Jackson's men gathered what they could carry, torched the remaining supplies, and fled. With flames leaping into the darkness, Jackson's forces moved west through the night to a reunion with the forces under Lee.

The fires at Manassas still smoldered on August 28 as the mass of Union troops arrived. Pope and his colleagues had no idea where the enemy had gone until word came that Confederates had been sighted on a ridge in the high hills to the west. The Federals did not know that Lee roamed nearby and that he had combined his force with the men under General James Longstreet, the devoted and talented leader referred to by Lee as "my old war horse." Over the next two days, Federal soldiers received another pounding in fighting that came to be known as the Second Battle of Bull Run, or Second Manassas. Pope mishandled the fighting, but some in Lincoln's Cabinet came to believe he was not entirely to blame. They felt that McClellan, with a portion of his army in Alexandria, could have done more to help. In response to a query from Lincoln as to the best course of action, McClellan wrote during the height of the battle that it might be advisable to leave Pope to "get out of his own scrape" while he focused on securing the capital. While the president pondered whether McClellan wanted Pope defeated, Cabinet members expressed fury. Chase privately called McClellan "an imbecile, a coward, and a traitor," and a chorus of critics called on Lincoln to remove him. The president was not ready to take that step. "Unquestionably he has acted badly toward Pope! He wanted him to fail. That is unpardonable. But he is too useful just now to sacrifice," he told an aide. "If he can't fight himself, he excels in making others ready to fight." The president told Welles, "McClellan has the army with him."

Lee prepared for another bold move. He thought the time was right for an invasion. The two Union armies still had not unified, their leadership appeared fractious, and the soldiers weakened and demoralized. "The purpose, if discovered, will have the effect of carrying the enemy north of the Potomac, and, if prevented, will not result in much evil," he wrote to Jeff Davis from a base about thirty miles west of Washington. His ambition contrasted sharply with his army's material circumstances. Just one year into the war, Lee's men struggled with a shortfall of wagons and too few healthy horses to pull them. Many wore rags for uniforms and thousands marched barefoot. His biggest concern was a dwindling supply of ammunition.

"The army is not properly equipped for an invasion of an enemy's territory. It lacks much of the material of war," Lee wrote Davis on

September 3. "Still, we cannot afford to be idle, and though weaker than our opponents in men and military equipments, must endeavor to harass if we cannot destroy them." Lee added another request for emphasis. "If the Quartermaster's Department can furnish any shoes, it would be the great relief. We have entered upon September, and the nights are becoming cool."

The next day, the army forded the Potomac and entered Maryland. Lee ordered all commanders to reduce their supplies to the minimum. This was in part to minimize the demands on the overtaxed animals the army needed to move cannons, ordnance, and food. "All cannoneers are positively prohibited from riding on the ammunition chests or guns," General Orders No. 102 stated. Questions about supplies arose again on September 7. Though the rebels had been treated kindly by Southern-leaning Marylanders, they still did not have enough food or animals. Many residents were unwilling to accept Confederate money. Lee grew more concerned, aware that a lack of supplies could hobble his remarkable and dedicated force every bit as much as fire from the enemy. "I shall endeavor to purchase horses, clothing, shoes, and medical stores for our present use," he wrote Davis, "and you will see the facility that would arise from being provided with the means of paying for them."

––––––

Washington no longer had serious qualms about its supplies. With logistical systems taking hold, the shortfalls the year before had been replaced by abundance. The main challenge was moving the materiel to the men in the field. The main fear was that field generals would not use what they had to crush the enemy. Lincoln complained that McClellan suffered from an ailment he called "the slows."

Meigs desperately wanted the army to make the most of what his department had made available. He obsessed over finding efficiencies. In September 1862 he turned his zeal on McClellan about the army's use of wagons. Questions about such lowly transport might seem trivial against the spreading carnage. Meigs knew better. Steamboats and railway offered remarkable advantages to the North, but supplies still had to get from wharves and depots to soldiers in the field. The wagon was the way. Meigs admired the regulation army model known as the Conestoga. It had been refined over the years on the western plains. Stout and lumbering, it had interchangeable parts that could be repaired in camp with portable forges. Each wagon had a tool box in front, a feed trough in back, and an iron "slush bucket" for grease hanging from the rear axle. Freight was protected by a canvas cover. Drawn by four to six horses, a wagon could move 2,800 pounds of supplies over good roads in good weather. A team of six mules could carry more than 3,700 pounds, plus about 270 pounds of forage.

The army's problem was that the wagons had to be managed properly, and in the rush to war, no one had established clear guidelines for their use. The wagon trains that followed the armies reached absurd proportions, causing chaos and slowing nearly every movement. They carried every kind of comfort: stoves, kettles, pans, chairs, desks, trunks, valises, knapsacks, tents, floorboards, and any other conveniences. Loaded in this way, the wagons could go about two and a half miles per hour over good roads. They could barely move on bad ones. By summer's end in 1862, Halleck, Meigs, and McClellan realized that the wagon trains sometimes created as many problems as they solved. Meigs now fixed on the matter of how to respond to requisitions from McClellan's officers. They had asked for far more stuff than their available wagons could deliver to the front lines. Meigs checked his ledgers. At Harrison's Landing, McClellan had thousands of wagons and ambulances and about five times as many horses and mules to pull them. Yet since then, the army had ordered still more horses.

In a stern letter to McClellan, on September 9, Meigs insisted on reforms. He prescribed no more than three wagons for stationary regiments to carry daily rations. Remaining wagons should be set aside for supply trains. He said that officers had to curb their appetite for comfort, including their use of the voluminous Sibley tents. Meigs felt they should make do with smaller, more portable "shelter tents." He was motivated in part by the cost of cotton, which was rising because of the war. Soldiers dubbed the small shelter a "dog tent," because that's what it seemed fit for; sometimes they stuck their heads out of the tents and barked like dogs. The name for the small shelters eventually became "pup tent." The quartermaster pegged the ideal use of wagons at about one for every eighty men, roughly the standard adopted by Napoleon. He noted that the Army of the Potomac used about one wagon for every thirty-four men, an untenable arrangement. "The extra wagons, now filled with officers' baggage, should be emptied, and the officers compelled to move without this unnecessary load," Meigs wrote. "None but the stringent authority of the commander of the army can carry out this reform, and, until it is done, the army will not be a movable one, and will not be effective."

In a related push for mobility, earlier Meigs had circulated a French proposal for the organization of a light, highly mobile "flying column" of troops that would lighten the burden on the army's logistical system and diminish the need for wagons and animals. The paper, prepared by a contractor to the French army, prescribed columns with two thousand infantry, four hundred cavalry, two pieces of artillery, and fifty horses. Soldiers would carry eight days of their own rations, including coffee, tea, sugar, rice, seven pounds of "sea biscuits," and "desiccated and compressed vegetables." The paper said the soldiers would be divided into squads, the members of which would share the burden of carrying equipment, including sections of shelter tents. In theory, the flying columns created a nimbler force, at least in the short run. Wagons loaded with additional supplies could follow in the rear. "Alarm the enemy, break up his camps, and keep always advancing," the paper said.

In distributing the document, Meigs suggested further that such squads take along hand mills for grinding corn, with the aim of lessening the burden on the Quartermaster Department to provide flour for bread. He wrote that such innovations might prove interesting to "some of our intelligent officers" and "may bear fruit." He was right. A year later, in Special Orders No. 65, the Army of the Potomac established a special board to examine the reforms. After experimentation and refinements, the board found the flying column system workable. At Meigs's urging, Rufus Ingalls, chief quartermaster of the Army of the Potomac, began adopting variations of the system in future campaigns.

There's no mistaking Meigs's goal in all of this. He wanted to burn away the fat in a young army and render it a lean and fast-moving force.

As Lee moved north in early September 1862, Federal fighters needed to be more mobile than ever. Lincoln felt the rebel army had to be confronted and destroyed. The president had more than the military threat in mind. He wanted a victory to reassure despondent Northerners, whose confidence and support wavered precariously. As one New Yorker wrote in his diary, "The nation is rapidly sinking just now, as it has been sinking rapidly for two months and more." The president also had to offset diplomatic efforts by the Confederacy to win recognition from France and England as an independent country. Lincoln saw a chance to crush the enemy, if only he could get McClellan to move. "God bless you, and all with you," Lincoln wrote the general, "Destroy the enemy, if possible."

For his part, Lee thought a thrust into Maryland might force the White House into a bind. The North could accept Confederate appeals for independence, or it could be blamed for continuing a devastating conflict. Lee hoped his maneuver would bolster the efforts of "Peace Democrats" in the North's coming elections. But luck seemed to be on the Union's side. On September 13 a Union corporal near Frederick, Maryland, saw an envelope on the ground that contained Lee's plans for the campaign, Special Order 191, wrapped around three cigars. It was the greatest intelligence coup of the war, a single document spelling out the positions of Lee's divided forces. About midnight, McClellan sent a dispatch to the president. "I have all the plans of the rebels, and will catch them in their own trap," he wrote. "Will send you trophies."

Had McClellan moved immediately, he might have decimated Lee, whose disjointed army still straddled the Potomac. Instead, McClellan hesitated under the impression that enemy forces outweighed his own. The delay gave Lee time to gather his troops near Antietam Creek, not far from the town of Sharpsburg. McClellan massed his men there as well. On September 16 he took still more time to examine Lee's lines and put his units into what he considered proper positions. The bloodiest day of the war began the next morning with the *pop-pop* of occasional firing, a sound that soon blossomed into an encompassing roar. By sunset, the death toll set a single-day record for the conflict: more than 3,650 dead. Another 17,300 were wounded. Lee intended to plunge into the fight again the next morning, but his officers convinced him that would be misguided. He ordered a retreat back across the Potomac. No one on the Union side moved to stop him. McClellan claimed later that he had planned on resuming the fight but felt compelled to bury the dead. He also said his men needed rest and that he saw "long columns of dust" to the south that he said proved rebels were arriving to reinforce Lee. "This army is not now in condition to undertake another campaign nor to bring on another battle," McClellan reported to Washington. "Not a day should be lost in filling the old regiments."

Much of Washington writhed with the constricted hope that McClellan would go on the offensive. "The country is becoming very impatient at the want of activity of your army, and we must push it on," Halleck wrote three weeks after the battle. "There is a decided want of *legs* in our troops. They have too much immobility, and we must try to remedy the defect." Lincoln visited the army to try to understand McClellan's hesitation. On his return to Washington, he directed Halleck to order McClellan to cross the Potomac, fight the enemy, or drive him south before the roads became impassable in fall rains.

And now McClellan turned to an old excuse, contending the Quartermaster Department had let him down. The army could not move because it had not received enough horses, clothing, or other supplies. McClellan said he had done what he could with what he had been given. The department had worked feverishly to support the force in Maryland. If some men did not have new boots, it was not for want of supply. One depot in Washington alone issued an average of 25,000 pairs a week from a supply of more than 116,000 on hand. McClellan's well-provisioned men tarried while Lee's forces moved swiftly south. The rebels were bloodied, exhausted, and in rags, but they moved. "History records but few examples of a greater amount of labor and fighting than has been done by this army during the present campaign," Lee wrote Davis during the march south. "The number of bare-footed men is daily increasing, and it pains me to see them limping over rocky roads."

Stanton felt compelled to examine McClellan's claims. He put to Halleck a set of pointed questions. Halleck responded with a scathing report that defended Meigs and derided McClellan. He said the army had not made many of the requests that McClellan claimed were not fulfilled. Records showed forty-eight thousand pairs of boots and shoes had been delivered to McClellan at Harpers Ferry on the twenty-first and that ten thousand more were on the way. If they did not get to every man in time, some blame was due to the natural friction generated by large supply networks. "I am sick, tired, and disgusted with the condition of military affairs here in the East," Halleck wrote a friend. "There is an immobility here that exceeds all that any man can conceive of."

For his part, Rufus Ingalls downplayed questions about a lack of clothing. In doing so, he also expressed unease about being stuck in the middle of a fight between Meigs and McClellan. Meigs gently upbraided him in a note that articulated the support role he thought quartermaster men ought to play in the war. "[T]he Quartermaster-General would regard it as a great misfortune, if not a great crime, to have any controversy grow up between it, or its officers, and the generals commanding armies," Meigs wrote. "The Quartermaster-General desires to accomplish this, and will not allow any controversy to arise."

For all the frustration, Lincoln could at least lay claim to a victory at Antietam. He had been waiting for such a moment all summer. He wanted to use a positive development to announce his plan to free the slaves living in rebellious states. On September 22, 1862, he issued the preliminary Emancipation Proclamation, set to take effect at the beginning of the new year. The proclamation gave formal weight to a practice well under way in the field. Though Lincoln did not go into the war to emancipate, he turned to it now to accelerate the demise of the Confederacy. According to historian James McPherson, "Emancipation was a *means* to victory, not yet an end in itself."

Meigs welcomed the announcement. His views about slavery had evolved, just as he had changed and grown over the last two years. His ambivalence was gone. He thought that freed black soldiers might spur slaves to rise up and join the Union, and he said so in clear terms. He hoped they would form "a dark & threatening cloud which will burst in tempest overthrowing Jeff Davis and his white 'nation.'"

CHAPTER 26

Hope Wanes

On November 5, 1862, Lincoln ordered Halleck to relieve McClellan of command and named Major General Ambrose Burnside as his replacement. Although Burnside had performed poorly at Antietam, Lincoln hoped that he would take the fight to Lee. Burnside wanted to please the president, but he stumbled from the start. Instead of moving directly south as expected, Burnside decided to head east toward Fredericksburg, Virginia. He worried that a southern thrust could not be supported properly by the single-track railways available to him in the other direction. Halleck initially opposed the change and went to talk to Burnside, taking along Meigs and Brigadier General Herman Haupt, chief of construction and transportation for the US Military Rail Roads in Virginia, to weigh the logistical questions. Halleck reluctantly agreed with Burnside, who then rushed his army toward Fredericksburg. Everyone felt that swift movement was essential to gaining an advantage. "Movement in everything and everywhere is essential. Trains must not stand still," Haupt wrote Burnside. "[T]he time for this should be measured by minutes, not hours."

Their plan was subverted by miscommunication. Burnside expected to receive pontoons from Meigs to support a temporary bridge across the Rappahannock River. Halleck and Meigs thought that Burnside intended to use a shallow ford upstream of Fredericksburg to cross the river. So they made no arrangements for the pontoons then. As a consequence of the confusion, Burnside's advance was delayed for weeks, giving rebel forces time to gather behind the town, on a ridge known as Marye's Heights. On December 13, 1862, two days after the army finally crossed the river, he ordered the troops to attack a sunken road at the base of the heights. Their target turned out to be a rebel stronghold. Burnside ordered wave after wave of troops against it. Union casualties soared by the hour, almost equaling the losses at Antietam. As one historian wrote, it was "a futile, wild, fantastic, direct slam by Federals against the exceedingly well entrenched Confederates."

The hapless general later displayed a grace and humility that distinguished him from McClellan. In the aftermath, questions about the culpability of Meigs or Halleck in the planning mishap faded away. "For the failure of the attack, I am responsible," Burnside said in a report about the fiasco. The bloodletting left him shaken. Weeks went by without any follow-through. Lincoln, Stanton, Meigs, and others in Washington grew impatient and angry. The public lost heart, meanwhile, and the newspapers howled for action. Meigs decided to cajole Burnside and on December 30 penned a letter that illuminated yet again the myriad roles he played during the war, including manager, accountant, planner, counselor, and scold. "My Dear General," he wrote, "You were good enough to say that you would be pleased to hear from me, and I venture to say a few words to you which neither the newspapers nor, I fear, anybody in your army is likely to utter. In my position as Quartermaster-General much is seen that is seen from no other stand-point in the Army."

Meigs offered something of a tutorial about present circumstances. He identified the war economy as a key concern. The Treasury could barely stay ahead of creditors, he said, and the government's line of credit was becoming too big for the market to bear. The Quartermaster Department, meanwhile, was losing its grip on commodity prices. As demand for hay and oats rose, so did their costs. Unless something changed, Burnside would be obliged to retire from the field and disperse his animals to save them from starvation. The quartermaster general told Burnside that his army was still strong, even though it was losing men to sickness and disability. His animals were well fed and healthy. The weather was still good. Meigs warned that the nation's appetite for war was waning. The people needed another victory, and they needed it now.

"Every day weakens your army; every good day lost is a golden opportunity in the career of our country—lost forever. Exhaustion steals over the country. Confidence and hope are dying," Meigs wrote. "The gallantry of the attack at Fredericksburg made amends for its ill success, and soldiers were not discouraged by it. The people, when they understood it, took heart again. But the slumber of the army since is eating at the vitals of the nation. As day after day has gone, my heart has sunk, and I see greater peril to our nationality in the present condition of affairs than I have seen at any time during the struggle."

While the letter was heartfelt, Meigs lacked authority to make a direct order here, and Burnside chose to ignore the advice.

———

In January 1863, lawmakers condemned the lack of progress in the war. Some sought scapegoats. One of these, Senator James Lane of Kansas, claimed in a speech on the floor of the Senate that he knew the culprits behind Union failures. They were West Point graduates. Lane had played a role in the bloody tumult that gave birth to the state of Kansas. He considered the military academy a training ground of disloyalty. He said he could not think of a single graduate who had shown "a ray of genius" during the war. He went further. West Point not only controlled the government "with iron shackles," but also one of its graduates was a traitor within. That would be Meigs, longtime friend of Jeff Davis. Lane described the quartermaster general as the very embodiment of "West Point pro-slaveryism."

Though the allegations irritated Meigs, he had faced down demagoguery before the war, and he still had powerful friends in the Senate. One of them, Senator Henry Wilson of Massachusetts, chairman of the Committee on Military Affairs, offered a tart defense on his behalf. "A question has been raised here in regard to the loyalty of General Meigs, and why? It is said that he was Jeff Davis's friend, and Jeff Davis was his patron," Wilson said. "I do not think there is anything in that. Jefferson Davis stood by General Meigs when John B. Floyd undertook to crush him. Floyd was not only a traitor but a thief, and he left the Government only when there seemed nothing more for him to steal. Davis was not a thief, but a traitor to the country . . . as to the loyalty of General Meigs, I do not think there is a man in America who has a right to question it."

As to the allegations that Meigs supported slavery, Wilson pointed to the quartermaster general's annual report of the previous year. "General Meigs was among the first men engaged in this war who declared it to be the true policy of the Government to organize the black men of the South for military purposes." The report called on the nation's leaders "as clearly and as broadly as any man in America has ever laid it down, that the slaves of rebels should be used to save our periled country."

————

Meigs had too much to worry about to focus long on political chicanery. Among other things, he was concerned about keeping up with the army's insatiable demand for horses. Union forces relied on the animals to a degree that might be hard to imagine now. It needed horses and mules to maintain its very existence. The numbers in play were remarkable. Armies with about 426,000 men would soon have nearly 114,000 horses and 88,000 mules. That's not counting the creatures sidelined by illness, wounds, or fatigue. Until now, Meigs had been lucky in meeting the demand. At the beginning of the war, Northern states had almost 5 million horses on hand. Enough were available even to offset the corruption among dealers who sold the government old, lame, and even blind animals. For many months, the prices remained steady, with horses delivered to Washington at the cost of about $125 each. But lately the market price had crept up close to $185, putting stress on both the Treasury and Meigs.

The quartermaster general thought that an obvious alternative was to encourage the army to confiscate horses in enemy territory, even though regulations permitted such taking only under limited circumstances. He thought it was irrational that Southerners were permitted to keep such an important resource. To Meigs, horses were as valuable as cannons or gunpowder. Given the number of animals the department routinely provided, he was skeptical when McClellan claimed, in October 1862, that his men could not chase Stuart's cavalry in Pennsylvania because of a lack of horses. Meigs examined his records and found that the Army of the Potomac, in fact, had recently received more than a thousand horses over six weeks, at a cost of $1.2 million. Meigs wrote a testy letter to Stanton, answering McClellan's allegations and underscoring the urgent need for better management. He said the cavalry would not need so many new mounts if McClellan's soldiers took better care of the ones they had. "The efforts of a quartermaster alone are not sufficient to prevent abuse, suffering, overwork, or neglect. Every commander, from the highest to the lowest in rank, from the commander of an army to the chief of the smallest detachment to which a wagon is attached, has a direct interest in the condition of the stock."

Meigs then turned his wrath on Major General William Rosecrans, another West Pointer and Army Corps of Engineers officer, who had recently assumed command of the Army of the Cumberland in Tennessee. Meigs heard little from Rosecrans until a night in January 1863 when Rosecrans made an urgent request for five thousand horses, armor-plated boats, and five thousand repeating rifles. Rosecrans was anxious to mount an infantry force to supplement his cavalry, which had turned in a mediocre performance just days before in the Stones River Campaign in Tennessee. His telegram went directly to the war secretary, who gave it to Halleck, who passed it on to the quartermaster general. "Major-General Rosecrans complains that his requisitions for horses to mount infantry regiments are not properly filled," Halleck wrote.

Meigs chafed at the note. It was one thing for Rosecrans to surprise him with a massive requisition, he thought, but it was another to go over his head and then suggest he was falling short on his responsibilities. "General Halleck informs me that you complain that your requisitions for horses for mounting infantry are not filled, and desires the evil removed," the quartermaster wrote Rosecrans. "Upon whom have you made the requisitions? I have no information on the subject from you or from the quartermaster of your command. Inform me, that I may act in the matter." The exchange, on January 14, 1863, touched off a cranky correspondence that lasted months. In the midst of everything else, the two stubborn West Pointers struggled for the upper hand. They lectured each other on warfare and management. Rosecrans would not be put off by Meigs. On January 15 he upped his request to eight thousand mounts, complaining that rebel cavalry were getting the best of his army. He suggested that Meigs take contracting shortcuts to fill gaps in his forces.

Meigs remained skeptical. He thought that the expense and effort demanded by Rosecrans's requests would sap the government unnecessarily, with no obvious benefit. He wanted more time and data to decide. In the meantime, he urged Rosecrans to take what he needed from the enemy. "It will take some time to get eight thousand horses, unless you can seize them in the field of your operations," he said. "Why do you not send your infantry in wagons for forced marches to intercept cavalry?" One can see Rosecrans rolling his eyes: A desk-bound general pushing tactical suggestions from a warm office in Washington? "Your dispatch received; thanks," he wrote back. "Have no wagons to spare, and these are cumbersome. In these narrow roads can't travel across the country. Would do well on Pennsylvania avenue."

Rosecrans kept at it for weeks. By April, his lecturing took on a didactic tone, and in some cases he sounded remarkably like Meigs. "Cheap horses for service absolutely necessary is the worst possible plan, and this is tenfold worse when service is military," he wrote. "The cost of feeding poor horses and bring them here is as great as that for good ones." Still, the quartermaster general refused to take shortcuts with the law or the contracting process. He knew that Congress would rage at any hint of manipulation or corruption. He told Rosecrans the law required contracts and public bidding.

Meigs eventually acknowledged a crucial shortcoming of his system, saying there were not nearly enough knowledgeable inspectors to cull out the lame animals that contractors continued to fob off on the government. He asked Rosecrans to identify disabled horsemen who could serve as inspectors for the army. He also proposed an idea that might have been more than mere black humor: "Inspection by faithful cavalry officers is the only remedy I can find, unless General Burnside will, under martial law, hang one or two bogus and bribing contractors. That would improve the stock, I think."

———

Rosecrans received 18,450 horses and 14,607 mules in the winter and spring, bringing to more than 43,000 the number of animals accompanying his men. No other army had as many. Finally, fed up about the expense and waste, Meigs uncorked a long letter that stands as a rich example of his oeuvre. It covered so much terrain that he himself described it as a "dissertation." He drew on his department's data to show why Rosecrans's approach was costly and ineffective. One issue was the high number of lame horses that had been delivered to the army, only to be returned to quartermaster operations. Thousands had been sent back to Louisville. Meigs said the circumstances showed that Rosecrans simply asked for too many to be able to inspect them. Besides, Meigs said, the horses were overworked, underfed, and abused. Why did Rosecrans take his men and their horses on long marches with no clear purpose? "Such marches destroy the horses," he wrote. "We have over one hundred and twenty-six regiments of cavalry, and they have killed ten times as many horses for us as for the rebels."

He objected to Rosecrans's assertions that his twelve thousand mounted men were outnumbered by rebels five to one. That would mean the enemy had sixty thousand men on horseback. How was that possible? Meigs suggested the general had to be mistaken. He pushed Rosecrans to live off the land, take what he needed from the enemy, and destroy the rest. It was an approach that Meigs would promote to the end. "[N]ever to pass a bridge without burning it, a telegraph wire without cutting it, a horse without stealing or shooting it, a guerrilla without capturing him, or a negro without explaining the President's proclamation to him."

The War Department went on to establish a specialized Cavalry Bureau to improve the purchase and care of horses. Run in collaboration with the Quartermaster Department, the bureau created sprawling depots in St. Louis, Washington, and four other cities. Each had stables and veterinary hospitals. In short order, the supply and quality of horses reached new highs.

CHAPTER 27

"Fret Him and Fret Him"

As another lovely Virginia spring reached its fullness, the ragged, determined rebel army stirred in the state's Piedmont, a region that rises in great swells to a crest at the Blue Ridge Mountains. Camps came and went. Cavalry gathered near a town called Culpeper. It was early June 1863, and an awful blossoming of the two-year-old war was nearly at hand.

The Army of the Potomac occupied the terrain to the north along the Rappahannock River. Major General Joseph "Fighting Joe" Hooker now led the army. Lincoln gave him the job months before, after Burnside's belated offensive was stymied by torrential rainstorms, a debacle that came to be known as the "Mud March." Hooker was known as a morose schemer and drinker, but Lincoln thought he would fight. The president held on to that hope, even though Hooker had recently faltered at Chancellorsville. Far from living up to his nickname, "Fighting Joe" retreated in the face of a force almost half the size of his own. But if the battle marked one of Lee's greatest victories, he paid dearly for it. Stonewall Jackson, shot mistakenly by his own men, died of the injuries a few days afterward.

Hooker worried now that cavalry led by Stuart intended to attack his supply lines. He ordered his horsemen out to assess matters, and on June 9 they crossed over before dawn and caught Stuart's force sleeping. The fight at Brandy Station, with seventeen thousand mounted soldiers, was the largest cavalry battle fought on the continent. When the Northern cavalry withdrew, they took with them a rare victory. More important, they discerned that Lee was headed again into the North. The rebel army was moving out of Virginia in part because of its material needs. Lee knew that in a defensive posture, the South could not keep pace with the Union's logistical might. He recognized the growing disparity in the "numbers, resources, and all the means and appliances for carrying on the war." Union troops wore fresh uniforms and sturdy, factory-made boots. In camp they ate beef, pork and beans, and fresh bread. In contrast, the rebels generally made do with ragged uniforms or clothing handmade by sweethearts, wives, mothers, and slaves. Sometimes the rebels wore pants, shirts, and shoes they had taken from dead or captured Federals. They ate cornbread, and foraged greens and, with luck, wild game. The gap in manpower grew wider by the month. In Tennessee, Joseph Johnston wrote: "We are too much outnumbered everywhere." Such disparities provided cold comfort to Lincoln, who, with good reason, worried continually about the quality of his generals. They brought him few victories.

On June 12 the president wandered over to Meigs's office to see if the quartermaster would join him for a ride on horseback. He wanted to learn more about the cavalry from Meigs. He also needed to air his thoughts about Hooker, whose withdrawal after Chancellorsville had been a grave disappointment. "Never, as long as I knew him, did he seem to be so broken, so dispirited, so ghostlike," the journalist Noah Brooks wrote about the president then. During the outing, Lincoln asked Meigs to join him again the next day for a demonstration of a new incendiary shell at Hooker's headquarters on the Potomac River. When the time came, the men boarded a tugboat and headed down the river. They got only as far as Alexandria when word came that Hooker had canceled the demonstration. The enemy seemed to be stirring, according to a Union observer in a surveillance balloon who had seen reinforcements arriving at rebel camps.

Hooker wired Lincoln and said he wanted to make a rush on Richmond. The president urged him to remain focused on engaging Lee's army. "Fight him, too, when opportunity offers," the president wrote. "If he stays where he is, fret him and fret him." Within days, federal troops began stalking the Army of Northern Virginia, keeping Washington at their back. The rebel forces maintained the initiative, and on June 14 they surrounded a Union garrison at Winchester, which barely escaped. The rebels took twenty-three cannons, more than three hundred horses, and hundreds of wagons filled with food and quartermaster supplies. Long lines of Confederate fighters began crossing the Potomac.

As this second invasion got under way, rumors spread and panic washed over the northeast region. Now the rebels were at Hagerstown, Maryland, it was said; now at Chambersburg, Pennsylvania. In Pittsburgh, fourteen thousand citizens manned defensive trenches. Stanton was so concerned Lee might be heading to Philadelphia that he ordered authorities to impress steamboats and barges to spirit away gun-making equipment. Meigs got involved more directly in the support of the Army of the Potomac than at almost any other time during the war. He moved to ensure preservation of equipment left behind by the sudden evacuation from the army's headquarters at Aquia Creek. In a telegram to Ingalls, now a brigadier general, Meigs said he counted at least 126 railcars that traversed the line between Aquia and Falmouth, Virginia. He did not want them to fall into enemy hands, and he did not want them destroyed unless absolutely necessary. He suggested dumping them into shallow water so that Union forces could retrieve them later. Ingalls was not to burn any wharves, warehouses, or property. If the place were overrun, Meigs said, gunboats could pummel everything into splinters at the last moment.

Meigs also focused on demands created by an emergency proclamation from Lincoln that called on Maryland, Pennsylvania, Ohio, and West Virginia, recently admitted as a state, to muster a hundred thousand militia. He ordered his men in Pennsylvania to hire transportation rather than buy it. He said they should fix prices in advance. "The people should have just compensation," Meigs wrote, "but should not be allowed to make speculation out of the Government." As he attended to these details, Meigs pondered the fundamental reason for the conflict. He concluded that it was the sin of slavery. "God does not intend to give us peace again until we expiate our crime," he wrote to his father. "Until the last shackle is stricken from the wrist of the black man."

———

The close involvement of Meigs in the preparations came at a price for his subordinates. Prone to irritability, he became an ogre when he saw incompetence or hesitation in his men. Now he erupted in anger when he learned that someone had sent a wagon train of supplies north out of Washington without an armed escort. The timing of the train's departure could not have been worse. The flamboyant Stuart and his horsemen were off on a romp around the Army of the Potomac. The rebel cavalry engaged Union forces in Maryland at River Road, just outside Washington, and then near Rockville. They made off with 150 wagons and 900 mules. In a flash of anger, Meigs sent a harsh letter to the hardworking Ingalls. "Last fall I gave orders to prevent the sending of wagon trains from this place to Frederick without escort," he wrote on June 28, 1863. "The situation repeats itself, and gross carelessness and inattention to military rule this morning cost us." The note troubled Ingalls, who fired off a note back to Meigs. "I had nothing to do with its escort," he said. "I only hope our losses may not be greater. We are deficient in cavalry now. All will be done that is possible." That response seems to have soothed Meigs.

Hooker, meanwhile, was relieved of his command after he complained he had been asked to do too much in the face of a superior force. Corps commander Major General George Meade, a West Point graduate and an engineer in the old army, took command. He put the Army of the Potomac into motion on a path that would soon take it to a prosperous crossroads town in Pennsylvania called Gettysburg. Confederate forces were headed in the same general direction. Rumors asserted that Gettysburg had a shoe factory, and they desperately needed shoes. Fighting broke out on July 1 when the rebels happened upon Union cavalry at the town. Through verve and good sense, the small Union force stood pat. They occupied good, high ground just to the south, at a place called Cemetery Hill. What might have been a skirmish became a full-blown conflagration as divisions from both sides poured in.

Drawing on lessons learned from earlier campaigns, along with the experiments with flying columns, Ingalls and Meigs directed the long wagon trains well out of the way of the troops. Baggage and tents were not stored near the fighting. Soldiers carried only a small amount of food, and ammunition was delivered at night, mostly by wagon. Troops rarely saw the operations that sustained them. Ingalls established a temporary depot twenty-five miles behind Union forces, at the head of a small rail line and a road leading to Baltimore. Supplies also started arriving at Frederick, on the B&O rail line. Both locations served as communications hubs for the army, with telegraph lines to Baltimore and Washington. Riders conveyed messages from Baltimore to Westminster and then to Meade's headquarters at Gettysburg. To make the most of local railways, Stanton called on Brigadier General Haupt, the military railroad chief in Virginia, who received authority to do whatever he thought necessary to keep supplies moving to the war fighters. Though Haupt's chain of command went up to Meigs, and he depended on the Quartermaster's Department for funding and labor, Stanton and Meigs allowed him to operate mostly as he saw fit. Haupt was a railroad engineer in private life and another of the war's dependable, creative, and hardworking heroes. The year before, he had moved the great piles of supplies to Manassas. He seemed almost a conjurer in the way he had rebuilt a spindly looking railroad bridge near Fredericksburg. So thought Lincoln, anyway. "That man Haupt has built a bridge four hundred feet long and eighty feet high, across Potomac Creek, on which loaded trains are passing every hour, and upon my word, gentlemen, there is nothing in it but cornstalks and beanpoles," Lincoln said.

Haupt rushed to Harrisburg and Baltimore, where he met with political leaders and railroad executives. He decided that only one line got close enough to the battlefield to be of use, a sparse operation out of Baltimore called the Western Maryland Railroad. It had just one track and four locomotives, and it lacked water stations, sidings, and turntables to maneuver the engines. The line typically ran just four trains each day that terminated at Westminster, where Ingalls established his depot. Haupt estimated the army needed at least thirty trains each way. He addressed this apparent impossibility with a few swift moves. First, he took control of the tiny railroad, under federal legislation approved the year before. Next, he ordered a trainload of railroad construction workers up from Alexandria and called on other rail lines to supply locomotives and cars. Then he put into motion an elegant system that ran around the clock. Five trains with ten cars each ran in convoys, one after the other in a long line. The trains carried in ammunition, weapons, and other supplies to wagons waiting at Westminster. They returned to Baltimore with wounded soldiers. Haupt estimated that 150 cars could go through every twenty-four hours, as long as they were unloaded promptly and there were no accidents. It was an ingenious solution to a problem that could have hobbled the Union army. Haupt later gave credit to the underappreciated railroad construction corps. "These men are not in a position to acquire military distinction or rewards, but I would fail in my duty if I omitted to signify to you my high appreciation of the labors, services, courage, and fidelity of the corps for construction and transportation in the department of US Military Railroads."

The efforts of Haupt, Ingalls and Meigs, along with thousands of others who provided the labor and transportation, ensured that the Union had more than enough supplies to see it through the momentous days at Gettysburg.

Those three days: The massing of Union men and guns on the high ground at Cemetery Hill. The savage combat at the Peach Orchard, Devil's Den, and Little Round Top. The ill-fated charge by George Pickett and his Virginians.

In those three days, the rebels reached the zenith of their cause, and the Union stood firm, well armed, well clothed, and well fed. "They began the fight, but we have repulsed them at all points," Ingalls wrote to Meigs. "This entire army has fought with terrible obstinacy, and has covered itself with glory." Even as the battle raged, Meigs prepared for the aftermath, arranging new wagons for supplies and remounts for the cavalry. On July 4 he asked Haupt to work closely with a private delivery firm that offered the services of its wagons and men to help move the wounded off the field. Meigs cautioned Haupt to set aside his compassion if necessary and remain focused on the greater goal, capturing and destroying Lee's army. The pursuit took precedence over the wounded. "Let nothing interfere with the supply of rations to the men and grain for the horses."

Meigs and all of Washington hoped in vain that Meade's army would catch up to Lee before he could slip out of the North. Days went by. On July 14, resigned to another lost opportunity, Meigs ordered Haupt south. "Withdraw all your construction corps from Pennsylvania railroads and bring them as quickly as possible to Alexandria. Lee has crossed the Potomac." The quartermaster general would not move on entirely without mopping up the blood-drenched terrain, where bodies lay, horses wandered, and weapons rested on churned-up dirt. He ordered several quartermaster men to oversee collection of huge amounts of materiel left behind by both armies, including muskets, ammunition, cartridge boxes, knapsacks, clothing, and more.

Captain W. Willard Smith, an aide to Halleck, was among them. He joined throngs of medical personnel, journalists, and onlookers from miles around who flooded into town. Smith discovered that collecting the gear was harder than he had expected. People came in "swarms to sweep & plunder the battlegrounds" of souvenirs. Some took guns, bayonets, and other equipment by the wagonload. One man made away with a six-pound cannon and lowered it into a well. Others took horses and mules, cutting out or burning away the US brand on the animals to obscure evidence of their thefts. When Smith and his men tried to retrieve the supplies, guilty residents professed ignorance. The captain confiscated a military coat and a pile of suspect tools from one man who claimed the tools were his and that he had paid for the coat with a loaf of bread. "I told him if he could prove that he owned the tools I would return them, but that I would not return the over coat, and that he ought to be ashamed to rob a Soldier who had come here to fight for him," Smith wrote Meigs.

Smith eventually arrested scores of looters and put them on the grim work of burying the bodies of men and horses. More than 24,000 muskets and rifles, 10,000 bayonets, 2,400 cartridge boxes, sabers, belts, and hundreds of other items were retrieved eventually and made available to the army.

―――――

Meigs relished his department's performance at Gettysburg. He had another reason to be proud that summer. John Meigs had graduated from West Point, at the head of his class, and joined the Army Corps of Engineers. He was assigned to Major General Robert Schenck, with responsibility for constructing entrenchments to defend Baltimore. Schenck gave him a thousand laborers and two companies of infantry. Before long, John received new orders directing him to defend the railroad lines in the vicinity of Harpers Ferry. The young Meigs had an idea related to ironclad boats that his uncle and father helped launch a year earlier, urging Schenck to fortify several railcars in the same way, sharp angles and all. "Against any but the largest bodies of troops, these defensive cars would be a perfect protection to the points where they might be placed," he wrote.

Schenck agreed. He asked J. W. Garrett, president of the B&O, to fortify five railcars in the manner of the river ironclads, and five more as bulletproof rifle cars. Garrett assigned three hundred of his men to the job, and they worked six days straight to deliver them. The monitor cars were enveloped by iron plates fixed at 45-degree angles. They had openings for cannons and loopholes for rifles, with an entrance through a trapdoor in the floor. John Meigs named them, navy style, in honor of recent Union victories, including Antietam and Gettysburg.

Schenck sent John Meigs and sixty men to Harpers Ferry on the rail lines. John's job was to protect workers repairing the damage caused by rebels. Fighting began as soon as he arrived. He silenced the rebels with mortar fire. On July 8 John wrote to Meade and his commander, seeking permission to go beyond the limits of his orders. "I am not afraid of the heavy masses of the enemy," he wrote to the busy

Meade. "May I build the bridge to-morrow and go on?" Schenck urged him to slow down and remain focused on his assignment. "Remember that the duty assigned you is not to seek a fight, but to help keep open and protect the railroad."

John also wrote to his father from a post he called "Headquarters Iron Clads." He gushed about the mission. He said he was especially proud of measures he took to deceive the enemy. It seems he painted the words *Govt Stores* on the sides of the bulletproof cars. "When Johnnie Reb comes up to them and sees the little shutters drop out of their ports and the whole thing suddenly transformed into an in-approachable blockhouse, I think he will be astonished," John Meigs wrote. Two days after the letter, John got into a scrape when he was or-dered to join a small force reconnoitering Confederate positions across the Potomac. During a fight, two dozen Union soldiers along with their commanding officer were taken prisoner. John escaped on foot, losing a borrowed horse.

CHAPTER 28

"Exhaustion of Men and Money"

Far from Gettysburg, the Union triumphed in Mississippi. Grant and William Tecumseh Sherman led those fights, in campaigns that foreshadowed an intensified, grinding war in the east. Grant pushed his men through swamps and heat before laying siege to Vicksburg. Trapped for weeks, soldiers and civilians resorted to eating rats. The rebel army capitulated on July 4, with the surrender of thirty thousand soldiers, nineteen generals, and almost two hundred pieces of artillery. It would stand as one of the most important victories of the war. Sherman then drove the rebels out of Jackson, the state capital.

Meigs admired the toughness of those men. In an overview of the military situation, commissioned that summer by Seward, Meigs applauded their willingness to cut free of communications and supply lines. Such aggression gave the Federals extraordinary flexibility of maneuver, while lightening the load on the army's strained supply apparatus. He praised Grant's reliance on freed slaves as soldiers and laborers, saying the "newly raised negro regiments showed great valor and devotion, and forever in this country dispelled all doubts as to the capacity of this oppressed race for the defense of their newly acquired liberty." Most of all, he drew attention to the campaign's impact on the balance sheet of the logistical war. By capturing half of Mississippi, Grant and Sherman blocked the supply of beef cattle to the rebels in the east and prevented Richmond from sending weapons, food, clothing, and reinforcements to the west.

A Vicksburg woman, writing in her diary on July 4, hinted at the importance of this great divide. She was awed by the vitality of

Union forces, "these stalwart, well-fed men, so splendidly set up and accoutered . . . Civilization, discipline, and order seemed to enter with the measured tramp of those marching columns; and the heart turned with throbs of added pity to the worn men in gray, who were being blindly dashed against this embodiment of modern power."

Meigs told Seward he thought that Union victory in the war was assured. Some two hundred thousand square miles of land had been taken from the Confederacy during the war, the equivalent of territory the size of France. The Union had twice as many fighters in the field and a far larger pool of replacements to tap. Meigs had faith in that force, saying that long marches and hard fighting had tempered the men. He wrote that Grant, Sherman, and other bold generals gave them clear direction. And behind them all was a powerful war machine that drew on secure domestic sources to supply nearly all of the clothing, equipment, and food needed by the mammoth Federal force. In contrast, he told Seward, Richmond had to import much at great cost to sustain itself.

"The National Government enjoys the highest credit, with abundant resources in money, in men, and in material," Meigs wrote. "Its armies everywhere outnumber the rebel forces, who are all in retreat. Every rebel port is blockaded, besieged, or possessed by the national arms. The Confederacy is divided by the Mississippi, all whose fortresses are in our hands, and whose waters are patrolled by a hundred war steamers."

Still, Meigs warned Seward that the Union faced tough going until the end, saying that the rebels "are a gallant people and will make stern resistance, but it is the exhaustion of men and money that finally terminates all modern wars."

Behind his optimism, Meigs was becoming angrier about the Confederacy and its leaders, including former friends. His emotions flared on August 17, 1863, about the time he was delivering his report to Seward. He learned that Union Commander George W. Rodgers, a relative of Louisa's, had died of wounds suffered from cannon fire during a naval attack on Charleston Harbor. Meigs dwelled on the loss in an eleven-page letter to his father that underscored his fury. He turned again to the stark themes of his Christian upbringing to frame the war as a rite of national atonement. "Can all this devotion, this sacrifice, this courage, this patriotism be wasted?" Meigs asked in the letter. "Will God allow this sacred blood to be poured upon the ground & not accept it as an expiation of the national sins?"

———

On August 28, 1863, Meigs rode into the hills west of Washington, making his way to the sprawling camp of the Army of the Potomac, just north of the Rappahannock River. It was the first of several journeys that took him out of the capital for nearly four months, longer than at any other time during the war. He did his part for the Union in the field, as it faced another of the great threats—and then indulged in his passion for hunting. Judging from his dispatches, it was one of the most exciting and satisfying times of the war for Meigs. Wherever he went, Meigs observed mammoth, sometimes awe-inspiring operations. At the Army of the Potomac camp, he looked at a veritable city of white cotton tents, a scene made hazy in places by camp smoke. Conestoga wagons stood in straight lines in the fields not far from the horses and mules that would pull them. Scores of cannons gleamed in the hot sun. Men ate and laughed and slept and marched, as soldiers in camp always do. During the visit, Meigs looked on as General Meade received a ceremonial sword for his performance at Gettysburg.

On his return to the capital, he received orders to visit the principal armies in the middle states and the South. Planned stops included depots at Memphis, Vicksburg, and St. Louis, along with Rosecrans's Army of the Cumberland. Stanton wanted Meigs to watch the soldiers on parade and examine the supplies provided by his department, including the baggage, clothing, ammunition, and wagons. His mission soon changed, and then changed again. First, he was redirected to Louisville to investigate a contracting scheme involving immature mules. In Louisville, he received a telegram ordering him to leave for Chattanooga, Tennessee. A ferocious battle was under way just southeast of the city, near a stream called Chickamauga Creek. Stanton wanted Meigs to help bring order to the Army of the Cumberland and send back reports about the action.

Drawing on sparse details, Meigs initially thought the Federals might have the advantage. It turned out the battle posed a grave threat, not only to Union forces led by Rosecrans but also to the North's entire position in the region. Only the heroic performance of General George H. Thomas averted annihilation. Under his cool leadership, federal soldiers fended off an onslaught by Confederate forces under Braxton Bragg. Rosecrans and the rest of his Union army fled to Chattanooga. Thomas rallied the remaining troops, buying time for Rosecrans and earning the nickname the Rock of Chickamauga. The fighting was over before Meigs arrived, but he found a perilous situation. Both sides had lost more than a quarter of their forces to casualties, more than thirty-four thousand in all. The battered Union forces rested in strong, well-provisioned camps throughout the town, but their sense of security was short lived. Bragg's men cut the rail line to the federal supply base in Nashville and occupied nearby Lookout Mountain, which towers 1,500 feet over Chattanooga, along with Missionary Ridge, an impregnable-seeming position 500 feet high. Meanwhile, Lieutenant General James Longstreet's corps, on loan to Bragg from the Army of Northern Virginia, took control of the valley and the south bank of the Tennessee River. The rebels resupplied themselves with weapons, ammunition, and shoes taken from the Union dead. The Federals had to content themselves with what they had. A single mountain path provided the only way to bring in supplies. Meigs saw that the path, which barely qualified as a road, would become a quagmire after a little rain. Rosecrans was trapped.

For two days, Stanton and his aides in Washington read the dismal dispatches in which Rosecrans attempted to explain the reasons for the debacle at Chickamauga. "I know the reason well enough," Stanton quipped roughly. "Rosecrans ran away from his fighting men and did not stop for thirteen miles." It was now late on September 23, 1863.

The war secretary realized that Washington had to do something extraordinary to help, regardless of the bungling that had created the mess. Chattanooga served as a railway hub in the region. The Union had to hold it to maintain control of Tennessee. Future operations deeper into the South depended on it. Stanton called for an emergency planning session and went to Lincoln's cottage at the Old Soldiers' Home to retrieve the president. Working through the night, the group resolved to reinforce Rosecrans with men drawn from the Army of the Potomac. They selected the Eleventh and Twelfth Corps for the job, giving the command to Hooker.

Now everyone asked the same question: How could they get the men to Chattanooga in time? For the answer, Stanton turned to the military railroad corps, one of the North's greatest logistical weapons. Under the leadership of Colonel Daniel McCallum, the railroad operators would achieve something no one had done before, something that few thought was possible. McCallum was an engineer and a poet. He distinguished himself before the war as a railroad executive. In 1862 he became director and superintendent of military railroads in the United States. He had already worked wonders during the war. Under his leadership, the rail lines under Union control soared from 7 miles to more than 2,100 miles. He would oversee construction of 26 miles of bridges. His mission now involved moving twenty-three thousand fighting men, their horses, artillery, and supplies about 1,200 miles, all in one swoop. Halleck declared that such a movement was not possible. McCallum said it could be done in two weeks. Many people jumped in to help. Garrett, president of the B&O Railroad, contributed 194 troop cars and 44 stock cars. Garrett also sent telegraphs ahead to make arrangements for the various stages. He stayed in constant contact with McCallum.

Meigs served as field organizer in Tennessee. He made financial arrangements to move the soldiers on a railroad between Louisville and Nashville. Hooker and his officers quickly gathered their troops at Manassas Junction and Brandy Station. The soldiers carried only what they needed for the trip and the following few days. That included forty rounds per man and two days' cooked rations. Commissary and quartermaster men arranged to provide coffee and sugar during the journey. Planners made sure that the trains moved in the dark to conceal them from rebel spotters in distant hills, and cautioned commanders to protect details about the planned stops: Wheeling, West Virginia; Columbus and Dayton, Ohio; Indianapolis, Indiana; Louisville, Kentucky; and, finally, Nashville, Tennessee. To confuse the enemy, officers received orders to say they were headed to Memphis. Somehow it all came together. By five o'clock on September 26, McCallum reported that nearly all the trains and troops and supplies were on their way west and south, thanks especially to Garrett and the other railroad men. Stanton was ecstatic. "A thousand thanks to you," he wrote to McCallum.

———

The hot dust in Chattanooga whipped through the Union encampments. It had not rained for two months. Any shade disappeared as the men cut down trees for their fortifications and fires. The grass withered and turned gray. Food trickled in, at least until the rains began in early October, and then the hunger grew as the river rose and mud sucked at the wheels of supply wagons. Soldiers debated whether it had been better broiling in the sun or dying a cool, damp death through starvation. One wagon driver became so troubled by the mud on the single path he had to follow, that instead of beating his mules in the usual manner, he sat still in his seat and wept. The two armies faced each other from trenches and log fortifications. They were so close in places that some stopped shooting at one another. It seemed inhuman to take quiet aim at a man whose eyes they could still see at twilight. Men on both sides called their trenches gopher pits. They joked with one another even as giant shells, launched from rebel siege guns, shrieked overhead. They dueled with songs, "Dixie" from the Southerners and "Hail Columbia" from the Northern boys.

The logistical challenges facing the quartermaster corps were nearly overwhelming. Thousands of mules died from starvation and the work of hauling in rations for fifty thousand men and forage for the starving horses, many of which no longer had strength enough to pull artillery. Mule carcasses lined the rough road all the way to Bridgeport, Alabama, where the Union army had a boatyard and maintained supplies. Rebel cavalry made a devastating attack on the tenuous supply line. The attack, on October 2, destroyed more than three hundred loaded wagons. The rebels killed or captured 1,800 mules. The army, with enough ammunition for less than a day's fighting, hung on "by the merest thread." Meigs scrambled in his usual way. He urged Stanton to send more mules, in part to support Hooker's arriving men. He guided pioneer troops who had put two abandoned sawmills into action, spitting out lumber for bridges, boats, and fortifications. He oversaw the inventory of equipment and metal from a large foundry and a destroyed bridge, stuff that was eventually transformed into rolling mills for rail lines.

Meigs wrote often to Stanton, and their correspondence showed a growing trust—even signs of affection. In one note, the gruff war secretary went beyond military protocol to express his appreciation of Meigs's efforts. "Your very interesting reports have been received, and I thank you much for the intelligence conveyed," Stanton wrote. "The army transportation advised by you to be forwarded is now being shipped by rail as fast as possible, and will be pushed forward with the utmost speed. 'All quiet on the Potomac.' Nothing to disturb autumnal slumbers. Your friends here are well. All public interest is now concentrated on the Tennessee and at Chattanooga."

On October 16, with the situation fast deteriorating, the army created a new military division that encompassed Tennessee. Grant, hero of Vicksburg, was put in overall command. He relieved Rosecrans and placed Thomas, the Rock of Chickamauga, in command of the Army of the Cumberland. In an exchange of telegrams, the two new leaders discussed the army's dire state. "Hold Chattanooga at all hazards," Grant said. "I will be there as soon as possible. Please inform me how long your present supplies will last, and the prospect of keeping them up." Thomas reported there wasn't much. They had perhaps two weeks before they would have to abandon Chattanooga. "We will hold the town until we starve," he told Grant.

Meigs traveled to Louisville to meet Grant and Stanton and then accompanied Grant on the return trip. Grant focused on feeding his men, and that meant improving his supply line. A key to this was the construction of a steamboat that could ply the upper Tennessee River, which could not be reached easily from downstream because of thin water at Muscle Shoals, Alabama. A quartermaster man, Captain Arthur Edward, had responsibility for building the boat. Meigs arranged for delivery of specialized supplies, including boilers and engines that were floated down the Ohio River and shipped by rail to the boatyard at Bridgeport, on the upstream side of Muscle Shoals. Mechanics and carpenters hustled down from the North to help out. The quartermaster team built the steamer from a flat-bottomed scow outfitted with pontoons, a new steam engine, a rough pilothouse, and a paddle wheel. The team fashioned a cabin from a rough frame and covered it with canvas. With the boat nearly complete, Grant launched a stealthy campaign to take key points on the river. At three in the morning on October 27, 1,400 men floated silently nine miles down the Tennessee on other pontoon boats, surprising the rebels at Brown's Ferry. The Union force dismantled those boats and used the pontoons to build a bridge. Hooker's men, waiting in reserve near rail lines outside of Chattanooga, moved to protect the bridge.

On October 29 the handcrafted steamboat *Chattanooga* steamed upriver. It moved barges holding thousands of rations, including pork and hard bread known as crackers, along with tons of forage for the animals. The boat stopped at Rankin's Ferry and Kelley's Ferry, triggering jubilation among the hungry soldiers. They proclaimed the boat, along with the newly opened roads, a "cracker line" of deliverance. "Their joy at seeing the little Steamboat and scows afloat and loaded with rations can be faintly imagined—hardly described; they shouted and danced on the bank of the river like crazy men," one quartermaster man recalled later.

———

Near the end of November, the replenished Union army began its push. The troops marched out of their lines in strict formation, as though on parade. More Union fighters followed, including twenty-five thousand of Thomas's men. The rebels, lulled by the long siege, mistook it for a drill. Those on the front lines found themselves overrun by Union forces in a snap. "It was a surprise in open daylight," Meigs wrote in a dispatch to Stanton that was soon published in newspapers. Sherman and his army arrived from the west and took a bridgehead several miles upriver of the city. Then Hooker pushed his men up Lookout Mountain. The Federals climbed and fought through rain and mist. Most of the fighting occurred above a mass of low clouds. Meigs was enchanted. Here was an imaginative desk general on a rare jaunt in the field who was on hand for one of the remarkable days of the war. He called it the "Battle Above the Clouds." "At nightfall sky cleared, and the full moon, the 'hunter's moon,' shone upon the beautiful scene," he wrote in his dispatch to Stanton. "Till 1 a.m., twinkling sparks upon the mountain side showed that picket skirmishing was still going on; then it ceased."

By the morning of November 25, the Stars and Stripes flew from the peak of Lookout Mountain. The fight continued. Southerners still jammed Missionary Ridge, and they commenced a cannonade on Union positions. All day long, big guns on both sides barked and spit fire. Infantry probes went up the ridge with limited success. Grant now ordered a general advance. He did not intend for the men to go far. They scrambled higher and higher on their own initiative, over rifle pits and through a hailstorm of shell, grape, and musket fire. Some fainted. All of them became soaked in sweat. They feared if they stopped, they would die. Meigs almost could not believe what unfolded before him. "With cheers answering to cheers," he wrote, "the men swarmed upwards." One Union leader later put the surge into perspective: "What so often is uttered in eloquent speeches in comfortable *salons,* in State House, and in halls of Congress, 'Victory or dead,' was here an uncomfortable reality."

Grant, Meigs, and other leaders eventually followed the foot soldiers to the crest of the ridge. The Federals redirected captured guns and rebuilt log breastworks as barricades. Bragg's disintegrating army fled the carnage. Union soldiers shouted, wept, and danced with emotion as they absorbed the new reality. Meigs looked around at the field and gave thanks for witnessing what he called the "great battle of the Rebellion."

"Total defeat; they are driven from the field, and these impregnable positions are stormed by our volunteers," he wrote that night before bedding down. "It was a glorious sight. I am rejoiced—I took part in it—a memorable day."

Meigs collected war souvenirs that littered the ground. One man recalled that the quartermaster created a veritable "curiosity shop" of rebel bullets, bayonets, and cartridge boxes. Meigs later accompanied Grant and other generals on a visit to the top of Lookout Mountain. Meigs drank from a spring and filled his canteen. Then he rode off, found a covey of partridges, and, relishing a passing chance to hunt, shot three of them with his pistol. On orders from Washington, Meigs eventually made his way to Nashville, Louisville, and then, after the New Year, home.

CHAPTER 29

"A Beauteous Bubble"

In January 1864 Montgomery Meigs received another warm welcome home. Stanton, Chase, and Lincoln met him at the White House before he joined a stellar crowd at a dinner party that included Seward, congressmen, and Supreme Court justices. None of it sat well with him. He yearned to be back in the field. The cold nights, daily excursions, and simple food in Tennessee had suited him, all of it a "relief from the dreary monotony of office labor." The sojourn afield had spurred doubts in his mind about his role in the war. Was the job of quartermaster the best he could do? Did people understand the important work of his department? The public was dazzled by stories of fighting generals, and he understood that against their exploits, the toil of administrators did not shine so brightly.

The administrative demands in Washington hit him like a hailstorm. One task required him to focus on a faltering effort by Lincoln to create a colony for freed slaves on Île à Vache, an island near Haiti. The president pushed the idea partly as a political solution to appease anti-black forces in the North that opposed emancipation, but the colony foundered quickly. Meigs arranged for a ship, *Maria L. Day*, to retrieve several hundred famished colonists and carry them to Washington, to "be employed and provided for at the camps for colored persons around that city." Before long, Meigs asked Stanton for permission to join an offensive planned for the spring. The war secretary refused, saying the quartermaster was too important to the war's administration to be spared. Meigs also sought a promotion, asking his father to reach out to influential friends in Pennsylvania, in the hope they might intercede.

As if seeking reassurance of his value, he went to the Capitol and inspected the progress of the work. The great dome was nearly finished, with its crowning feature, the statue of *Freedom,* recently installed. It looked as magnificent as he had envisioned. He was satisfied he could rightly claim a great share of credit for the success of the domes—but only a share. Walter deserved acclaim for his role in the design and execution as well. "The great dome of the Capitol was the conception of Thomas U. Walter. But it was Captain Meigs whose skill in engineering guided its construction," wrote the historian Russell Weigley. "[A]nd if the dome displays a grace of line which is the mark of the architect of Girard College, it possesses also a sturdy dignity and reassuring stability which reflect the mind and character of its chief engineer." The Architect of the Capitol, the office responsible for the operation and preservation of the Capitol complex, now agrees with that assessment. "While Thomas U. Walter is credited as the architect of the Capitol Dome, his world-renowned design could not have been accomplished without Montgomery C. Meigs."

In any event, the new dome was an inspiration. Poet Walt Whitman, who served as a nurse in the District during the war, thought it sublime. "I shall always identify Washington with that huge and delicate towering bulge of pure white, where it emerges calm and lofty from the hill, out of a dense mass of trees," he wrote in a dispatch for the *New York Times.* "A vast eggshell, built of iron and glass, this dome—a beauteous bubble, caught and put in permanent form." Whitman offered an unintentional tribute to Meigs's engineering efforts, saying that the derrick might be a fitter emblem of the nation's character than the statue *Freedom.* "[T]here is something about this powerful, simple, and obedient piece of machinery, so modern, so significant in many respects of our constructive nation and age, and even so poetical."

Meigs also visited the bridge at Cabin John, known as Union Arch. With the scaffolding removed, Meigs experienced the full effect of the smooth, imposing curve of stone. It was perhaps the favorite of his creations. "It stands successful—the greatest masonry arch in the world," he wrote in his diary. "[W]ater flows through it; there is little leakage.

A stone bears the inscription—Union Arch. Chief Engineer Capt. Montgomery C. Meigs. U.S. Corps of Engineers. Esto Perpetuo."

Meigs added in his diary: "It is a great monument."

————

On May 4, 1864, the Army of the Potomac began its great Overland Campaign into the Confederacy. It would culminate nearly a year later with the fall of Richmond, but only after what Grant described "as desperate fighting as the world has ever witnessed." The numbers associated with the offensive—the supplies, the men, the deaths—remain notable. The force included nearly one hundred thousand infantry, fifteen thousand cavalry, and six thousand artillery men. They had rested in a comfortable camp north of the Rapidan River. They showed strength and discipline, and they had confidence in Grant, who was now lieutenant general of all Union armies, the first to hold that title since George Washington. Meade served as commander of the Army of the Potomac.

The quartermaster corps performed admirably here. They deployed 4,300 wagons to carry an immense supply of pork, crackers, coffee, salt, and sugar, along with mess kits, ammunition, and baggage. On hand to draw the wagons were 23,000 mules. More than 30,000 horses carried cavalry soldiers and pulled the artillery. Beef cattle followed on the hoof, to be butchered as needed. Grant later estimated that if put into single file and spaced properly, the train would have extended the seventy miles or so from the crossing on the Rapidan to the city of Richmond. Thanks to Rufus Ingalls, chief quartermaster of the Army of the Potomac, each wagon bore corps badges, division colors, and brigade numbers, along with markings that described its contents.

Ingalls adopted a strict method for using the wagons. As soon as they were emptied, they generally would be sent to the rear for resupply with identical provisions. Apart from creating a new level of efficiency, his system addressed one of the great logistical burdens of the war, the feeding of animals. Instead of having to carry tons of forage for themselves, the animals often ate when they returned to depots. Grant tells us in his memoir, "There never was a corps better organized than was the quartermaster's corps with the Army of the Potomac in 1864." Even so, the force moved slowly. Its path took it over terrain etched by streams and widely covered by thick forests. It squeezed over narrow roads in the direction of Chancellorsville. Grant intended to go after Lee wherever he happened to be. He aimed to attack with overwhelming numbers and then attack again, leaving Lee no chance of dividing his force and sending reinforcements elsewhere. As Grant told Sherman in the run-up to the campaign, he wanted all Northern armies, from Mississippi to South Carolina, to move against their rebel foes in a coordinated way. He wanted the armies to damage any enemy resources used to carry on the war. Sherman, fierce, temperamental, and energetic, stood ready to do so. His three armies—in Chattanooga, northern Alabama, and southern Tennessee—made a simultaneous move toward Atlanta. He wanted his combined force of 112,000 men to cause as much damage as possible and take or destroy the city railways. He was in a "savage frame of mind," as one historian noted.

The Army of the Potomac soon encountered three of Lee's corps coming from the west. Almost 102,000 Federals engaged an estimated 61,000 rebels in the tangled undergrowth of a region in Virginia known as the Wilderness. The fight in the dim light beneath the pine, oak, and hickory trees took on a nightmarish quality. Coherent maneuvers were not possible, and many units blundered into the enemy. Gunshots ignited brush fires. The smoke obscured an already murky battleground. Men perished in the flames. Grant pressed on. He requested 5 million rounds of ammunition for the infantry and asked Washington to "rake or scrape together" new soldiers to replace the dead and wounded. James McPherson, the great historian of the Civil War, called it a "a new kind of relentless, ceaseless warfare," fueled by what Lincoln called Grant's "dogged pertinacity." There was no escaping that it came with an unprecedented cost in lives. Army of the Potomac casualties after the first week exceeded the Union losses in any other week of the war until then, some 32,000 dead, wounded, and missing men.

Maj. Gen. Philip Sheridan, whose rapid rise through the ranks was fueled by his aggression, echoed Grant's relentlessness. With 10,000 cavalry soldiers, he carved a path toward Richmond, inviting an attack from the smaller rebel cavalry force under Jeb Stuart. They lived largely off what they found and destroyed railroads, trestle bridges, and telegraph lines along the way. At one rebel depot, Sheridan's men dismantled or torched 100 railcars, 2 locomotives, and 1.5 million rations, including 200,000 pounds of bacon, according to Sheridan's estimate. A showdown came at Yellow Tavern, several miles from the Confederate capital. Union fighters armed with modern fast-firing carbines riddled many of the enemy cavalry and dispersed the rest. Stuart was mortally wounded.

Now there was rain, day after day of rain. The Army of the Potomac slogged through the mud to do battle near Spotsylvania Court House. The fighting there became almost crazed. "To give some idea of the intensity of the fire, an oak tree 22 inches in diameter, which stood just in the rear of the right of the brigade, was cut down by the constant scaling of musket-balls," one general reported. Civilians on both sides kept close track of these grim events through press accounts. In the North, it was widely thought the end of the war might be drawing near. "News continues very good," one man wrote in his diary. "May it prove *true*, also." It was not yet true. The end was not as near as many hoped. The fighting and the dying would go on and on that summer. After a month, the number of casualties reached 44,000 for the Union and perhaps 25,000 for the defensive-oriented Confederate force (a number that cannot be fixed for certain because of an unreliable Southern tally). One after another, the dead and infirm were ferried by quartermaster wagons and ambulances to Fredericksburg. And still Grant pressed on.

Behind it all, legions of supply workers, sometimes operating in the line of fire, provided steadfast support. For the crossing of the James River, army engineers built what was one of the longest floating bridges in the history of warfare, a 2,200-foot-long structure composed of 101 wooden pontoons. It enabled the crossing of a line of 3,500 beef cattle and a wagon train 35 miles long. The quartermasters, meanwhile, had to hustle to keep pace with the destruction of horses. In the first six months of 1864, the Army of the Potomac received almost 40,000 cavalry horses, representing two complete remounts.

Meigs went into the field again to help out as a set of eyes and ears for Washington. He traveled to Bermuda Hundred, Virginia, to assess the force under General Benjamin Butler, whose army was supposed to move toward Richmond. Butler had been bottled up in a defensive position. Meigs did what he could before leaving for Belle Plain, a rude landing on the Potomac south of Aquia that Grant used as a supply depot during the Overland Campaign. Meigs aimed to improve operations at the makeshift port, which seemed as congested at times as New York Harbor. As he sorted out those difficulties, a Patent Office clerk who had dedicated herself to helping Union soldiers received permission to travel to Belle Plain and then to Fredericksburg, which Union forces had occupied. The clerk, Clara Barton, was horrified by scenes of unrelenting agony. Wagons carrying the wounded bounced over rough roads and slogged through the pink clay mud at Belle Plain. In Fredericksburg, men lay so thick on the streets, exposed, untended, and unfed, that cavalry horses could not pass. Barton rushed back to Washington and reported to Senator Henry Wilson, who reached out to Stanton with a warning. Bring order to the chaos, Wilson said, or the Senate would find a way to do so. Stanton ordered Meigs to take command of both Fredericksburg and Belle Plain. He gave the quartermaster wide latitude to do whatever he needed. Meigs moved quickly, ordering homes in Fredericksburg opened to Union troops. He made sure they were fed and received care. He pushed for the army to clear guerrillas from along the river. The ability to use river transport ended the need to carry the wounded to Belle Plain by springless wagons over rough roads, an ordeal that killed some of them.

The wounded who made it to the landing were transported in steamboats to Washington. In less than a month, the city's hospitals took in eighteen thousand new patients. Many of them died in short order, and then the corpses stacked up faster than they could be buried.

A stench drifted over the city like smoke. Meigs had to provide the answer to a grim, practical question: Where would all the bodies go?

———

Care of the dead became a responsibility for the Quartermaster's Department early in the war, when Secretary Cameron had called on the department to help commanders keep track of soldiers who died at hospitals and take note of where each was buried. Cameron mandated that Meigs create a "registered headboard" at each soldier's grave. That mandate was extended to the field a few months later, when army officers received orders to secure land near battlefields to inter the dead. In July 1862 Congress authorized Lincoln to create national cemeteries for servicemen. As the war ground on, finding burial sites became a monumental challenge. By the spring of 1864, the pine and rosewood caskets passed through Washington in a seemingly unending flow. On May 13 a cemetery on the property of the Old Soldiers' Home ran out of room. Nearly 6,000 soldiers had been interred there in less than three years. Another 2,000 had been buried at Harmony Cemetery and elsewhere in the vicinity of Washington. Added to that were burials of more than 4,100 deceased former slaves.

Meigs knew already where he wanted to direct these "waves of sorrow," as the journalist Noah Brooks put it. He would create a cemetery on the Arlington estate of Robert Lee's family, a beautiful spread of land in hills on the south side of the Potomac, overlooking the capital. Lee's wife, Mary, and the family fled the estate in the spring of 1861. In the first few years of the war, Union troops used one part of the property as a camp, while the federal government used another part to house and educate former slaves. The land was put up for auction after the Lee family failed to pay—effectively was not permitted to pay—a $92.07 tax bill. The federal government bought it for $26,800. The burials at Arlington began in May, with the interment of Private William Christman, twenty-one, a Pennsylvania infantryman who had contracted the measles and died at Lincoln General Hospital in the District. Meigs referred to the land as the "new cemetery," even though it had not been formally established. On June 15 he toured the property before asking Stanton for permission to use it as the next national cemetery. In a brief letter, Meigs recommended "that the land surrounding the Arlington Mansion, now understood to be the property of the United States, be appropriated a National Military Cemetery, to be properly enclosed, laid out, and carefully preserved."

With Stanton's approval, Meigs sketched out his plans that same day for Brigadier General D. H. Rucker, the chief quartermaster of the Washington depot. The cemetery would occupy two hundred acres along the lines sketched out in a scale map drawn and signed by Meigs. Bodies that had been buried on the property during the space crunch in May were to be reburied close to the mansion. Locating the cemetery at Arlington was at root a logical decision. The land was close to Washington's hospitals and easy to access. But there's little doubt that Meigs's bitterness about Robert Lee's defection factored into the choice. As he wrote several months later, he wanted Lee and other Confederate leaders tried and executed "by the government which they have betrayed [and] attacked." News of Meigs's plan for Lee's former home stirred vengeful cheers from newspapers in the North. "How appropriate that Lee's land should be appropriated to two such noble purposes—the free living black man whom Lee would enslave, and the bodies of the dead whom Lee had killed in a wicked cause!" one story said.

The number of burials mounted quickly, with nearly three thousand by summer's end. The sad stories of the soldiers buried there and elsewhere in Washington at the time offer a haunting catalogue of death during the war. Most were young men under thirty, born in all parts of the United States, as well as in towns in Germany, Ireland, England, France, and a host of more exotic locales, including Russia, Persia, and Mexico. They succumbed to gunshots, cannon fire, and bayonet wounds; diseases that included dysentery, typhoid, and diphtheria; infections contracted during surgeries; and the blunt physical or emotional shock of losing a limb. Contrary to Meigs's order, the officers in charge of Arlington initially dug graves far from the Lee mansion, where they had established their offices. When Meigs caught wind of their insubordination, he set matters straight. Twenty-six graves soon surrounded Mary Lee's beloved rose garden, just steps from the place in the yard where, in warm weather, she liked to sit and read. As if to sharpen the point, Meigs soon dug a mass grave nearby, a huge pit to hold the bones of unidentified soldiers. He took pride in Arlington and hoped that Americans would understand his role in its creation. He later put his name in gilded letters on one of the archways leading into the place.

CHAPTER 30

A Vulnerable Capital

In June, as Grant lay siege to Petersburg, several miles south of Richmond, Lee secretly dispatched a force under Lieutenant General Jubal Early on a bold mission. Early was to protect Lynchburg from a Union threat and then move north to clear out the lightly defended Shenandoah Valley. If he succeeded, Lee told him, he was free to pursue fleeing Union troops into Maryland. Lee thought that a threat to Washington or Baltimore might spur Grant to send troops, weakening the main body of his army. Or he might make a rash attack on the rebels, opening up opportunities for counterattack. Lee also had in mind the pressing need for food, clothing, and animals. He told Early to go after any "military stores and supplies that were deemed of sufficient importance to warrant the attempt."

Reports of the rebel raiding force arrived in Washington at a time when few were inclined to believe them. It was early July 1864, scorching hot and dusty. Congress remained in session, wilting through the legislative process. City residents, long used to false alarms, expected the reported threats to dissipate like a summer storm. Besides, they had other matters to worry about, including the upcoming presidential election. Many voters were appalled by the losses that came with Grant's campaign, leading some pundits to predict that the Democratic candidate, former Major General George McClellan, might soon occupy the White House. Lincoln himself assumed that could be the outcome.

As details filtered into the city, fears about Early's force began to take root. Observers reported seeing a rebel force estimated at twenty thousand moving through the Shenandoah Valley. It supposedly included horsemen, infantry, and artillery. On July 4 the telegraph line to the west went dead, and word arrived from railroad men that Federals had evacuated Harpers Ferry. Could the Confederacy be launching a third invasion? Though initially skeptical, Stanton sent out two forces to reoccupy Harpers Ferry and scout the situation on the Potomac near Point of Rocks, Maryland. After the soldiers departed, he realized the capital was vulnerable to attack. The city had strong physical defenses. More than 50 forts and 22 batteries straddled key points along a thirty-seven-mile perimeter on both sides of the Potomac. The forts, cleverly constructed of earth and logs, could hold 643 field guns and 75 mortars. Trenches linked many of them together. Meigs, Totten, and two other engineers had earlier studied the fortifications at Stanton's request and found them sound.

The real problem was manpower. The fortifications required at least twenty-five thousand infantry and nine thousand artillery corps to man them. Grant's demands that spring had nearly dried out the well of talent in the region. Fewer than ten thousand men remained on hand to fight the rebel force. Some of these men, recent recruits known as hundred-days men, had not been trained properly and did not even know how to march, much less aim and fire their guns. Others were debilitated by illnesses or wounds.

Early advanced north through the Shenandoah Valley and then pushed across the Potomac. On July 6 his force captured Hagerstown, Maryland, where officers extracted $20,000 from the locals, calling it payment for recent Union depredations in the Shenandoah Valley. His men drove into Frederick on the morning of July 9 and made a $200,000 "levy" on residents. They also took nearly a thousand horses and destroyed fifty miles of railroad track. The invaders encountered federal forces outside of Frederick. Major General Lew Wallace, with reinforcements rushed north by Grant, made a stern show of resistance near the Monocacy River, where the roads to Washington and Baltimore converged. He delayed the rebels but could not stop them. Early continued his advance on the nation's capital.

———

On July 4, 1864, Congress approved a reorganization plan for the Quartermaster Department. The vote affirmed the validity of Meigs's incessant complaints about the need for more people. He and others would later consider the reorganization one of the war's great administrative successes. It gave the department more clerks and enabled Meigs to fire cheats and incompetents more easily. On the same day, Meigs learned the White House intended to promote him for his service during the war. Though pleased on both counts, he considered those matters less important than Early's mission. Meigs knew as well as anyone the numbers and the quality of war fighters in the vicinity, wanting in both cases. He saw an opportunity for himself. If the Quartermaster Department could be mustered to meet the threat, he might be permitted to lead men in battle. On July 9 Stanton seemed to open the way for Meigs, telling the army it could draw on the department's clerks, workmen, and officers in Washington and Alexandria. The next day, Meigs handed out guns. As he was preparing for action, Halleck quashed his hopes, ordering the clerical force to guard shops, supplies, and public buildings. Meigs could not let go of his wish to help, so he offered his services to an officer directly involved in managing the forts. He argued that even if his men did not have fighting experience, they would look strong in the trenches, and so deter or delay the enemy. The officer accepted the help, and Meigs, at long last, received a field command.

By now, Early's footsore men had set up camp just to the north of Rockville, several miles from the District. On July 11 they made another hard, hot march directly at the capital, triggering a stampede of Marylanders down the Seventh Street Road, on foot and in wagons filled with household goods. As threatening as they appeared, many of the rebels fell out of their lines, exhausted and covered in dust. They shot at the Federals but did not mount a full-on attack. Meigs's clerks, meanwhile, rushed up to Fort Slocum, in northwest Washington. They arrived after dark, manned the rifle pits, and lay on their weapons in readiness. Two houses smouldered after being burned to the ground by Union troops, who wanted to remove any cover for rebel sharpshooters. Meigs admired the fields and rolling hills and farmhouses. He slept in an orchard, wrapped in a poncho, his horse tethered to an apple tree. Before dawn the next morning, he woke to the sound of lowing cows and braying mules. As he rallied his men, Meigs learned that the homes of his friend Montgomery Blair and Maryland governor Augustus Bradford had been torched by the Confederates. The quartermaster general received command of Federal forces at Fort Slocum, Fort Totten, and Fort Stevens, which happened to straddle the rebel path into town. Despite their inexperience, and just as Meigs predicted, they formed an imposing barrier behind the earthworks.

Working under Major General Alexander McCook, who had been given command of Washington's defenses, Meigs organized the clerks, invalids, and others into a division of almost five thousand men. As they cleared away timber and brush in front of their position, the enemy appeared at Fort Stevens. Like so many, the Battle of Fort Stevens unfolded in a haphazard way. Union leaders did not know that the summer heat had exhausted many rebel soldiers. Southern officers seemed overly impressed by the capital's defenses. In a report to Richmond, Early described them as "very strong and constructed very scientifically." He pressed his men into artillery fire that came from almost every forward angle. As the day wore on, veteran fighters from the Army of the Potomac's Sixth Corps arrived and stepped into the fray. Perhaps the most extraordinary thing about the scene was the presence of the president of the United States. Lincoln had restrained himself from giving tactical orders during the crisis, but he could not resist the chance to see the fighting. For the second day in a row, he rode his carriage to the front line, accompanied by his wife, Welles, and others.

The president stood on a rampart and watched as national troops marched out and exchanged fire with the rebels down in the valley. Now and then bullets thudded into the earthen berm, kicking up dust. Lincoln remained undaunted, even when sniper fire hit a surgeon standing three feet away. A chorus of men urged him to take cover. "Get down, you damn fool," said Captain Oliver Wendell Holmes, according to legend. (The quote cannot be verified. But six decades later, Holmes, then a Supreme Court justice, recalled seeing the president at the fort.) General Horatio Wright, commander of the Sixth Corps men, started to order the president down and then balked when he considered the absurdity of pulling rank on the commander in chief. He offered Lincoln an ammunition box to sit on. The president lowered himself. He would not sit, though, and he bobbed up periodically to see what was going on, exposing himself to danger each time.

When the rebel force withdrew, Lincoln cheered along with everyone else. The Union had repelled the enemy decisively, while suffering 280 casualties. For Meigs, the sultry day marked a high point in his career, and not only because he finally led men under fire. During the fighting, a War Department courier handed him a letter from Stanton. As of July 5, it said, the quartermaster had been brevetted major general for "distinguished and meritorious services to the present War." Puffed up by the experience, Meigs issued a statement, General Orders No. 2, that praised his men "for the alacrity and zeal with which they organized and moved to defend the capital, insulted by traitors. The rebel army, under tried and skillful leaders, has looked at and has felt the northern defenses of Washington. These looked ugly and felt hard. They left their dead unburied, and many of their wounded on the way by which they retired. They will not soon again insult the majesty of a free people in their nation's capital." He gave it a dateline: "Headquarters Meigs' Division."

In the war's Western theater, the armies under Sherman moved steadily closer to Atlanta. They fought at Dalton, Resaca, Rome, and Allatoona Pass, Kennesaw Mountain and so on, moving east and south through rugged, densely wooded terrain. Every movement depended on support from the railroad construction corps, whose achievements would seem implausible had they not actually occurred. The supply line began far back at Nashville. It extended 151 miles to Chattanooga. The railcars carried provisions, clothing, gear for the men, and forage for the animals. As at Gettysburg, the empty cars were then used to ferry back the sick, wounded, and discharged soldiers, as well as refugees and prisoners of war. The supply line later snaked its way toward Atlanta, 136 miles farther along the Western & Atlantic Railroad. The rebels attacked and destroyed sections of both lines repeatedly. They twisted the iron tracks and burned the timber cross ties. With supply trains barely keeping pace with the army's needs, Sherman began excluding passengers to make room for food and other supplies. When clergy and others complained, Sherman said, "[C]rackers and oats are more necessary to my army than any moral or religious agency."

The Construction Corps distinguished itself by keeping the trains moving through vast stretches of enemy territory. In the lead was McCallum, the wizard behind the move of Union men during the siege at Chattanooga. He directed separate units of his men to work their way from both Nashville and Chattanooga and meet midway, fixing rails and building new water towers and telegraph stations. When they moved toward Atlanta, the men repaired damaged track as they came to it. Meigs ordered the completion of the rolling mill in Chattanooga that he and his men began working on during the siege the previous fall. The mill enabled them to straighten 50 tons of rails each day, far more quickly and at a far lower cost than manufacturing and shipping the rails from the North. The railroad workers rebuilt more than a dozen bridges that summer. One of them, over the Oostanaula River, was still burning when repairs began. Work was delayed for a time because the iron rails were too hot to handle.

They made an even more impressive showing at the Chattahoochee River. It took the corps just four days to rebuild the 780-foot-long, 92-foot-high bridge over the river. All told, the logistical work during the campaign was among the most impressive of the war. Rail lines in the region under Union control rose to 956 miles from 123 miles a year before. The number of cars shot up to 1,500 from 350.

On September 2 Sherman took Atlanta. "So Atlanta is ours, and fairly won," he wrote in a dispatch the next day.

Sherman showered the quartermaster operations with praise. Never once was there a shortfall of provisions, forage, ammunition, or any other essential supplies, he said. At no point were the construction workers more than five days behind the commanding generals. Sherman calculated that it would have taken almost thirty-seven thousand wagons to carry the same loads as the railroads, in the same stretch of time. "Bridges have been built with a surprising rapidity, and the locomotive whistle was heard in our advanced camps almost before the echo of the skirmish fire had ceased," he reported, adding that the bridges "were built in an inconceivably short time, almost out of material improvised on the spot."

———

More than a dozen cities honored Sherman's march with hundred-gun salutes. Even as the guns thumped approval, Meigs prepared for the next stage of Sherman's advance, pressing his people hard to maintain the momentum. He was as busy as ever when, on October 3, Stanton added to the workload. He sent Meigs to New York to inspect supply operations there. The war secretary had heard nasty rumors about another contracting scheme. Meigs caught the train to New York that same evening, about the time one of his worst fears became a reality. His son John was shot dead on a back road in the Shenandoah Valley.

John, twenty-two, had been working as an engineer with a new force called the Army of the Shenandoah, which was formed in response to Early's recent campaign. Federals under Phil Sheridan had ravaged the valley, taking or destroying two thousand barns filled with hay, seventy flour mills, and no fewer than three thousand sheep. Sheridan named John his chief engineer. Though still green, the young man knew all the important roads and streams west of the Blue Ridge and, like his father, showed talent as a mapmaker. John and two aides were returning to camp along a country lane when they came upon three men. It was raining. The other men wore capes or coats that obscured their dress.

John Meigs apparently identified them as Union colleagues, when, in fact, they were rebels.

The exact details of what came next might never be known. Sheridan tells us in his memoirs that he was told the rebel guerrillas called on Meigs and the assistants to surrender. According to this version, Meigs offered no resistance. That story differs from one offered by a man claiming to have been one of the rebels at the scene. He said later that John Meigs pulled a gun and fired. (In examining the gun later, Montgomery Meigs found that it had been fired.) Federal soldiers discovered John's body sprawled on the ground. He lay on his back, one bullet wound in the head, the other in his heart. His left arm stretched above his head, the right extended at his side, a handgun nearby.

When Meigs heard the circumstances, he concluded that John had died in an ambush, not in an honest fight. Meigs was convinced that enemies had targeted John and considered it an act of murder. "And so has perished my first born a noble boy—gallant generous gifted—who had already made himself a name in the land," Meigs wrote in his pocket diary. "A martyr in the cause of liberty." Sheridan ordered his men to burn all houses within five miles, giving the job to a twenty-four-year-old general named George A. Custer, who would gain infamy a decade later for leading 266 officers and men to their annihilation in the Battle of Little Bighorn against the Lakota, Arapaho, and other Indian tribes. On October 7, John Meigs's body was moved to Washington.

The next day, Lincoln, Stanton, and others joined the family for a funeral service at Oak Hill Cemetery Chapel. Stanton called him "one of the youngest and brightest ornaments of the military profession." A few days later, Montgomery and Louisa buried John's remains in a place alongside Charlie and Vintie. They planted ivy at the base of an oak tree nearby. (John's body remained there until 1880, when Meigs transferred it to a family plot at Arlington. For his grave, Meigs commissioned a poignant sculpture depicting John's body as it was found, sprawled out on the ground.)

Neither Montgomery nor Louisa gave in completely to grief. They had too much to do and too many people depending on them. "Dear Mont grieves for him most deeply and tenderly, but has so much pride in remembering what he *was* and so much patriotism which encourages him to remember the holy cause, in which our happiness was sacrificed that he does not give way to despondency," Louisa wrote to an aunt. "He has a courageous & noble spirit, & since our loss is *irremediable*, he feels that we must look forward to that Eternity where we hope to meet our dear son with those who have gone before him, not upon a past which can never return to us."

But Meigs never really moved on. The reservoir of bitterness about the war and the defection of his former friends and colleagues only deepened. He offered a $1,000 reward for information about his son's killer, fixing his obsession on several guerrillas. Among those in his mind was Colonel John S. Mosby—known as the Gray Ghost—the commander of irregular Confederate cavalry in the Blue Ridge country. He thought of the killers as infamous "villains" who had committed "murder" on that country road. He vowed to identify them and hold them responsible for snatching away his son in whom Meigs had invested his highest hopes. "I never did know an equal & and I never shall find one other like him," he wrote his family. Decades later, Mosby disputed any notion of murder. He said John Meigs died in a fair fight at a hard time. "When they came to the Shenandoah Valley to win glory in the Northern Army, they could not have expected to engage in the pastime of killing us without running the risk of getting killed themselves. They took their chances: we did the same."

CHAPTER 31

The Refit at Savannah

Long after the war, Sherman enjoyed describing how the Union's ability to repair rail lines demoralized his enemies. He liked one story in particular, an apocryphal tale about a chat between two rebel soldiers. As the story went, the rebels had just destroyed a tunnel and blocked Union trains. One soldier blithely predicted that, as a consequence, the Northern forces would retreat. The other just shook his head. "Oh, hell," said the listener, "don't you know that old Sherman carries a duplicate tunnel along?"

The rail lines helped amplify and extend the North's power during the campaign to Atlanta. But the time had come to move on, to cut free of such support. Staying in Atlanta required devoting too many resources to protecting the line of supply, an effort that was sapping his army. So Sherman and Grant traded thoughts about a seemingly outlandish alternative. Sherman would send all his wounded men back to Chattanooga, tear up the rail line to Atlanta, and then would "move through Georgia, smashing things to the sea." Sherman, more fervently even than Meigs, believed that Federals had to pursue a hard, encompassing war. He wanted to crush the Confederacy's spirit and cripple its ability to continue fighting. Grant consented, and on November 12, 1864, Sherman summoned the soldiers involved in the defense of the railways. Then his army, some sixty thousand of the Union's fittest men, marched away. Great black columns of smoke rose into the sky behind them as Atlanta burned. On their way out of the city, soldiers sang a chorus of "Glory, glory, hallelujah!" It was a confident, well-fed force that had been tempered by hardship and success. The last questions about the country's leadership had been answered in recent days with Lincoln's reelection, an outcome attributable in part to Sherman's success in Atlanta and the vote of the soldiers.

The force brought relatively few wagons. Sherman encouraged his men to forage liberally and to take or slaughter mules, horses, hogs, and other animals. The Union rules for war had changed. Gone was the sense of delicacy about civilian interests. The army cut a broad swath through the fertile state, some thirty miles on either side of its path to the sea, causing perhaps $100 million in damage, or roughly $1.5 billion now. "This may seem a hard species of warfare, but it brings the sad realities of war home to those who have been directly or indirectly instrumental in involving us in its attendant calamities," Sherman said. It fell to Meigs to ensure that the men received supplies at its terminus, even though no one in Washington knew for sure where that would be. Sherman planned to head to Savannah. Meigs reckoned it was possible Lee would pull out of Petersburg and confront Sherman's army, forcing it toward Pensacola. So he arranged *two* refits.

Meigs respected Sherman, who in turn had great confidence in the quartermaster. It was said that upon receiving one dispatch from Meigs—scratched out in his wretched script—Sherman endorsed it with these words: "The handwriting of this report is that of General Meigs, and I therefore approve of it, but I cannot read it." If Sherman did not completely grasp the complexity of the supply system, he was confident the Quartermaster Department would provide what his men needed. For weeks, Meigs and hundreds of his subordinates worked feverishly to gather and ship food and equipment. In December civilian captains guided steamers and other boats through savage winter storms to Port Royal Harbor, near Hilton Head, South Carolina, the staging area for the refit at Savannah.

The quartermaster men then faced the problem of getting the supplies into Savannah Harbor. For four years, Georgians had clogged the harbor with every kind of obstacle. Meigs summoned a special wrecking party from the Florida coast, marveling as it cleared a path with "ingenious equipment which modern science has contrived." The triumphant army reached Savannah on December 21. They had waded through swamps, destroyed railways, burned down houses, herded cattle, and slept under the stars. They left friends along the way in scattered graves that marked the army's course. And now they received an unlikely gift: a new wardrobe. On the boats and in warehouses were tens of thousands of new boots and shoes, greatcoats, fresh shirts, trousers, and underwear; blankets, camp kettles, pans, axes, spades, and shelter tents; wagons, whippletrees for wagon horses, harnesses for mules; leather, wax, and even needles and thread.

Meigs regarded the refit at Savannah as one of his department's finest accomplishments. In an exchange of letters with Sherman, however, he focused his praise on the army's recent march. To Meigs, it demonstrated like never before the viability of warfare untethered from supply lines. He was especially taken by the fact that Sherman's men found forage for their animals rather than relying on costly deliveries from the North. In a Christmas Day response, Sherman thanked Meigs for his support. "I beg to assure you that all my armies have been admirably supplied by your Department," Sherman wrote, adding: "I am sometimes amazed at the magnitude of its operations."

To many Northerners, Sherman now embodied the great meshing of men and management and verve that marked his army's sweep through Georgia. In their cheering, perhaps understandably, the civilians did not pause to consider what lay behind Sherman's great achievement. "To his admirers he looked modern, and Americans were nothing if not modern," the historian Charles Royster wrote in a study of Sherman. "His success came from decisiveness, speed, efficiency, statistics, sophisticated logistics, long-range planning, large-scale operations, and thorough results."

———

Though Meigs was immersed in the logistical challenges, he received an honor for work unrelated to the war. On January 5, 1865, the National

Academy of Sciences swore him in as a member. Congress had formed the group two years earlier to provide advice to the government about science and technology. Among the fifty charter members were several of Meigs's friends and fellow Saturday Club members, including Bache and Henry. With his induction, at age forty-eight, Meigs became one of the first elected members—a noteworthy achievement for a part-time scientist, technologist, and tinkerer.

The next day, he and Stanton traveled to Savannah to confer with Sherman about the next stage of his army's movement. War leaders wanted to maintain the momentum at all costs. Grant asked Meigs to provide grain and commissary supplies to Sherman with the least delay possible. Meigs pushed his people hard. He also continued to keep a close watch on spending. As he had throughout the conflict, he worried about government debt and the impact on the Northern economy. The armies under Grant and Sherman continually ordered supplies at the last moment. Such requests precluded planning, and that meant added expense. Meigs was most concerned about the cost of shipping. Nearly everything had to be delivered by sea, with Northern ships cycling in a constant stream along the East Coast. Grant's siege force required a virtual armada to keep it supplied, including 190 steamers, 60 tugs, 40 sailboats, and 100 barges. The cost of shipping forage reached $1 million a month during the winter. Those vessels comprised a mere subset of the Quartermaster Department's ocean fleet, which in the last year of the war included 719 vessels that cost more than $92,000 a day on average to operate. The department operated another 599 vessels for river transport. The demand for ships and boats was so acute that Meigs sometimes resorted to taking newly made vessels from private shipping companies. He urged Sherman to give him as much time as possible to prepare when ordering supplies.

Union leadership decided against a direct attack on Charleston, one of the great rebel strongholds during the war. It opted instead for a more daring plan—marching inland, cutting off the city from supplies and then attacking. Sherman's army trudged through sand and swamps in South Carolina, terrain that many military men regarded as inaccessible. Charleston soon fell. The army pushed on, tearing up railroads as it went. In Columbia, soldiers torched much of the city and destroyed huge caches of the Confederacy's remaining gunpowder and cartridges. Once again, Sherman's army needed to be "reclad and reshod." To help prepare for this refit, Meigs had ordered two divisions of the railroad construction workers to travel by rail from Nashville to Baltimore, and then by ship to the Carolinas. They traveled with the army and soon repaired two rail lines headed inland from the North Carolina coast. Those lines were supplied with railcars and engines shipped from the North or captured by the army. When the right wing of Sherman's force arrived at Goldsboro, on March 22, 1865, they replenished themselves with rations and clothing from yet another field depot established by the quartermasters. Every soldier received a complete outfit. Wagons were repaired, covered with new canvas, and filled with supplies. The animals were fed with forage shipped in from the North.

With the Confederacy imploding, Sherman wanted to resume moving as quickly as possible. "I think I see pretty clearly how, in one more move, we can checkmate Lee," he wrote to Grant. Meigs joined the army in North Carolina. As he and Sherman sorted through logistical matters, news filtered into camp that 80,000 of the 125,000 men under Grant's command had moved out of the trenches at Petersburg. Then came word about the battle at Five Forks, a crossroads in Dinwiddie County, Virginia, on the far right of Lee's line. Lee declared that Five Forks had to be held in order to protect the last rail line into Richmond, but it fell quickly to Sheridan's men. Lee telegraphed Davis that Richmond must evacuate, triggering chaos in the Confederate capital. Leaders fled as soldiers destroyed river bridges and torched the city's business district.

Meigs boarded a boat and made his way north, visiting a supply depot in Morehead City. On April 5 he stopped at Wilmington, North Carolina, taking time to make drawings of Fort Fisher, which had fallen to combined Union naval and ground forces after a long campaign. He was delighted to learn that the Confederate government had fled from

Richmond. In Washington, War Department clerks hollered the news out of office windows, people rushed into the streets, and the army launched into an eight-hundred-gun salute. "Richmond Is Ours!!!," the *Evening Star* bellowed under a joyful headline: "The News—The Glorious News."

Meigs heard the best report while aboard a boat that was anchored off the tip of the Virginia Peninsula. Lee and twenty-seven thousand of his men had surrendered to Grant at Appomattox Court House. Meigs made his way to City Point, Virginia, the hive of supplies and operations that Grant used as his headquarters. He began shutting down the war machine that he had such a great hand in building. For the first time in nearly four years, he suspended all orders for mules, horses, wagons, clothing, and equipage. Though Meigs was ebullient about victory, he also was bitter about the cost. He hoped that those responsible for the "murder of my son and the sons of hundreds of thousands" would be tried and executed.

He considered traveling home by way of Richmond, wanting to see for himself the fallen house of his enemy. He chose instead to join Grant and his staff and go to Washington. When he arrived, on April 13, he went to Louisa and the children. Afterward, he visited the War Department. He and Stanton shared happy stories about recent events until Grant arrived, and then Stanton greeted him effusively. Meigs also visited Secretary of State Seward, who was at home in bed recovering from a carriage accident. The next day, Good Friday, Meigs went to his office and then on to services at Saint John's Church, across from the White House. He made the rest of the day into a holiday with his wife and children, as the city bubbled with happiness. Flags adorned most buildings, and residents and visitors alike paraded through the streets, some of them accompanied by marching bands. "The country is drunk with joy," Meigs wrote in his journal.

———

That night, as Meigs relaxed with his family, bad news arrived by military messenger. He grabbed a handgun, threw on his coat, and rushed into the dark. The streets were filling with people who had heard rumors that an assassin had shot President Lincoln at Ford's Theatre, where he had gone to see the play *Our American Cousin*. An assailant also had attacked Secretary of State Seward, still in bed at home. Meigs met Stanton and Welles in the lower hall of Seward's Lafayette Square home. He learned that Seward was unconscious and bleeding from knife wounds. Seward's son Frederick, bludgeoned while trying to defend his father, had slipped into a coma.

Stanton asked Meigs to clear the house of any nonessential people. Stanton and Welles wanted to leave immediately to find the president. Meigs implored the war secretary to stay put, for his own safety and the good of the country. Stanton ignored the suggestion and asked Meigs to join them. Meigs relented and called on soldiers to stand on either side of the carriage. A city judge sat up front with the driver and an army officer held on to the back as they hurtled through Washington. Tenth Street outside the theater was packed with an apprehensive and angry crowd. Lincoln had been carried across the street to a red brick townhouse owned by a tailor named William Petersen and his wife, Anna. Stanton, Welles, and Meigs walked up a flight of steps, went through a long hall, and found the president on a bed in a back room.

Lincoln breathed slowly and deeply and looked calm and striking. He had only a few hours to live. The small room was filled with Cabinet members, politicos, friends, and family, all of them pale with grief. No one spoke except for Stanton, who quietly directed the army's search for the assassins. The near-silence was broken when Mary Lincoln came into the room from another part of the house. She kneeled beside the bed, took her husband's hand, and sobbed. The eyes of everyone in the room shimmered with tears. A rainstorm sent rivulets of water coursing down the windows, in "dreary sympathy" with those inside. At midnight, on authority from Stanton, Meigs broke briefly from the scene to order the army to go on high alert, turn out in the capital, and double the number of guards at government facilities. Then, along with the others crowded around the president, he waited. Lincoln died at 7:22 a.m.

"The murderers have not been arrested," Meigs wrote in his diary later that day. "J. Wilkes Booth, actor, murdered the president."

———

On Tuesday, April 18, the mourners moved slowly through the East Room of the White House, one quietly after another by Lincoln's body. They paused, looked at his face, and then passed by, crying and moaning, as at the loss of a father or a friend. Meigs went to the Capitol, on orders from Stanton, and began preparing for a lying-in-state. The next day, as Lincoln's funeral procession made its way from the White House, the quartermaster general led a large contingent of department employees, including railroad construction corps members. When the president's body arrived at the Capitol, Meigs directed its placement in the rotunda.

Meigs thought the president's embalmed body was well preserved. Gone was the discoloration and swelling around his eyes that emerged on the morning of his death. Despite his anger and grief, he was proud of the setting and thought the dome's interior looked magnificent. Mourners began flowing by the casket in a constant stream, entering the rotunda through the great east door and exiting through the west. In the evening, Meigs darkened the space with drapery over the windows. The next morning, a group of men—a military honor guard, Lincoln's Cabinet, and generals Grant, Meigs, and Rucker—moved the body to a funeral car at the railroad depot. Alongside Lincoln's casket, they placed a smaller one holding the body of his eleven-year-old son, Willie, who had died of a typhoid-like illness in the dark days of early 1862. Father and son were to be buried together in Springfield, Illinois.

As the funeral train rumbled west, Stanton asked Meigs to accompany Grant to North Carolina, where Grant was to take command of operations that would close out the war. Stanton said that Meigs had no time to spare. Could he pack and get to Alexandria before Grant's boat departed? The haste was related to an unauthorized act by Sherman. Instead of demanding unconditional surrender from Joseph

Johnston, Sherman entered into negotiations for what amounted to a truce. The apparent presumption of Sherman to take on political responsibilities infuriated Stanton and others in the administration. The agreement had to be undone as soon as possible. Meigs went home, grabbed a clean shirt, a poncho, and a valise. Before Meigs boarded the boat, the gruff war secretary, brimming with emotion, embraced and complimented him. "No better officer or more faithful soldier lives," Stanton told Meigs.

CHAPTER 32

The Journey Home

The war was finally over. To mark the North's victory, Meigs suggested the Union armies gather in Washington at the end of May for a final grand review. Soldiers bivouacked in the hills near the city, around campfires that glittered at night like new stars. Northerners flooded into the city by train and boat and carriage to witness the spectacle. The Army of the Potomac went first, looking crisp and disciplined as it moved in marching salute past President Andrew Johnson and the Cabinet. Sherman's western army followed the next day. They had a looser-limbed style suggestive of their pioneer roots and the different kind of war they had been fighting.

Next came the task of demobilization. The men of the army had to be discharged, paid, and transported home. Once again, the Quartermaster Department managed. In forty days, some 233,000 men, 12,800 horses, and 4 million pounds of baggage traveled across the border between war and civilian life. Many went west to Louisville, St. Louis, and Cincinnati. Others passed through Baltimore and then on to Harrisburg or northeast through Philadelphia. By winter, a second wave brought the diaspora's total to 800,000. The department's transportation branch had never been busier. The logistics were akin to those needed for the massive offensives of the previous year—save for the absence of gunfire and the strange finality of it all. Meigs sensed grandeur in this migration. The government sent the men back to "every hamlet and village of the States north of the Potomac and Ohio Rivers, and restored to their homes, the labor of the war over, to return to the pursuits of peaceful industry which they had left at the call of their country in her hour of need."

Those journeys brought an end to the war for the living. Much more still had to be done for the dead. The bones of tens of thousands of Northern men lay in forests, fields, and shallow graves on battlefields across the South. Their stories had to be documented, their passing marked. For Meigs, Stanton, and others, it stood as a matter of honor. Not long after Grant and Lee met at Appomattox, a Northern theologian named Horace Bushnell framed the war in a way that resonated with many in the North. The half million deaths were "the price and purchase-money of our triumph," Bushnell wrote. "[In] this blood our unity is cemented and forever sanctified."

Meigs seems to have embraced this notion. His own losses, his empathy for the parents who had lost their own boys, and his Christian devotion helped sustain him during his last great challenge as a war manager. Even as he delivered the survivors home, Meigs launched the campaign to identify and inter the bodies still in the field. He delegated much responsibility at first to Captain James M. Moore, an assistant quartermaster who supervised development of Arlington. Moore was not well known, but he was competent, dedicated, and energetic. His push to find the remains of Union men was among the most important of several under way at the time. On June 7, under Special Orders No. 132, he traveled to battlefields in the Wilderness and at Spotsylvania Court House. Men under his command scoured the landscape for remains. For two weeks, they buried and reburied bodies and bones. They had no difficulty deciding where to build new cemeteries. They efficiently chose the places of the greatest carnage. In some trenches, the bones of Northern and Southern men were intermingled. Moore's men marked each grave with a headboard, neatly painted with the man's name, rank, and regiment. When the identities could not be determined, they painted "Unknown U.S. soldier" along with a date of the battle. As hard as they worked, the burial crews could not complete their work immediately. Rotting bodies and Virginia's heat sometimes forced them to wait.

The next assignment sent Moore to Camp Sumter, the notorious Confederate military prison in Andersonville, Georgia. Thousands of Federals, forced to live in trenches and little caves carved out by hand, died there of exposure, disease, and starvation. The crew and its supplies departed Washington for Savannah by ship on July 8. In Savannah, they had to scramble to find a way to travel inland. The railroads were in a shambles and they could not find enough wagons to carry them. Ten days after arriving, they procured a boat, traveled to Augusta, and found a working railroad. For six days, they crawled through Georgia on rickety tracks, seldom going faster than twelve miles per hour. Men dressed in rebel uniforms would board the train at stops and want to talk. Some of the Southerners seemed genuinely aggrieved about the treatment of Union prisoners, especially at Andersonville. "[A]ll of them candidly admitted it was shameful, and a blot on the escutcheon of the South that years would not efface," Moore wrote to Meigs.

At Macon, the small force joined with a company of cavalrymen and the 137th Regiment of US Colored Troops. Nothing prepared them for what they found at Andersonville. The Union dead lay in trenches about three hundred yards from the camp stockade. Dirt barely covered the men, many of them naked and stacked like cordwood. In some places, rain had washed away all but a few inches of soil. With help from records secretly maintained by an enlisted prisoner of war, Moore eventually identified the names, ranks, and dates of death of 12,010 men; another 450 others remained unidentified. The burial crews worked from early morning until dark, laboring through oppressive heat that sickened some of them. Moore blocked out fifty acres for the cemetery, and his men laid out pathways and planted trees and flowers. They made bricks and then used them to create gutters to drain rainwater. They sawed 120,000 board feet of Georgia pine to make the grave markers.

News about the conditions enraged Northerners. Clara Barton had traveled to the prison to see the conditions for herself. On August 17, in a ceremony to commemorate the place as a new national cemetery, she raised the Stars and Stripes. Moore's men fired a salute and sang songs.

Moore hoped the new cemetery would serve as testimony to the hell that can be unleashed by war. "Nothing has been destroyed. As our exhausted, emaciated, and enfeebled soldiers left it, so it stands to-day as a monument to an inhumanity unparalleled in the annals of war," Moore wrote Meigs. "The ground is filled with the holes where they had burrowed in their efforts to shield themselves from the weather, and many a poor fellow, in endeavoring to protect himself in this matter, was smothered to death by the earth falling upon him."

Moore's men eventually found and interred more than fifty thousand bodies across Georgia, Virginia, and Maryland.

———

Despite Moore's achievements, Meigs grew frustrated in his effort to create a master list of the dead. Commanders had not always kept track of their missing and killed, despite clear orders to do so. Facing the demands of fighting and moving, officers often took advantage of a loophole that required action only "so soon as it may be in their power." In the fall of 1865, the quartermaster directed the department to produce "a special report to his office of the localities and condition of cemeteries, with reference, especially, to their exact location, condition, place of deposit, and condition of records, with recommendations of the means necessary to provide for the preservation of the remains from desecration; and whether the site should be continued, and the land purchased, or whether the bodies should be removed to some permanent cemetery near."

He called on another quartermaster officer—Lieutenant Colonel E. B. Whitman, of the Military Division of the Tennessee—to greatly expand the search for bodies from Georgia to Mississippi. Under Whitman, hundreds of men, operating in effect as forensic sleuths, traced the paths that the armies had followed. They received unstinting support from the War Department. "To ask," Whitman said later, "was to receive." His exploring party set out from Nashville in March 1866, with pack mules, camp gear, and provisions. They stopped at Corinth, Vicksburg, and Atlanta, and then followed Sherman's route to the sea.

At key locations, the scouts formed skirmish lines and swept over battlefields, a process that sometimes took up to a week. They took note of every grave they found. The unit distributed circulars—the headline read "Important Information Wanted"—to former Union surgeons, chaplains, soldiers, and quartermaster men. They also reached out to Southern citizens. Whitman and his men visited more than three hundred places. They found more than forty thousand graves and took note of more than ten thousand names that had been written on rude markers, cut into nearby trees or recalled by residents. They gathered information about twenty-eight thousand other men from the hospitals that had maintained records. The work brought the awfulness of the war to life for Whitman. "It revealed the sad fact, and brought it to notice, that the entire country over which the war had extended its ravages was one interminable grave-yard."

By late 1866, more than three dozen national military cemeteries anchored battlefields across the country. They held the remains of almost 105,000 Union soldiers—with many more to come. Meigs calculated the cost of removing and reburying the bodies at about $9.75 each. He continued to compile his list of dead, driven by the belief that every man who lost his life in the service of democracy deserved to be remembered. As Whitman's scouting mission came to a close, penny-pinchers in Washington insisted on using cheap wooden headboards. Others suggested cast-iron markers showing only a number to identify the soldiers. Meigs wanted the cast-iron markers to be plated with zinc to prevent rust, and each to bear the soldier's name. He thought these men deserved to be remembered by the living. The survivors of the great national cataclysm needed this fundamental observance to move on. "I do not believe that those who visit the graves of their relatives would have any satisfaction in finding them ticketed and numbered like London policemen, or convicts," Meigs wrote. "Every civilized man desires to have his friend's name marked on his monument."

CHAPTER 33

"Dogs to Their Vomit"

Not long after the war, Major General Robert Allen, the talented quartermaster in the Trans-Mississippi theater, spoke to members of Congress about the Quartermaster Department's role in the Union victory. He recalled the struggle to transform chaos into order while contending with an onslaught of criticism. "I must be permitted to remark that history furnished few, if any, examples of armies so great traversing territories so wide and having their every want at every step supplied."

Meigs understood where he stood and what he had done, and he did not want to leave those days behind. Never again would he have so much power or stand so near the center of such a vital enterprise. He had to move on, and for now that meant attending to administrative chores. Congress soon passed a law limiting the standing army at 75,000. Meigs let go thousands of employees and dismantled military depots that had anchored bases of operations everywhere in the field. The department held fire sales of 207,000 horses and mules, 4,400 barracks, hospitals, and other buildings and mountains of irregular or damaged clothing. Meigs also shed the great fleet the department had amassed. The number of ocean transports shrank more than tenfold to 53 vessels. He sold off all 262 riverboats left in service.

As he managed this contraction, Meigs could not get his emotions in order. He nurtured his grievances against those who had betrayed the country. He could not come to grips with the deaths of so many young men, including, of course, his beloved son John. Even if he had wanted to move on, he simply could not. Soon after the war's end, Varina Davis wrote to Meigs from Georgia. She wanted to visit her husband, Jeff Davis, who was being held in a cell at Fort Monroe. She hoped that with Meigs's endorsement, Stanton might intervene. Stanton said it was up to him. Meigs told himself that he understood her suffering; she simply wanted a measure or two of comfort. Yet he could not bring himself to respond to her, the wife of a former friend who had helped Meigs in uncounted ways. He merely sent word through channels that Jeff Davis was faring well enough. "Poor woman she has been guilty of a great crime," Meigs wrote to his father. "Even the blood of my son slain by her husband's hired murderers does not shut up my compassion."

Alfred Rives, the brilliant aqueduct engineer who had worked under Meigs's supervision on the Washington Aqueduct before the war, sought a reunion. Meigs spurned him, saying he would not "see any of those gentlemen who had deserted their country & joined the party who murdered my son with any satisfaction." His rancor toward the South deepened during the debates about reconstruction and rights of freed slaves. He believed that given an opportunity, white Southerners would strip freed slaves of the freedom they had won. Repeatedly he urged Congress to remain vigilant. To help former slaves eke out a living and guarantee them a measure of economic freedom, he urged lawmakers to give each family five acres of land. "The emancipation of the negro slave is incomplete as long as, being without land, he is at the mercy of his former master." His lobbying came to nothing. President Andrew Johnson showed no interest in the cause. In his frustration, Meigs predicted Southerners would resume their oppressive ways and return "like dogs to their vomit. They can not enslave but they will outrage & oppress. Their hearts are not changed."

By the end of 1866, the war caught up with Meigs. He often felt unwell. His legs swelled. Each breath came hard. A doctor diagnosed his ailment as a form of typhoid. At age fifty-one, he had to take a break. In early 1867, Meigs took a short sick leave. His family recommended more and, stubborn as he was, Meigs agreed. He and Louisa settled on a plan to tour Europe. In late May, the War Department gave Meigs extended leave, putting General Rucker temporarily in command. His friends applauded the change. To open doors in Europe, Seward gave his friend a letter addressed to American diplomats. The letter gave Meigs much credit for the Union victory. "The prevailing opinion of this country sustains a firm conviction which I entertain, and on all occasions cheerfully express, that without the services of this eminent soldier, the National cause must either have been lost or deeply imperiled in the late Civil War."

The family traveled abroad for a year. For the first time in many years, Meigs relaxed as he and Louisa absorbed the great art and architecture that had, through reproductions, inspired so much of his work on the Capitol. When he returned, he found his job in Washington a steady if sometimes boring routine. Now he was responsible for much of the "military peace establishment." If the challenges fell far short of what he craved, he could at least keep watch for interesting, sometimes tumultuous, developments as the nation turned its eyes again to the west. Settlers needed the protection of soldiers, and the soldiers needed supplies from the Quartermaster Department. Meigs became preoccupied with Native Americans and their resistance to the waves of white people occupying their tribal lands. He displayed little empathy about the plight of American Indians. Instead, still bitter about the war, he focused on blocking their access to modern repeating rifles. "As a measure of humanity to our own men, whom they murder, and to our own women, whom they violate with all the aggravations of savage barbarity, the supply of arms to any Indian, not a citizen of the United States, should be prohibited by legislative enactment, under severe penalties," he wrote. "The arrow is a sufficiently effective weapon in the chase of the buffalo."

Meigs also shouldered the tedious task of settling claims relating to confiscations of property from border state residents during the war. The department reforms in July 1864 required him to establish that persons making the claims had been loyal at the time. He eventually oversaw adjudication of nearly thirty-four thousand cases worth $40 million. All through the postwar years, he also monitored the national cemeteries and the graves of fallen soldiers. Congressional support for that work came and went, and Meigs's proposal for zinc-plated iron markers languished. In the meantime, the cemeteries fell into disrepair, and "the wooden head boards have been set up as they fell from decay, or they have been replaced by numbered stakes." Meigs resisted a congressional mandate to use marble or granite as markers. He thought they cost too much. It is our good fortune that Congress ignored him and appropriated $1 million for the placement of sturdy headstones on every grave. The standard markers now present a familiar, elegant profile to cemetery visitors. Cemetery crews did not finish the project until 1881, when virtually all the graves of Civil War soldiers had received markers.

———

As the new decade approached, Meigs itched to create and build. Slogging through administrative work was not enough. It never was. In 1869 and 1870, with his personal finances well in hand, he began making designs for a family home in the capital. He let his imagination romp, making drawings with illusionary murals, Roman doorways, and rooms framed by columns. The house, built on Vermont Avenue, was fireproof. It had a simple exterior, a mansard roof, and a wide porch. High ceilings and brick-and-mortar floors framed the interior. A fireproof circular staircase connected the upper and lower floors. A library had room enough for several thousand books, including texts about history, science, and the military. The house became an anchor for his children and grandchildren, whom he liked to amuse with stories or by showing them how to plant flowers in "grandmother's garden." He once summoned the grandchildren and told them to stand around a box in the yard. Just when they settled down, he gave the box a kick. Snakes slithered in every direction, the children squealed, and he had a big laugh, telling them the snakes were there to eat bugs, not them.

Meigs offered designs for a museum building at the University of Michigan and laboratories at Pennsylvania's Dickinson College. After Congress appropriated money to pay superintendents to keep watch over the national cemeteries, Meigs began drafting plans for a model "lodge" to house them. In 1870 he sought advice from Frederick Law Olmsted, the landscape architect, who suggested that the cemeteries ought to "establish a permanent dignity and tranquility." Meigs designed small homes in a popular style at the time known as French Second Empire. The prototypical version was L-shaped, with a half basement below, sleeping quarters above, and a mansard roof. They could be made of brick or stone, depending on supplies available to local builders. One of the first lodges went up at the Battleground National Cemetery, which Meigs created on a square acre not long after the Battle of Fort Stevens for Union soldiers who died there. Dozens of the lodges still stand in cemeteries across the country.

In another collaboration with Olmsted, Meigs drafted plans for a huge military warehouse in Jeffersonville, Indiana. Designed with utility in mind, it includes attractive details such as arches built into solid brick walls and Tuscan-style pilasters. Meigs estimated the cost at 5.5 cents per cubic foot of storage room. He also had a hand in designing cottages that served as housing for commissary sergeants at Fort Whipple, now known as Fort Myer, in Arlington, Virginia.

In 1877 he turned his attention to a new museum for the Smithsonian Institution. It had received a huge donation of objects from the Philadelphia Centennial Exhibition in 1876. The old Castle did not have enough room to hold the expanded collection. Meigs attended the Centennial as an exhibitor and won an award for two of his drawings of bridges. The board of regents, still led by Joseph Henry, asked him to study public museums in Europe and apply his findings to the new space in Washington, called the National Museum Building, now known as the Arts and Industries Building. His plans called for a square, fireproof building. An architectural firm, Cluss and Schulze, later refined plans and made the final drawings. Meigs served as the consulting engineer, visiting the site almost daily to make inspections of the work.

The Smithsonian broke ground for the building in April 1879. It had an open floor plan, a rotunda, large arched windows, and eight towers. Perched on top are allegorical statues that depict *Columbia Protecting Science and Industry*. The National Museum Building embodied the spirit of Montgomery Meigs in one important respect. It is still considered to be the least expensive permanent building ever erected by the federal government.

CHAPTER 34

"Soldier, Engineer, Architect, Scientist, Patriot"

Meigs took to the road more often in those years. From 1869 to 1874, in his official capacity as quartermaster general, he went on inspection tours to Texas, the Southwest, and California. Once, he rode the Northern Pacific Railway to the Red River and then headed to Denver. On other trips, he traveled to the West Coast, stopping at San Francisco and Los Angeles. On at least one of these journeys, he took his son Montie along. In 1875, on special orders, he had returned to Europe to study the military operations of other countries, with a particular focus on quartermaster operations. He savored this trip, in part because it gave him time to paint. He focused on churches, steeples, shorelines, and clouds in watercolor renderings that show the finesse of an energetic man who has calmed down.

Something else made the journey memorable. Meigs began using a new technology called a typewriter. An inventor named Christopher Lathem Sholes had recently begun mass producing the first practical model. Suddenly, readers of Meigs's letters did not have to decipher them. Meigs described the typewriter as "a wonder of invention, and a triumph of human ingenuity and brains, over the stupidity of dead metals, that the thing does so quickly and so well. Writing twenty words a minute, the action of the living fingers and their diverse and complicated muscles, is another wonder."

We learn from his letters that he met with German emperor William I and senior military leaders. He described the people, the clothes he wore, the maneuvers he observed, and some of the lavish social events he attended. He exclaimed about the wealth that surrounded him, and in a note to Louisa, he drew a diagram of the dinner table. "It is impossible to imagine the brilliant appearance of a gathering for an imperial dinner, all in new fresh clothes, blue, light blue, scarlet, green and white with the breasts covered with decorations and epaulettes and shoulder and gilt or silver shoulder knots."

His affection for his wife jumped out of each note. "Ever your loving, MCM," he wrote. Not long after Meigs's return, Louisa began feeling poorly. She tired easily, and her heart troubled her constantly. In March 1879 her lungs became congested. She would never fully recover. When she died, in the fall, they had been married for almost four decades. Meigs thought that she looked more beautiful than when they'd met—"as time allowed the good & great soul to stamp itself on" her features.

The changes kept coming. On February 6, 1882, President Chester Arthur ordered Meigs to retire. He was sixty-five, three years beyond retirement age. Others had waited in the wings for the top post, including Rucker and the inimitable Ingalls. In a statement to the officers in his department, Meigs offered an old soldier's glowing memories. He wanted them to remember:

> The corps has seen great changes since I entered it. It has been expanded till, leavened by the knowledge and spirit and integrity of the small body of officers who composed it early in 1861, it showed itself competent to take care of the supplies and transportation of a great army during four years of most active warfare.
>
> It moved vast bodies of soldiers over long routes; it collected a fleet of over 1,000 sail of transport vessels upon the great rivers and upon the coast; it constructed and equipped a squadron of river iron-clads, which bore an important part in the operations of the army in the West, and after having proved its practical power and usefulness, was accepted by the navy, to which

such vessels properly belonged; it supplied the army while organizing and while actively campaigning over long routes of communication by wagon, by rail, by river, and by sea, exposed to hostile attacks and frequently broken up by the enemy; and, having brought to the camps a great army, it, at the close of hostilities, returned to their homes over a million and a quarter of men.

It is now reduced to the proportions of a peace establishment, containing only sixty-four officers of the staff and about two hundred acting assistant quartermasters who hold their commissions in the line. During this time the corps has applied to the wants of the army over nineteen hundred and fifty-six millions six hundred and sixteen thousand dollars and has used this vast sum, nearly two thousand millions, with less loss and waste from accident and from fraud than has ever before attended the expenditure of such a treasure.

One last project carried Meigs into old age. The federal Pension Bureau needed a new building, and Congress took the unusual step of naming Meigs to build it. The number of bureau employees had soared to keep pace with the needs of Civil War veterans and the families of those who had died. By the early 1880s, the Pension Bureau dispersed almost a quarter of the nation's revenues. It was another unexpected chance, enabling him to apply ideas that developed during his European trips. And it turned out to be his final and most important architectural contribution.

Meigs's design drew on the Farnese and Cancelleria palaces in Rome, Renaissance masterpieces he saw during his trip with Louisa. With its great rows of windows and clean lines, the design foreshadows a revival of "Renaissance classicism" that would soon flourish in the buildings of New York City. Plans showed a building that was far larger than the Roman models—400 feet long, 200 feet wide, and almost 152 feet high. It had four floors. Meigs relied on brick and iron instead of stone and timber. In deference to instructions he received from Congress, the building was virtually fireproof.

Just as he did with the Cabin John Bridge, Meigs went beyond his mandate and used the project as a chance to innovate. He aimed to create a modern, well-ventilated space that would be bright, healthy, and pleasant for the workers. Wherever possible, he sought to supplement traditional building methods with modern techniques, such as the use of metal trusses. For the site, he selected the north end of Judiciary Square.

Over the next five years, Meigs kept watch on the details of construction. He documented each stage with photographs, which show layers of red bricks rising steadily over time, more than 15 million in all by the end, making it the largest brick building in the world at the time. It is a wonder inside, a surprise that has to be experienced to be understood. A gigantic courtyard rises more than four stories high. A water fountain sits on the main floor. One hundred forty-four columns form the perimeter on the first and second floors. Behind them are offices. Eight colossal columns rise seventy-five feet from the courtyard. They remain among the tallest in the world. Each is made with tens of thousands of bricks and plastered over and painted to resemble marble. A shed roof, chosen for its economy, tops it off.

Meigs once calculated that the space holds 4 million cubic feet of air. The volume of air inside was key to his goal of air-conditioning the place. He came up with an innovative scheme involving vents in the walls that allowed fresh air in, and hot air to rise up and escape. His theory about the space turned out to be true, as the courtyard served as a natural chimney. Meigs claimed a great public health achievement here, saying his tabulations showed that the number of sick day claims by clerks plummeted after they moved into the Pension Building. To enable clerks to store and move records, Meigs designed an elevated rail track that carried baskets containing up to 150 pounds of documents. The track fed a hand-operated elevator that moved the documents to lower floors. He built shafts to house a hydraulic elevator for disabled veterans. They remained empty because no money was available at the time to buy and install the lifts. Meigs took care to honor Civil War soldiers. He commissioned a three-foot-high terra-cotta frieze that wraps around the outside of the building. Meigs hired Caspar Buberl, the same Bohemian artist who'd created *Columbia* for the Smithsonian Museum Building. He drew on disparate sources for the design, including the ancient Parthenon and the photographic studies by Eadweard Muybridge. The frieze depicts Federal infantry, cavalry, artillery, navy, quartermaster, and medical units. To ensure Buberl got the details right, Meigs arranged for soldiers in fighting uniforms to march by the artist.

For the building's west entrance, Meigs insisted the frieze honor freed slaves. One panel depicts a black man driving a wagon pulled by mules. Meigs told Buberl, "He must be a Negro, a plantation slave, freed by war."

The Pension Building was big, brash, and controversial. Some people loved it. Others derided it. Still others joked, calling it Meigs's "Old Red Barn." Sherman or Sheridan is said to have cracked that the building was fine but for one thing. "Too bad the damn thing is fireproof." Tastes change, and by 1985, the great brick pile was so admired that it was transformed into the home of the National Building Museum. The *New York Times* architecture critic was awed when he visited, calling it "one of Washington's greatest (and least known) pieces of monumental architecture . . . [It] will stand as a potent reminder of the ability of architecture to transcend the mundane and create truly powerful drama."

———

Meigs continued to crackle with energy and verve. While working on the Pension Building, he served as a regent of the Smithsonian Institution, as "a citizen of Washington." In 1885, he became a member of the executive board, "always present, painstaking, and eminently judicious." Inevitably, though, his pace slowed, and in his last few years, he embraced a peaceful routine. He had his books, a workshop, and children and grandchildren to keep him busy. He thought often about the dome and the aqueduct. He reflected on the war, his memories fresh, vivid, inescapable. In late 1887 or early 1888, a publisher invited him to write about the relationship between Lincoln and Stanton. The request came in response to allegations from McClellan, who claimed that Stanton, Chase, and others had schemed against him to take advantage of Lincoln's "complete ignorance of war." He said Lincoln lost faith in him before the Peninsula Campaign, undermining his chances.

Meigs did not want to take on the project, in part because he did not consider himself a good writer. An agent eventually convinced him that he "had special opportunities to know the truth" because of his close proximity to the president and war secretary throughout the war. Besides, McClellan's claims irritated him. In his essay, published after his death in the *American Historical Review*, Meigs related new details about the Fort Pickens adventure and the momentous war councils in early 1862, when Lincoln and his advisors sorted out what to do with McClellan. He remained an admirer of Stanton despite criticism of him from some quarters after the war. "Many military names from this War will live in History but Lincoln's and Stanton's will outlast all but Grant's," he wrote. "Between Lincoln, Stanton, and Grant, I believe there was never a dispute."

Meigs did not get out much anymore, in part because one of his legs was bent with rheumatism. He remained sharp, and habitually wore crisp white shirts and ties as he sat in a favorite armchair, his legs up, "and read and read and read." In a habit begun decades earlier, he filled scrapbooks with letters, photographs, engineering papers, and newspaper stories, some about him. Now and then a veteran would stop at the house, and Meigs, still sharp and interested, was able to recall details about the man's regiment and its war record. One day, a scruffy looking man appeared at the front door, claiming to be a veteran. He was ushered in.

"Well, what is your service?" the general asked the visitor.

The man did not answer.

"Where did you serve?" Meigs asked.

The man remained silent.

"What action were you in?" Meigs said.

Finally, the visitor answered, "Well, fact is, General, I never did no fighting. I just followed the races."

Meigs, still gruff and prone to irritability, took the answer as an insult. He rose from his chair, grabbed the man's neck and trousers, and pushed him down the hall and out of the door. "The idea of that fellow coming to see me," he said to his granddaughter, who watched the episode unfold.

Early on January 2, 1892, Meigs died of influenza after a short illness. He was seventy-five. His body lay in the library of his home, a tattered old flag at the base of his casket. Honorary pall bearers from the army, Smithsonian, and National Academy of Sciences came on January 5 and carried it to St. John's Church, just across from the White House, where Meigs attended services and served as a lay leader. Two hundred cavalry and artillery soldiers marched with his casket across the Potomac River to Arlington Cemetery, pausing at the old Lee mansion, where they placed the casket in a room and waited as a crowd of onlookers dispersed. Then they toted it to a spot high in the hills, next to where Louisa and John were interred. They put it into a sarcophagus that Meigs had designed. With an inscription carved into its base, Meigs offered the world another reminder of the passions that fueled him and the roles that he had embraced with pride: "Soldier, Engineer, Architect, Scientist, Patriot."

The army issued general orders to mark his death and honor his service. "The Army has rarely possessed an officer who combined within himself so many and valuable attainments, and who was entrusted by the Government with a greater variety of weighty responsibilities, or who has proved himself more worthy of confidence," the orders said. "There are few whose characters and careers can be more justly commended, or whose lives are more worthy of respect, admiration, and emulation."

But the world was already beginning to forget the man who so wanted to be remembered. "M. C. Meigs stands high with those who know him, but his merits have not been, I think, appreciated by the public as they ought to have been," former Secretary of Treasury Hugh McCulloch, the last man to occupy that post in the Lincoln administration, and a Saturday Club friend of Meigs's, lamented several years later. "The civil war in the United States could not have been prosecuted by the Government with the smallest hope of success, had not the Union armies been properly provided and cared for by the Quartermaster's Department. Fortunately for the country, there was at the head of this department M. C. Meigs."

Acknowledgments

Several years ago, I went for a regular Sunday walk with my family on the C&O Canal, to the northwest of Washington, DC. We normally followed a path of crushed stone alongside the water, not far from Great Falls. But on this day we went another way, walking on what seemed to be a two-track road through the woods.

I was poking along, giving my son Cormac a chance to keep up, when I noticed a railing off to the side. It seemed out of place in the forest. When I looked more closely, I saw that the rail guarded an open well. There was enough light down below my feet to illuminate words carved into a stone: "Capt. M.C. Meigs" and "Chief Engineer" and "Anno Domini 1857." It didn't make sense to me. I recalled Meigs vaguely, from a college history course, as a general in the Civil War. Why would a stone memorial refer to him as captain? Why in a well? And why there? I lingered over the matter for a moment and then tucked it away in my mind for another day. Such questions often come and go. But not this time. More than a year later, I began searching for answers. What I found has delighted me ever since—and shaped the book you hold in your hands.

My effort to write the story about M. C. Meigs would not have gone far without the generosity of a great number of researchers, historians, curators, colleagues, friends, and other sharp readers, who tolerated my questions, guided me to documents, and offered uncounted suggestions for improving my manuscript. I can only hope they know how much I appeciate their efforts.

Among others, I am indebted to Barbara Wolanin, Stephen Berry,

Mark Wilson, Peter Cozzens, Douglas L. Wilson, Robert M. Poole, Amy Elizabeth Burton, Elizabeth Terry Rose, Mary A. Giunta, Thomas Jacobus, Eric Hintz, Guy Gugliotta, David Voreacos, Craig Tracy, Ken Webb, and (Ret.) Gen. Montgomery Meigs, a descendent of M. C. Meigs and a senior lecturer at the University of Texas. I owe special thanks to Michelle Krowl, a historian and researcher at the Library of Congress who guided me through the Meigs family files and offered valuable ideas, and to Bill Dickinson, whose enthusiasm about Meigs is infectious and whose suggestions sent me in many interesting directions. David Thomson, a PhD candidate in history at the University of Georgia, read the manuscript behind me for historical accuracy. Louisa Watrous—another descendent of M. C. Meigs—was unstinting with encouragement, assistance, and family documents. Thanks also to Daniel Holt, John Lonnquest, Matthew Pearcy, and James Garber for their suggestions.

Along the way, I received help from the Lincoln Studies Center at Knox College and the folks at Cornell University Library who maintain an invaluable online reservoir of the Official Records of the Union and Confederate armies. The Lemelson Center for the Study of Invention and Innovation at the Smithsonian National Museum of American History provided a small financial stipend that helped me take time off from work to examine its wonderful files.

I drew on the work of many other scholars and writers. That includes two earlier, admirable studies: *Quartermaster General of the Union Army: A Biography of M.C. Meigs*, by Russell F. Weigley; and *Second Only to Grant: Quartermaster General Montgomery C. Meigs*, by David W. Miller. I learned much from essays by Sherrod East, including *The Banishment of Captain Meigs*. Also illuminating and engaging were the essays in *Montgomery C. Meigs and the Building of the Nation's Capital*, edited by William C. Dickinson, Dean A. Herrin, and Donald R. Kennon. Mark Wilson's *The Business of Civil War: Military Mobilization and the State, 1861–1865,* and Erna Risch's *Quatermaster Support of the Army* provided data and insights that added greatly to my story.

For details about the Civil War and nineteenth-century America in general, I relied on the extraordinary work of James McPherson in his

Battle Cry of Freedom: The Civil War Era and of Allan Nevins, including the volumes comprising his *Ordeal of the Union, The Emergence of Lincoln,* and *The War for the Union.* Margaret Leech's magnificent *Reveille in Washington* gave insight into the nation's capital during the war. For the life of John Meigs, I turned to Mary A. Giunta's poignant book, *A Civil War Soldier of Christ and Country: The Selected Correspondence of John Rodgers Meigs, 1859–64.* I learned more than I knew possible about the capital's water system from Harry C. Ways Jr.'s fascinating book, *The Washington Aqueduct 1852–1992.* Guy Gugliotta's *Freedom's Cap: The United States Capitol and the Coming of the Civil War* provided keen insights about Jefferson Davis and the struggles between Meigs and Walter, the labor they and others poured into the Capitol and the significance of those efforts to the nation. I also drew on the terrific, interesting *History of the United States Capitol: A Chronicle of Design, Construction, and Politics* by William C. Allen.

The backbone of *The Quartermaster*—at least until Lincoln calls on Meigs to serve as quartermaster general—is the transcription of some 2,800 pages of the shorthand journals that Meigs kept while supervising work in the nation's capital before the war. This is a story in itself. The transcriber was William Mohr, a shorthand specialist who retired in 1989 as official reporter of debates for the U.S. Senate. In 1991, Mohr began working closely with a group of smart, dedicated folks to make sense of Meigs's seemingly inscrutable shorthand journals after they came to the attention of Richard Baker, Senate historian, and Barbara Wolanin, curator for the Architect of the Capitol. A ten-year-long effort to transcribe and publish the journals included specialists from the Architect of the Capitol, the Senate Curator, the Senate Historical Office, and the Library of Congress. I relied primarily on the complete transcript of Meigs's journals. I also drew on *Capitol Builder: The Shorthand Journals of Montgomery Meigs, 1853–1859, 1861,* edited by Wendy Wolff, an engaging, abridged version of the transcript that includes related observations.

Thanks to Amy Rennert for helping so ably as my agent and advisor, and to Alice Mayhew, my editor at Simon & Schuster, for her guidance and spot-on editing and advice. Alice and her talented colleague, Stuart Roberts, helped me at every step during the long haul to the book's completion.

I cannot express enough gratitude to the *Washington Post*, the news organization that has sustained me for more than a quarter-century. I owe much to former owner, Don Graham, a remarkable man and a great steward of the newspaper through both good and hard times. Thanks to our current owner, Jeff Bezos, the *Post* has new life. I am indebted to a long line of editors who have helped me and taught me along the way. Lynn Medford, the former editor of the *Washington Post Magazine*, and David Rowell, her deputy, gave shape to the article that became the seed of *The Quartermaster*. I owe much to investigations editor Jeff Leen for his counsel, ideas, and steadfast leadership.

And, finally, thanks to my dear wife, Amy, for her wisdom and love.

Notes

xi *"I do not know one"*: Abraham Lincoln, June 5, 1861, *Abraham Lincoln Papers at the Library of Congress,* http://memory.loc.gov.

xi *"Without the services of this"*: William Seward, May 28, 1867, letter in Henry B. Meigs, *Record of the Descendants of Vincent Meigs* (Baltimore: John S. Bridges, 1901), 258.

xi *"The logistical demands of the"*: James McPherson, *Battle Cry of Freedom* (New York: Oxford University Press, 2003), 325.

xi *"Meigs should be given"*: Allan Nevins, *The War for the Union,* vol. 2 (New York: Charles Scribner's Sons, 1960), 471.

CHAPTER 1: RIGID DUTY

5 *Montgomery Cunningham Meigs*: Henry L. Abbott, *Memoir of Montgomery C. Meigs 1816–1892,* in National Academy of Sciences Biographical Memoirs (Washington, DC), www.nasonline.org.

5 *They lived not far from the Savannah River*: Russell F. Weigley, *Quartermaster General of the Union Army* (New York: Columbia University Press, 1959), 19.

5 *So they returned to Philadelphia*: S. Emlen Meigs in *Vincent Meigs,* 269.

5 *Sometimes in the summer*: Montgomery C. Meigs, *The Shorthand Journals of Montgomery C. Meigs, 1853–1859, 1861, Complete Transcript,* vol. 4 (Washington, DC: US Government Printing Office, 2001), 7 (hereafter cited as GPO).

5 *Montgomery was bright and affectionate*: Louisa Meigs notes copied in letter to Montgomery Meigs, July 14, 1874, Montgomery C. Meigs Papers (Washing-

ton, DC: US Library of Congress, Manuscript Division), shelf 18,202, reel 12 (hereafter cited as LOC).

6 *The stories begin*: Henry Meigs, in *Vincent Meigs*, 7.

6 *He told the children*: John Forsyth Meigs in *Vincent Meigs*, 231–32.

6 *Montgomery Meigs would credit:* Montgomery Meigs letter, September 3, 1888, Meigs Papers, LOC, shelf 18,202, reel 16.

6 *He dreamed of going*: Weigley, *Quartermaster General*, 22.

6 *He was accepted*: Abbott, *Memoir*, 315, and *Army Corps of Engineers: A History* (Alexandria, VA: Office of History, Headquarters, US Army Corps of Engineers, 2008), 17–20.

7 *Meigs studied mathematics*: Barbara A. Wolanin, "Meigs the Art Patron," in *Montgomery C. Meigs and the Building of the Nation's Capital,* ed. William Dickinson, Dean A. Herrin, and Donald R. Kennon (Athens: Ohio University Press, 2001), 134.

7 *He complained about*: Weigley, *Quartermaster General*, 29.

7 *In 1836 Meigs*: Meigs West Point journal, Meigs Papers, shelf 18,202.1, reel 11; *George W. Cullum's Biographical Register of the Officers and Graduates of the United States Military Academy*, 846, http://penelope.uchicago.edu.

7 *In the summer of 1837*: Rick Britton, "What a Beautiful County It is," *Robert E. Lee on the Mississippi,* Lee Family Digital Archive, Washington and Lee University, http://leefamilyarchive.org/reference/essays/britton/index .html.

7 *Meigs admired Lee*: A. L. Long, *Memoirs of Robert E. Lee* (Secaucus, NJ: Blue and Grey Press, 1983), 44.

CHAPTER 2: PATIENCE AND PERSEVERANCE

9 *Meigs began a long*: Meigs, *Shorthand Journals*, vol. 2, September 4, 1855.

9 *The project posed*: Kelli W. Dobbs, Rebecca J. Siders, *Fort Delaware Architectural Research Project* (Center for Historic Architecture and Design, University of Delaware, 1999), 1–10.

9 *On Pea Patch*: Weigley, *Quartermaster General*, 35.

10 *"I am a"*: Mark R. Wilson, *The Business of Civil War* (Baltimore: Johns Hopkins University Press, 2006), 63.

10 *In 1839 Meigs received*: *Cullum's Biographical Register*, http://penelope.uchi cago.edu.

10 *Montgomery and Louisa*: Meigs, *Shorthand Journals*, vol. 2, September 4, 1855; Sherrod E. East, *The Banishment of Captain Meigs* (Washington, DC: Historical Society of Washington, DC, 1940), Vol. 40/41, 98.

11 *The defenses were part*: Reynolds Farley, *Christ Church*, www.detroit1701.org /ChristChurch.html#.VhO5kLRViko.

11 *he filled some*: Farley, *Historic Fort Wayne*, http://detroit1701.org/Fort%20 Wayne.html.

11 *Montgomery and Louisa*: Weigley, *Quartermaster General*, 45.

11 *The family relished*: Meigs, *Shorthand Journals*, vol. 2, August 27, 1855.

11 *In his inaugural*: James K. Polk, *Inaugural Address*, March 4, 1845, www.pres idency.ucsb.edu/ws/index.php?pid=25814.

12 *Soon after taking office*: R. D. Monroe, *Congress and the Mexican War 1844– 1849* (Abraham Lincoln Historical Digitization Project, 2000), http://lincoln .lib.niu.edu/biography4text.html.

12 *The war resulted in*: James M. McPherson, "America's 'Wicked War,'" *New York Review of Books*, February 27, 2013.

12 *The House approved*: Miller Center of Public Affairs, University of Virginia, *James K. Polk: Foreign Affairs*, http://millercenter.org.

12 *Meigs was unsettled*: Meigs, *Shorthand Journals*, vol. 1, October 31, 1853.

13 *Totten knew Meigs*: J. G. Barnard, *Eulogy of the Late Joseph G. Totten, Annual Report of the Board of Regents of the Smithsonian Institution 1865* (Washington, DC: US GPO, 1865), 137–72.

13 *Totten lives on*: *Memoir of Joseph Gilbert Totten*, J. G. Barnard (National Academies of Sciences, 1866), 89, www.nasonline.org.

13 *It was the brainchild*: S. P. Langley, *A Biographical Sketch of James Smithson* (Washington, DC: Smithsonian Institution, 1963), Smithsonian Institution Archives, *James Smithson: Founder of the Smithsonian Institution*, http://si archives.si.edu.

13 *A chemist and mineralogist*: Smithsonian, James Smithson and the Founding of the Smithsonian, www.si.edu/About/History.

13 *at the time*: National Register of Historic Places—Nomination Form, *Smithsonian Institution Building* (National Park Service), www.nps.gov/nr.

13 *For Meigs and others*: Harold K. Skramstad, *The Engineer as Architect in Washington: The Contribution of Montgomery Meigs* (Records of the Columbia Historical Society of Washington, DC, 1969–1970), 267.

14 Eastman was a: Henry R. Schoolcraft, *Historical and Statistical Information Respecting the History, Condition and Prospects of the Indian Tribes of the United States* (Philadelphia: Lippincott, Grambo, 1851); Charles E. Fairman, *Art & Artists of the Capitol of the United States of America* (Washington, DC: US GPO, 1927), 239–40.

14 *The paintings spurred*: Skramstad, *Architect in Washington*, 268.

14 *fearing he would*: Meigs, *Shorthand Journals*, vol. 1, December 25, 1854.

14 *Meigs thought it was ironic*: Ibid., August 5, 1858.

15 *He also made time to*: Weigley, *Quartermaster General*, 51.

15 *Even his hunting*: Meigs, *Shorthand Journals*, vol. 1, October 1, 1854.

CHAPTER 3: WHOLESOME WATER

16 *The fire started somewhere*: William Dawson Johnston, *History of the Library of Congress*, vol. 1 (Washington, DC: US GPO, 1904), 275.

16 *The library itself was:* Ibid., 23–25.

16 *In August 1814*: *Jefferson's Legacy: A Brief History of the Library of Congress*, www.loc.gov/loc/legacy/loc.html.

16 *Thomas Jefferson reseeded:* William C. Allen, *History of the United States Capitol: A Chronicle of Design, Construction and Politics* (Washington, DC: US GPO, 2001), 132.

17 *Officials took new precautions*: Benjamin Brown French, *Witness to the Young Republic: A Yankee's Journal, 1828–1870* (Lebanon, NH: University Press of New England), 223–25.

17 *"No public building"*: French, *Witness to the Young Republic*, 225.

17 *Jones told investigators*: Johnston, *History of the Library of Congress*, 275.

18 *Pretense and muck: The Seventh Census of the United States*: 1850.

18 *The Treasury Department: History of the Treasury Building* (Washington, DC, US Department of Treasury), www.treasury.gov/about/education/Pages/edu_fact-sheets_building_history.aspx.

18 *Off to the side*: Henry Adams, *The Education of Henry Adams* (New York: Literary Classics of the United States, 1983), 260.

18 *After his only visit*: Charles Dickens, *American Notes for General Circulation* (London: Chapman and Hall, 1842), 1: 281–82.

18 *It was a sluggish*: Joseph T. Kelly, *Memories of a Lifetime in Washington* (Washington, DC: Records of the Columbia Historical Society, 1930), 31/32: 117–49.

19 *The inadequacy of the water*: Harry C. Ways, *The Washington Aqueduct, 1852–1992* (Baltimore: US Army Corps of Engineers 1992), 1–3.

19 *Many of the city's*: Kelly, *Memories*, 123.

19 *"And as nothing"*: Millard Fillmore, *First Annual Message* (Santa Barbara, CA: American Presidency Project, 2012), www.presidency.ucsb.edu/ws/index.php?pid=29491.

19 *Congress's vacillation flowed*: Skramstad, *Architect in Washington*, 266.

20 *So Totten turned to*: Pamela Scott, *Capital Engineers: The U.S. Army Corps*

of Engineers in the Development of Washington, DC, 1790–2004 (Alexandria, VA: Office of History, Headquarters, US Army Corps of Engineers, 2011), 40–41; Meigs, *Shorthand Journals*, vol. 2, September 4, 1855.

20   *When he arrived*: Ibid., vol. 1, February 12–30, 1853, and Ernest B. Furguson, *Freedom Rising: Washington in the Civil War* (New York: Vintage, 2004), 53.

20   *He was to conduct*: Meigs report in *Senate Ex. Doc. 48, 32nd Congress, Second Session, Message of the President*, 8.

20   *It would take*: "The Potomac Aqueduct," *Baltimore Sun*, March 23, 1855, in Meigs, *Shorthand Journals*, vol. 2, 1855.

20   *With discipline and enough*: *Baltimore Sun*, March 23, 1855.

21   *He also rekindled*: Meigs, *Senate Doc. 48*, 10–11.

21   *Frontinus's memoir*: Sextus Julius Frontinus, Translated by Charles E. Bennett, *Frontinus: Stratagems* and *Aqueducts of Rome* (Cambridge, MA: Loeb Classical Library, Harvard University Press, 1925), 329–467.

21   *The Roman described*: *Frontinus*, 331.

21   *Frontinus wrote that*: Ibid., 455.

21   *He also shared this*: Ibid., xvii.

CHAPTER 4: AN AQUEDUCT WORTHY OF THE NATION

22   *Three months after*: Meigs, *Senate Doc. 48*, 55.

22   *The population soared*: Martin V. Melosi, *The Sanitary City* (Baltimore: Johns Hopkins University Press, 2000), 58.

22   *Meigs described how*: Meigs, *Senate Doc. 48*, 9.

22   *Washington had almost*: Ibid., 44.

23   *The system he had*: Ibid., 36.

23   *"If it is not good"*: Meigs letter to father, February, 12, 1853, *Meigs Papers*, LOC, shelf 18,202.1, reel 4; David W. Miller, *Second Only to Grant* (Shippensburg, PA: White Main Books, 2000), 19.

23   *After years of*: Harry C. Ways, "Montgomery C. Meigs and the Washington Aqueduct," in *Building of the Nation's Capital, 21*.

24   *In one of his first acts*: Allen, *United States Capitol*, 211; Guy Gugliotta, *Freedom's Cap* (New York: Hill and Wang, 2012), 126.

24   *During army service*: The Papers of Jefferson Davis, vol. 5, Rice University, *Chronology*, http://jeffersondavis.rice.edu.

24   *Like Meigs*: Gugliotta, *Freedom's Cap*, 31, 39.

24   *"Davis excelled in"*: Ibid., 221.

24   *Davis pressed Pierce*: Wendy Wolff, ed., *Capitol Builder: The Shorthand Jour-*

nals of Montgomery C. Meigs, 1853–1859, 1861 (Washington, DC: US GPO, 2001), xxix.

24 *It was a fantastic*: Weigley, *Quartermaster General*, 67.

25 *In reality, it was*: Glenn Brown, *Glenn Brown's History of the United States Capitol, Annotated Edition in Commemoration of the Bicentennial of the United States Capitol* (Washington, DC, US GPO, 1998), 186, 302.

25 *Before taking on*: Gugliotta, *Freedom's Cap*, 71.

25 *His best-known work*: Founder's Hall, Girard College, www.girardcollege.edu.

25 *After the fire*: Walter letter, January 27, 1852, in *Documentary History of the Construction and Development of the United States Capitol and Grounds* (Washington, DC: US GPO, 1904), 342.

25 *His ink and watercolor*: Allen, *United States Capitol*, 190.

25 *Despite his fine record*: House Proceedings, March 12, 1852, *Congressional Globe*, in *Documentary History*, 468–71.

26 *Contractors, lawmakers and*: Allen, *United States Capitol*, 211.

26 *He thought Walter*: Meigs in *Report of the Secretary of War*, December 1, 1853, 75.

26 *The two would fight*: Thomas U. Walter letter to friend, April 19, 1858, Walter letter book, Architect of the Capitol office.

26 *Meigs's plans*: Wolff, *Capitol Builder*, xxx; Brown, *Glenn Brown's History*, 374.

26 *To link the building*: Wolff, *Capitol Builder*, 788.

26 *His plans included*: Meigs in *Report of the Secretary of War*, December 1, 1853, 71–75.

27 *Meigs soon took aim*: Meigs, *Notes on acoustics and ventilation, with reference to the new Halls of Congress, by Captain M. C. Meigs, United States Corps of Engineers, May, 1853*, in *Report of the Secretary of War*, December 1, 1853, 80–84.

27 *The other, Joseph*: Hugh McColloch, *Men and Measures of a Half Century* (New York: Charles Scribner's Sons, 1889), 262.

27 *They expressed enthusiasm*: Joseph Henry letter to Meigs, Papers of Joseph Henry, vol. 8, May 6, 1853, 539.

27 *In the legislative*: Meigs, *Notes on acoustics*, 80; Brown, *Glenn Brown's History*, 210.

27 *The three men visited*: Meigs in *Annual Report, U.S. Capitol Extension Office*, October 22, 1853, in *Documentary History*, 586–91.

27 *he returned to Washington*: Meigs, *Shorthand Journals*, vol. 1, June 12, 1853.

28 *His masons went*: Jefferson Davis, Papers of Jefferson Davis, vol. 5, *1853–1855*, Lynda Lasswell Christ, ed. (Baton Rouge: Louisiana State University Press, 1985), 180; Meigs in *Report of the Secretary of War*, December 1, 1853, 74–75.

28 *He worried that*: Allen, *United States Capitol*, 222.

28 *England had used*: Edward Dobson, *A Rudimentary Treatise on the Manufacture of Bricks and Tiles* (London: George Woodfall and Son, 1850), 9.

28 *Meigs began counting*: Meigs, *Shorthand Journals,* vol. 1, May 21, 1853; see also Ex. Doc. 138 of the House of Representatives, 34th Congress, 1st Session.

28 *To ensure that he had*: Meigs, *Shorthand Journals,* vol. 1, July 27, 1853; Meigs in *Report of the Secretary of War,* December 1, 1853, 74.

CHAPTER 5: A RIVAL TO THE PARTHENON

30 *"I doubt whether"*: Meigs, Meigs in *Report of the Secretary of War,* December 1, 1853, 75.

30 *Some observers*: Fairman, *Art & Artists,* 139.

30 *Not only did he*: Receipts, Architect of the Capitol, May 14, 1853, for candles, and August 22, 1854, for sperm oil, Capital Extension 1851–1874, Record Group 43.

30 *He committed himself*: Weigley, *Captain Meigs and the Artists of the Capitol,* Records of the Columbia Historical Society, 1969–1970, 287.

30 *Like Capitol builders*: Meigs, *Shorthand Journals,* vol. 1, January 28, 1853; Meigs to Crawford in Fairman, *Art & Artists,* 143.

31 *Over the centuries*: Evan Hadingham, "Unlocking Mysteries of Parthenon," *Smithsonian,* February 2008.

31 *To be complete*: Allen, *United States Capitol,* 245.

31 *He said he wanted*: Weigley, *Captain Meigs and the Artists of the Capitol,* Records of the Columbia Historical Society, 1969–1970, 289–90.

31 *"In our history"*: Fairman, *Art & Artists,* 143.

31 *In contrast, Meigs*: Skramstad, *Architect in Washington,* 268.

32 *Called* Progress of Civilization: Scott, *Capital Engineers,* 54.

32 *"[A]nd thus quietly"*: Meigs, *Shorthand Journals,* vol. 1, October 31, 1853.

32 *He made a few*: Ibid., vol. 5, January 14, 1858.

32 *Charles, eight, passed*: Ibid., vol. 1, September 3, 1854.

33 *American cities "had become"*: Michael R. Haines, *The Urban Mortality Transition in the United States, 1800–1940,* 7, presented at the Demographic Forum 1999, Oslo, Norway, August 2000.

33 *Like other parents*: Michael McEachern McDowell, *American Attitudes Towards Death, 1825–1865,* December 1977, a dissertation at the Center for the Study of Pop Culture, Bowling Green University.

33 *They visited the boys'*: Meigs, *Shorthand Journals,* vol. 1, December 2, 1853.

33 *About his boys*: Ibid., October 22, 1854.

34 *To thwart him*: Allen, *United States Capitol,* 222–23; Meigs, *Shorthand Journals,* vol. 1, December 15, 1853.

34 *On January 3, 1854*: *Congressional Globe*, Senate, 33rd Congress, 1st Session, January 3, 1854.

34 *When Meigs arrived*: Meigs, *Shorthand Journals*, vol. 1, January 4, 1854.

CHAPTER 6: AMERICA'S CURSE

35 *He argued that*: Stephen Douglas, *Nebraska Territory*, *Congressional Globe*, January 30, 1854, Senate, 33rd Congress, 1st Session, 275; W. T. Sherman, *Memoirs of Gen. W. T. Sherman* (New York: Library of America, 1990), 245–51.

35 *He had watched*: Allan Nevins, *Ordeal of the Union*, vol. 2, *A House Dividing, 1852–1857* (New York: Charles Scribner's Sons, 1947), 223.

35 *This posed a*: Steven E. Woodworth, *This Great Struggle* (Lanham, MD: Rowman & Littlefield), 18–20.

36 *The book infuriated*: McPherson, *Battle Cry of Freedom*, 66.

36 *Over the furious*: Douglas, *Nebraska Territory*, *Congressional Globe*, January 30, 1854.

36 *Representative Abraham Lincoln*: Lincoln in Nevins, *Ordeal of the Union*, vol. 2: *A House Dividing*, 341.

37 *Meigs clearly did not*: Papers of Jefferson Davis, vol. 6, 6–7; Meigs, *Shorthand Journals*, vol. 1, April 20, 1854; Gugliotta, *Freedom's Cap*, 6–7; Scott, *Capital Engineers*, 60.

37 *Now Meigs became*: Meigs, *Shorthand Journals*, vol. 1, December 25, 1854.

37 *Most of all*: Ibid., June 8, 1854.

37 *Made of wood*: Allen, *United States Capitol*, 146–47.

37 *Crowning the building*: Allen, *United States Capitol*, 227.

38 *"I have in the"*: Meigs, *Shorthand Journals*, vol. 1, December 26, 1854.

38 *Meigs loved shooting*: Ibid., vol. 3, September 26, 1856.

38 *"For I am thus"*: Ibid., vol. 1, October 18, 1854.

38 *He managed even*: Papers of Jefferson Davis, vol. 5, 371.

38 *His accounting at*: Meigs, *Shorthand Journals*, vol. 1, November 2, 1854.

39 *He examined the friezes*: Ibid., October 28, 1854.

39 *After they "burst in"*: Ibid., October 25, 1854.

40 *"[T]ime is life"*: Isaac Pitman in Alfred Baker, *The Life of Sir Isaac Pitman (Inventor of Phonography)* (London: Sir Isaac Pitman & Sons, 1919), 286.

40 *Meigs started reading*: William D. Mohr, "The Shorthand Journals of Montgomery C. Meigs," in *Building of the Nation's Capital*, 123–26.

40 *"This is written"*: Meigs, *Shorthand Journals*, vol. 1, November 6, 1854.

40 *Meigs was "seduced"*: Ibid., December 25, 1854.

40 *His normal script*: Scope and Content Note, *Meigs Papers*, LOC, shelf 18,202, reel 1.

41 *He took pride*: Meigs, *Shorthand Journals*, vol. 1, December 31, 1854.

CHAPTER 7: THE SATURDAY CLUB

42 *Schaeffer had worked*: Meigs, *Shorthand Journals*, vol. 2, January 4, 1855.

42 *In the United States*: United States Patent and Trademark Office, *Table of Issue Years and Patent Numbers, for Selected Document Types Issued Since 1836*, www.uspto.gov.

42 *The British engineer Isambard*: Steven Brindle in *The Great Builders*, Kenneth Powell, ed. (London: Thames & Hudson, 2011), 90, 100–105; Margot Gayle and Carol Gayle, *Cast-Iron Architecture in America: The Significance of James Bogardus* (New York: W. W. Norton, 1998), 86–99.

43 *The Saturday Club*: Albert C. Peale in *Bulletin of the Philosophical Society of Washington*, vol. 14, 1900–1904 (Washington, DC: Philosophical Society of Washington), 317; Meigs, *Shorthand Journals*, vol. 2, January 4, 1855.

43 *A. D. Bache, the friend and*: Joseph Henry, *Eulogy on Prof. Alexander Dallas Bache* in *Annual Report of the Board of Regents of the Smithsonian Institution, Showing the Operations, Expenditures, and Condition of the Institution for the Year 1870*, www.history.noaa.gov/giants/bache.html.

43 *Another member was*: *Bulletin of the Philosophical Society of Washington*, vol. 14, 317.

43 *A passionate lepidopterist*: Kenneth Haltman, *The Butterflies of North America: Titian Peale's Lost Manuscript* (New York: Abrams, 2015).

43 *"The discussions were always"*: McColloch, *Men and Measures*, 262.

44 *As Meigs recalled it*: Meigs, *Shorthand Journals*, vol. 2, January 6, 1855.

44 *Along with at least*: National Academy of Sciences: The First 100 Years (Washington, DC: National Academy of Sciences, 1978), 106.

44 *The artist was*: Bernard Rabin and Constance S. Silver, in *Constantino Brumidi, Artist of the Capitol*, Barbara Wolanin, curator (Washington, DC: US GPO, 1998), 215.

44 *When he was thirty-five*: Wolanin, *Artist of the Capitol*, 14–16.

45 *He recalled when*: Meigs, *Shorthand Journals*, vol. 2, December 28, 1854.

45 *With Meigs's support*: Weigley, *Captain Meigs and the Artists*, 285.

45 *He secured permission*: Allen, *United States Capitol*, 265.

45 *The busts remain*: United States Senate, Art & History, www.senate.gov; US Senate Catalogue of Fine Art (Washington, DC: US GPO, 2002).

45 *Meigs eventually "dispensed":* Weigley, *Captain Meigs and the Artists of the Capitol,* 285.

46 *Meigs told Dickinson:* Meigs, *Shorthand Journals,* vol. 1, December 13, 1854.

46 *At her father's:* Edward B. Sewall, *The Life of Emily Dickinson* (Cambridge, MA: Harvard University Press, 1974), 444; Connie Ann Kirk, *Emily Dickinson: A Biography* (Westport, CT: Greenwood Press, 2004), 60–63.

46 *As for Stanton: Congressional Globe,* Senate, 33rd Congress, 2nd Session, February 21, 1855.

46 *On March 3, 1855:* Meigs, *Shorthand Journals,* vol. 2, March 3, 1855.

47 *He had abandoned:* Ibid., March 5, 1855.

47 *Meigs went home:* Ibid., March 4, 1855.

CHAPTER 8: THE WORKLOAD GROWS

48 *Meigs thought that some:* Meigs, *Shorthand Journals,* vol. 2, March 5, 1855.

48 *"He is evidently":* Ibid., March 7, 1855.

49 *About this time:* Ways, *Washington Aqueduct,* 53.

49 *In the spring of:* Meigs, *Shorthand Journals,* vol. 2, April 27, 1855.

49 *He asked his favorite:* Ibid., April 28, 1855.

49 *Meigs also admired:* Ibid., January 10, 1855.

51 *He described these:* Meigs letter to Jefferson Davis, November 26, 1855, National Archives, microfilm.

51 *He wrote that Walter's:* Meigs, *Shorthand Journals,* vol. 3, *Clippings* appendix.

51 *Meigs described how:* Meigs letter to Jefferson Davis, November 26, 1855.

51 *It worked well:* Ibid., vol. 2, December 10, 1855.

CHAPTER 9: ROWDY LOOKING

52 *But while admirers marveled:* Simon Brown letter in *New England Farmer,* June 25, 1856.

52 *Stories in the* New-York Daily Tribune: Meigs, *Shorthand Journals,* vol. 3, March 29, 1856.

52 *Meigs sought a:* Ibid., April 4, 1856.

52 *("Had God granted"):* George Templeton Strong in Robert C. Williams, *Horace Greeley: Champion of American Freedom* (New York: New York University Press, 2006), xvii.

53 *Meigs was not:* Meigs, *Shorthand Journals,* vol. 3, April 4, 1856.

53 *The Potomac is:* Ibid., April 11–12, 1856.

53 *The country was losing*: Nevins, *Ordeal of the Union*, vol. 2, *A House Dividing*, 544.

54 *The tensions were reflected*: Ibid., 427–28.

54 *The book, A Journey*: W. P. Trent in Frederick Law Olmsted, *A Journey in the Seaboard Slave States* (New York: G. P. Putnam's Sons, 1904), xxvii.

54 *As if to demonstrate*: McPherson, *Battle Cry of Freedom*, 152–53.

54 *The antislavery town*: Walter Stahr, *Seward: Lincoln's Indispensable Man* (New York: Simon & Schuster Paperbacks, 2012), 162–63.

54 *In Washington, congressmen*: Nevins, *Ordeal of the Union*, vol. 2, *A House Dividing*, 427.

54 *On May 8*: "The Herbert Trial," *New York Times*, July 14, 1856.

54 *Meigs was appalled*: Meigs, *Shorthand Journals*, vol. 3, May 8, 1856.

55 *Then violence seeped into*: Charles Sumner, *Congressional Globe*, 34th Congress, 1st Session, June 2, 1856, 1349–50; *The Crime Against Kansas Speech*, reprinted by *New-York Daily Tribune*, https://books.google.com.

55 *Sumner was a handsome*: Nevins, *Ordeal of the Union*, vol. 2, *A House Dividing*, 438.

55 *"Mr. Sumner, I have"*: *Congressional Globe*, 34th Congress, 1st Session, June 2, 1856, 1349–50.

55 *Brooks chose the cane*: David Herbert Donald, *Charles Sumner and the Coming of the Civil War* (Naperville, IL: Sourcebooks, 2009).

55 *A flamboyant proslavery*: Stephen W. Berry II, *All That Makes a Man* (New York: Oxford University Press, 2005), 58.

55 *Northerners saw it*: George Templeton Strong, *Diary of the Civil War, 1860–1865* (New York: Macmillan, 1962), 67.

56 *In the South*: Nevins, *Ordeal of the Union*, vol. 2, *A House Dividing*, 446.

56 *"If the northern men"*: Laurence Keitt letter to Susan Sparks, May 29, 1856, in Stephen Berry, *Laurence Massillon Keitt: Politics as Epic Poem*, www2.uncp .edu.

56 *He took on no debt*: Meigs report in 34th Congress, 1st Session, House of Representatives Ex. Doc. No. 139, 2.

56 *He named each vendor*: Meigs, 34th Congress, 1st Session, House of Representatives Ex. Doc. No. 139, 12–17, 56.

57 *Democrats selected James Buchanan*: Nevins, *Ordeal of the Union*, vol. 2, *A House Dividing*, 466–88.

57 *Nativist lawmakers*: Meigs, *Shorthand Journals*, vol. 3, April 29–May 1, 1856.

58 *"This ends the long agony"*: Ibid., October 16, 1856.

CHAPTER 1 0: ENERGETIC, OBLIGING, FIRM

59   *With change coming in*: Meigs, *Shorthand Journals*, vol. 4, February 7, 1857.

60   *Davis was stepping*: Papers of Jefferson Davis, vol. 6, 167.

60   *In one letter*: Meigs, *Shorthand Journals*, vol. 4, September 9, 1857.

60   *Another influential man*: Stahr, *Seward*, 158.

60   *Seward liked Davis*: Nevins, *Emergence of Lincoln*, vol. 1: *Douglas, Buchanan, and Party Chaos 1857–1859* (New York: Charles Scribner's Sons, 1950), 22.

60   *One day not*: Meigs, *Shorthand Journals*, vol. 3, August 15, 1856.

60   *It was a classic*: Stahr, *Seward*, 86, 363.

60   *Seward directed the group's*: Meigs, *Shorthand Journals*, vol. 4, February 10, 1857.

60   *He told Seward*: Ibid.

61   *On March 4*: James Buchanan, *Inaugural Address*, March 4, 1857, www.presidency.ucsb.edu.

61   *The House had*: Meigs, *Shorthand Journals*, vol. 4, March 4, 1857.

61   *Across from his perch*: Ibid.

61   *Photography was a*: Meigs, *Shorthand Journals*, vol. 3, August 22–23, 1856.

61   *In Massachusetts alone*: Beaumont Newhall, *The History of Photography* (New York: Museum of Modern Art, 1982), 30–32.

61   *About the time he*: Meigs letter to Jefferson Davis, January 28, 1856, Architect of the Capitol office, photography operation; Wayne Firth, A Chronology of Photography at the United States Capitol, 1856–2005 (Draft 11-22-2005), Architect of the Capitol, photography operations.

61   *Cheering him on*: Bulletin of the Philosophical Society of Washington, vol. 14, 1848, 324–25.

62   *Meigs's new boss*: Weigley, *Quartermaster General*, 79.

62   *To the degree*: Nevins, *Emergence of Lincoln*, vol. 1, 71–72.

62   *It dawned on him*: Meigs, *Shorthand Journals*, vol. 4, March 4, 1857.

62   *Signs of trouble*: Meigs letter to Floyd, April 14, 1857, Architect of the Capitol; Meigs, *Shorthand Journals*, vol. 4, April 14, 1857.

62   *He fired off*: Meigs letter to Floyd, April 6, 1857, Architect of the Capitol.

63   *Totten was flabbergasted*: Meigs, *Shorthand Journals*, vol. 4, March 4, 1857.

63   *Officers in uniform*: Nevins, *Emergence of Lincoln*, vol. 1, 121–23.

63   *"Our progress in"*: Abraham Lincoln letter to Joshua Speed, August 24, 1855, Abraham Lincoln Online, www.abrahamlincolnonline.org.

64   *They would also use*: Meigs, *Shorthand Journals*, vol. 4, June 11–13, 1857.

65   *"I fear no investigation"*: Meigs letter to Buchanan, July 3, 1857, in East, *Banishment of Captain Meigs*, 118.

65 *Floyd's games and machinations*: Meigs, *Shorthand Journals*, vol. 4, July 22, 1857.

65 *Floyd then added*: Ibid., November 16, 1857.

65 *The idea was repulsive*: Ibid., October 13, 1857.

65 *He realized his*: Papers of Jefferson Davis, vol. 6, *1856–1860*, 547.

65 *He resolved to "strive"*: Meigs, *Shorthand Journals*, vol. 4, October 13, 1857.

66 *He asked Davis if*: Ibid., December 9, 1857.

66 *One unsigned piece*: *Pennsylvania Inquirer*, December 17, 1857, in Meigs, *Shorthand Journals*, vol. 4, appendix.

66 *Still others lambasted*: Meigs, *Shorthand Journals*, vol. 5, May 18, 1858; Andrew Johnson, *Documentary History*, 688.

67 *The* Washington Evening Star *provided*: *Evening Star* (Washington, DC), "The New House Hall," December 17, 1857.

CHAPTER 11: AN INSCRIPTION FOR ALL TIME

68 *He focused on*: Meigs, *Shorthand Journals*, vol. 5, February 16, 1858.

68 *Meigs carried a pedometer*: Ibid., December 14, 1858.

69 *He had come to*: Ibid., January 14, 1858.

69 *Without seeking approval*: National Park Service, National Register of Historic Places Inventory—Nomination Form, *Cabin John Aqueduct M: 35–37*.

69 *When the captain*: Meigs, *Shorthand Journals*, vol. 5, April 3, 1858.

70 *He even wrote a*: Ibid., August 2, 1858.

70 *"If these are opened"*: Ibid., vol. 3, August 27, 1856.

71 *New disputes in Kansas*: Nevins, *Emergence of Lincoln*, vol. 1, 229–43.

71 *Aware of the game*: Meigs, *Shorthand Journals*, vol. 5, September 25, 1858.

71 *In June 1858*: *Documentary History*, February 22, 1860, 744–49.

71 *Meigs was disgusted*: Meigs, *Shorthand Journals*, vol. 5, June 17, 1858.

71 *He was riding*: Meigs, *Shorthand Journals*, vol. 5, August 5, 1858.

72 *Meigs seems to*: Ways, *Washington Aqueduct*, 44.

72 *One night, he turned*: Meigs, *Shorthand Journals*, vol. 5, December 21, 1858.

72 *Then, on January 3*: Washington Aqueduct annual report for fiscal 1859; Meigs, *Shorthand Journals*, vol. 6, January 3–4, 1859; *Evening Star* (Washington, DC), January 3–4, 1859.

73 *Two months earlier*: Nevins, *Emergence of Lincoln*, vol. 1, 402–3.

73 *With hundreds of lawmakers*: *Evening Star* (Washington, DC), January 4, 1859.

73 *The Kentuckian described*: John C. Breckinridge, *Congressional Globe*, 35th Congress, 2nd Session, January 4, 1859.

74   *Meigs was deeply*: Meigs, *Shorthand Journals*, vol. 6, January 4, 1859.

74   *Skylight illuminated the scene*: Ibid.

74   *The room was well*: *Baltimore Sun* article in Wolff, *Capitol Builder* (probably January 5, 1859).

75   *But after workers*: *Evening Star* (Washington, DC), January 5, 1859.

75   *"I wish you could"*: Weigley, *Quartermaster General*, 88.

75   *Three months later*: Ways, "Washington Aqueduct," 30–31.

75   *The Meigs household*: Meigs, *Shorthand Journals*, vol. 6, July 21 and August 1, 1859.

75   *Louisa once beat*: Mary A. Giunta, ed., *A Civil War Soldier of Christ and Country* (Urbana: University of Illinois Press, 2006), 1–2.

76   *He wanted to attend*: Weigley, *Quartermaster General*, 91.

76   *John had submitted*: Giunta, *Civil War Soldier*, 2.

76   *"I trust that while"*: Copy of Meigs letter to Floyd in Meigs, *Shorthand Journals*, vol. 6, June 25, 1859.

77   *On the afternoon of September 5 Meigs*: Ibid., September 5, 1859.

77   *"I trust that you"*: Weigley, *Quartermaster General*, 94.

CHAPTER 12: "EVERYTHING INTO CONFUSION"

78   *For readers in*: *Evening Star* (Washington, DC), October 17, 1859.

78   *In August, it*: John Brown in *Life and Times of Frederick Douglass*, electronic edition (Chapel Hill: Academic Affairs Library, University of North Carolina, 1999), 324–25, http://docsouth.unc.edu/neh/douglasslife/douglass.html.

78   *The reports from Harpers Ferry*: *Evening Star* (Washington, DC), October 19, 1859.

79   *By the time Lee*: Nevins, *Emergence of Lincoln*, vol. 2, 81–85.

79   *This was too much*: Weigley, *Quartermaster General*, 116.

79   *His views would change*: McPherson, *Battle Cry of Freedom*, 203.

80   *Floyd wanted to replace*: Meigs, *Shorthand Journals*, vol. 6, March 29–April 1, 1859; *New York Tribune*, September 21, in Meigs, *The Shorthand Journals*, vol. 6, appendix.

80   *Floyd insisted that Meigs*: *New York Times*, September 27, 1860.

80   *Meigs's meaning was clear*: Weigley, *Quartermaster General*, 98.

80   *On November 2, 1859*: Floyd letter to Meigs in Meigs, *Shorthand Journals*, vol. 6, November 2, 1859.

80   *Floyd claimed he sacked*: Brown, *Glenn Brown's History*, 372–73.

80   *To Meigs and others*: *New York Times*, September 27, 1860; Meigs, *Shorthand Journals*, vol. 6, November 9, 1859.

80   *"I have for the last"*: Meigs, *Shorthand Journals*, vol. 6, November 6, 1859.

81 *The dome was not*: Ibid., October 27, 1859.

81 *Meigs gathered his foremen*: Farewell statement by Meigs on November 2, 1858, in Wolff, *Capitol Builder*, 807.

81 *He was convinced*: Weigley, *Quartermaster General*, 99.

81 *He kept*: Mark A. Snell, *From First to Last: The Life of Major General William B. Franklin* (New York: Fordham University Press, 2002), 42–48.

82 *The Senate demanded*: Nevins, *Emergence of Lincoln*, vol. 2, *1859–1861*, 196.

82 *Floyd stood out among*: Ibid., 199.

83 *The Meigses generally considered*: Weigley, *Quartermaster General*, 117.

83 *In a backlash*: Brown, *Glenn Brown's History*, 507–8.

84 *In February 1860*: *Documentary History*, February 22, 1860, 744–49.

84 *Nobody really cared*: Wolanin, "Meigs the Art Patron," 163–64; Brown, *Glenn Brown's History*, 507.

84 *Now his idea was*: Historic American Engineering Record, National Park Service, HAER No. DC-21, http://cdn.loc.gov.

85 *The lawmakers proposed*: *Evening Star* (Washington, DC), *The Special Message of the President on the Civil Appropriations Bill,* June 28, 1860.

85 *To ensure that Meigs*: *Congressional Globe*, Senate, 36th Congress, 1st Session, June 12, 1860.

85 *"I deemed it impossible"*: *Evening Star*, Washington, DC, "The Special Message of the President on the Civil Appropriations Bill," June 28, 1860.

85 *He said Meigs*: Papers of Jefferson Davis, vol. 6, 360.

86 *"I do not permit myself"*: Jeremiah S. Black in East, *Banishment of Captain Meigs*, 129.

86 *He told Buchanan*: Meigs, *Annual Report for 1861, Report of Operations on the Washington Aqueduct*.

86 *The* New York Times *wrote*: "Affairs at Washington: The Dismissal of Capt. Meigs—The Reasons Secretary Floyd Not Able to Get the Money Political Affairs, *New York Times*, September 27, 1860, published October 6, 1860.

87 *People packed into*: Abraham Lincoln, Cooper Union Address, February 27, 1860, in *New York Times*, www.nytimes.com.

88 *Lincoln's chief opponent*: Miller Center, University of Virginia, *The Campaign and Election of 1860*, http://millercenter.org.

89   *In that session*: Nevins, *Emergence of Lincoln*, vol. 2, *1859–1861*, 282–86.

89   *Douglas was the only*: Miller Center, *Campaign and Election of 1860*; Nevins, *Emergence of Lincoln*, vol. 2, *1859–1861*, 276.

89   *Just before the election*: Meigs Pocket Diary, October 20, 1860, Meigs Papers, LOC, shelf 18,202, reel 2.

89   *He assumed Floyd*: Meigs letter to John Meigs, October 9, 1860, in Giunta, *Civil War Soldier*, 77.

89   *He didn't care*: Weigley, *Quartermaster General*, 109.

89   *It was a final*: East, *Banishment of Captain Meigs*, 132–33.

90   *He planned on*: Meigs letter to John Meigs, October 9, 1860, in Giunta, *Civil War Soldier*, 77.

90   *From Knoxville*: Meigs Pocket Diary, October 25, 1860.

91   *"We cannot tell yet"*: Strong, *Diary of the Civil War*, 59.

91   *Meigs, a Democrat*: Meigs Pocket Diary, November 15, 1860.

91   *"Dear Sir: As the"*: Meigs to Lieutenant General Winfield Scott, November 10, 1860, in *The War of the Rebellion: A Compilation of the Official Records of the Union and Confederate Armies*, ser. 1, vol. 52, pt. 1 (Washington, DC: US GPO), 3, at Cornell University Library, http://ebooks.library.cornell.edu (hereafter cited as *Official Records*).

91   *He said, "the temper"*: Ibid., 4.

91   *"At present both this"*: Ibid.

92   *"My Dear John"*: Giunta, *Civil War Soldier*, 84.

CHAPTER 15: FLOYD RESIGNS

93   *Events soon handed Meigs*: East, *Banishment of Captain Meigs*, 42.

93   *Floyd's reputation slid*: Nevins, *Emergence of Lincoln*, vol. 2, 347.

93   *In the following days*: Robert Anderson, *Official Records*, ser. 1, vol. 1, 105–6.

93   *In fact, Anderson's*: Nevins, *Emergence of Lincoln*, vol. 2, 368–69.

94   *Not only had the*: Wilson, *Business of Civil War*, 51–54.

94   *Then he endorsed*: The Supreme Court, *The Floyd Acceptances*, 64 US 7 Wall. 666 666 (1868), www.justia.com.

94   *The scheme surfaced*: Nevins, *Emergence of Lincoln*, vol. 2, 373.

94   *Northerners became further*: *Penny Press* (Cincinnati), January 24, 1860.

94   *"I desire to get"*: S. Adams, *Official Records*, ser. 3, vol. 1, 8–9.

94   *Near the end of*: William Wilkins et al., ser. 3, vol. 1, 15.

95   *They wrote to the*: Sarah Hutchins Killikelly, *The History of Pittsburgh* (Pittsburgh: B. C. Gordon Montgomery, 1906), 205.

95   *Buchanan did so*: Nevins, *Emergence of Lincoln*, vol. 2, 374–75.

95 *In early 1862*: *Official Records*, ser. 1, vol. 7, 254.

95 *Floyd's health soon failed*: John B. Floyd, Miller Center, http://millercenter.org.

95 *Years later, Ulysses*: Ulysses S. Grant, *Grant Memoirs and Selected Letters* (New York: Library of America, 1990), 206.

95 *Everywhere Meigs looked*: Meigs letters to John Meigs, November 17–25, 1860, in Giunta, *Civil War Soldier*, 80–84.

96 *After more than*: National Park Service, *Fort Jefferson*, www.nps.gov/drto /learn/historyculture/fort-jefferson.htm.

96 *They had already*: Meigs letter to John Meigs, December 17, 1860, in Giunta, *Civil War Soldier*, 85.

96 *He urged a unit*: Meigs Pocket Diary, November 22, 1860.

96 *Meigs also convinced two*: Weigley, *Quartermaster General*, 123–24.

96 *In January a steamship*: Meigs, *Official Records*, ser. 1, vol. 52, pt. 1, 1–3.

96 *In addition to*: Ibid., 5–6.

97 *Meigs was grateful*: Meigs letter to John Meigs, February 6, 1861, in Giunta, *Civil War Soldier*, 96.

97 *He shared his view*: Meigs, *Official Records*, ser. 1, vol. 52, pt. 1, 5.

97 *On February 13, 1861*: Meigs Pocket Diary, February 13, 1861; Washington Aqueduct annual report for fiscal 1861, 2.

CHAPTER 16: HE PLUCKED A LAUREL

98 *When Meigs returned*: Meigs, *Shorthand Journals*, vol. 6, February 20, 1861.

98 *"Meigs has been summoned"*: *National Republican* (Washington, DC), July 4, 1861.

98 *Holt recounted with glee*: Meigs, *Shorthand Journals*, vol. 6, February 21, 1861.

99 *He walked with Louisa*: Weigley, *Quartermaster General*, 129.

99 *It was regarded*: *Daily Dispatch* (Richmond, VA), July 22, 1861.

99 *Rumors of plots*: Margaret Leech, *Reveille in Washington, 1860–1865* (New York: New York Review Books, 1941), 40.

99 *The president-elect was*: Carl Schurz, "Reminiscences of a Long Life," March 1907, in *McClure's Magazine* 28 (New York: S.S. McClure, 1907), 461.

99 *Meigs cast it as*: Copy of Meigs letter to Captain William B. Franklin, February 25, 1861, in Meigs letter to father, February 27, 1861, Meigs Papers, shelf 18,202.1, reel 5; Allen, *United States Capitol*, 310.

100 *Judging from the prints*: Weigley, *Quartermaster General*, 131.

100 *"Exciting times, these"*: Meigs, *Shorthand Journals*, vol. 6, March 3.

100   *The inaugural procession*: Carl Schurz, "Reminiscences of a Long Life," *McClure's*, 461.

101   *"No time was wasted"*: Weigley, *Quartermaster General*, 132.

101   *quickly resumed*: Washington Aqueduct annual report for fiscal 1861, 6.

CHAPTER 17: A SECRET MISSION

105   *It was widely*: Stahr, *Seward*, 223.

105   *When Meigs arrived*: Meigs, *Copy of Private Journal*, March 29, 1861, in John G. Nicolay Papers, LOC, Manuscript Division.

105   *Lincoln and Seward*: Montgomery Meigs, *General M. C. Meigs on the Conduct of the Civil War* (Chicago: American History Review, 1921), 300.

105   *The president asked Meigs*: Meigs, *Copy of Private Journal*, March 29, 1861.

105   *Lincoln asked if Meigs*: Ibid.

106   *General Scott felt that*: E. D. Keyes, *Fifty Years' Observation of Men and Events* (New York: Charles Scribner's Sons, 1884), 282–84.

106   *They made lists*: Meigs, *Conduct of the Civil War*, 300.

106   *They found Lincoln sprawled*: Keyes, *Fifty Years' Observation*, 284.

107   *"I depend on you"*: Meigs, *Copy of Private Journal*, March 31, 1861.

107   *Whenever possible*: Copy of *Gideon Welles Diary* (extract), in John G. Nicolay Papers, LOC, Manuscript Division, 16; Meigs letter to Seward, April 6, 1861, *Official Records*, ser. 1, vol. 1, 368.

107   *Seward, who understood*: Meigs, *Shorthand Journals*, vol. 6, April 1, 1861.

107   *Meigs assured Seward*: Ibid.

107   *A veteran of the*: *New York Times*, July 14, 1863.

108   *Lincoln signed something*: Abraham Lincoln, April 1, 1861, *Official Records*, ser. 1, vol. 4.

108   *Over the next several*: Erna Risch, *Quartermaster Support of the Army* (Washington, DC: Center of Military History, 1989), 336.

108   *Organizers gathered nearly*: Meigs, *Conduct of the Civil War*, 301.

108   *After Seward told*: *Welles Diary* (extract), 17.

108   *When Secretary of War*: Welles, *Diary of Gideon Welles*, vol. 1 (New York: Houghton Mifflin, 1911), 64.

108   *Meigs sailed before*: Meigs, *Shorthand Journals*, vol. 6, April 1, 1861, April 7–9, 1861.

109   *During the voyage*: Meigs, letter to Seward, April 6, 1861.

109   *The trip south was*: Meigs, letter to Seward, April 10, 1861, *Official Records*, ser. 1, vol. 1, 368–70.

109   *The government would*: Meigs, letter to Seward, April 10, 1861, 369.

109 *"The dispatch and"*: Ibid.

109 *"This loyalty and"*: Ibid.

110 *On April 16*: Meigs, *Shorthand Journals,* vol. 6, April 16, 1861.

110 *"I see a bright"*: Ibid., April 25, 1861.

CHAPTER 18: A SOUL ON FIRE

111 *Meigs arrived back*: Meigs, *Copy of Private Journal,* April 1, 1861.

111 *It was a chaotic*: Senate history, *Soldiers occupy the Senate Chamber,* www .senate.gov.

111 *Enemy forces also*: Meigs, *Conduct of the Civil War,* 288.

111 *Panic had spread*: *Official Records,* ser. 1, vol. 2, 602; Nevins, *War for the Union,* vol. 1 (New York: Charles Scribner's Sons, 1959), 86–87.

111 *The president was in*: Meigs, *Copy of Private Journal,* May 3, 1861.

112 *"The extraordinary powers"*: Welles, *Diary of Gideon Welles,* vol. 1, 38.

112 *He told Montgomery Blair*: Meigs, *Copy of Private Journal,* May 4, 1861.

112 *He accounted for*: Ibid., May 10, 1861.

112 *Better to remain*: Ibid.

112 *Meigs thought his*: Weigley, *Quartermaster General,* 336.

113 *"The only possible reason"*: William T. Sherman letter to John Sherman, *The Sherman Letters* (New York: Charles Scribner's Sons, 1894), 122.

113 *He decided to decline*: Meigs, *Copy of Private Journal,* May 14, 1861.

113 *Filled with pent-up*: Ibid., May 15, 1861.

113 *In the coming weeks*: Smithsonian Institution, *Memorial Record of M.C. Meigs,* January 27, 1892, LOC, 18,202.1, roll 23.

113 *A drizzle was falling*: *Copy of Private Journal,* May 19, 1861.

114 *"His soul seems on fire"*: Louisa Meigs to Minerva Rodgers, May 26, 1861, Meigs Papers, LOC, shelf 18,202.1, reel 3.

114 *In a letter to*: Robert E. Lee letter, August 6, 1861, reprinted in *New York Times,* www.nytimes.com/1861/08/06/news/the-rebel-gen-lee.html.

115 *As the story goes*: James Albert Woodburn, *The Life of Thaddeus Stevens* (Indianapolis: Bobbs-Merrill, 1913), 600.

115 *Lincoln was insistent*: Doris Kearns Goodwin, *Team of Rivals* (New York: Simon & Schuster Paperbacks, 2005), xvi.

115 *"My dear sir"*: Lincoln letter to Scott, June 5, 1861, The Lincoln Papers at the LOC, General Correspondence, http://memory.loc.gov.

116 *Finally, the president*: Lincoln to Simon Cameron, June 10, 1861, Collected Works of Abraham Lincoln, University of Michigan, http://quod.lib.umich.edu.

116 *After the meeting, Meigs*: Meigs, *Copy of Private Journal,* June 13, 1861.

117   *Only two months*: Cameron, *Official Records*, ser. 3, vol. 1, 301–310; *Official Records*, ser. 3, vol. 2, 802.

117   *This outpouring triggered*: Lincoln, *Official Records*, ser. 3, vol. 1, 311–21.

117   *"On, to Richmond!"*: *New-York Daily Tribune*, June 29, 1861.

117   *The army quickly*: *Official Records*, ser. 3, vol. 2, 802.

117   *To create that system*: James A. Huston, *The Sinews of War* (Washington, DC: Office of the Chief of Military History, 1966), viii.

118   *Meigs was occupied by*: *Letters Sent by the Office of the Quartermaster General, June 9–December 31, 1861*, M745, Main Series, 1818–1870 (National Archives Microfilm Publication), roll 36.

118   *Secretary Cameron did not*: Risch, *Quartermaster Support*, 340.

118   *Meigs asserted himself*: Meigs, *Copy of Private Journal*, June 21–24, 1861.

118   *Like all the leading*: Baron Jomini in Martin Van Creveld, *Supplying War* (New York: Cambridge University Press, 1977), 1.

118   *Near the end of*: Meigs testimony, July 14, 1862, *Report of the Joint Committee on the Conduct of the War*, pt. 1 (Washington, DC: US GPO, 1863), 292–93.

118   *Lincoln wanted to*: Meigs, *Copy of Private Journal*, June 25, 1861.

120   *"I did not think"*: Ibid., June 29, 1861.

121   *The capital hummed*: Leech, *Reveille in Washington*, 103.

121   *Overhead, a balloon aeronaut*: *Evening Star* (Washington, DC), June 25, 1861.

121   *On Independence Day*: Meigs, *Copy of Private Journal*, July 4, 1861.

121   *That same day*: Abraham Lincoln, address to Congress, July 4, 1861, *Official Records*, ser. 3, vol. 1, 311–21.

121   *Lincoln said secessionists*: Lincoln, address to Congress, July 4, 1861.

122   *Everything seemed to go*: *Official Records*. ser. 1, vol. 2, 305–9.

122   *In truth, poor planning*: Nevins, *War for the Union*, vol. 1, 216–20.

122   *Meigs and his son*: *Official Records*, ser. 1, vol. 2, 376.

122   *Before John left*: Louisa Meigs letter to mother, July 25, 1861, Meigs Papers, LOC, shelf 18,202.1, reel 3.

122   *He decided to "go"*: Meigs, *Copy of Private Journal*, July 21, 1861; Louisa Meigs letter to mother, July 25, 1861, Meigs Papers, LOC, 18,202.1, reel 3.

122   *Along the way*: *Official Records*, ser. 1, vol. 2, 300.

123   *Men around him*: Meigs, *Copy of Private Journal*, July 21, 1861.

123   *Meigs saw evidence*: *Official Records*, ser. 1, vol. 2, 321.

124   *One bright moment came*: Ibid., 376.

124   *On July 23*: Ibid., 356.

125 *The men of the*: Nevins, *War for the Union*, vol. 1, 342.

125 *Many contractors operated*: *Harper's New Monthly Magazine* 29 (New York: Harper & Brothers Publishers, 1864), 227–31.

125 *They sold sand*: *Congressional Globe*, House, 37th Congress, 2nd Session, 710–11.

125 *A muckraking reporter*: "The Fortunes of War: How They Are Made and Spent," *Harper's New Monthly* 29 (New York: Harper & Brothers Publishers, 1864), 227–31.

126 *A satirical song*: *Vanity Fair*, September 21, 1861.

126 *Government employees enabled*: "The Frauds on Government," *Cleveland Morning Leader,* February 10, 1862.

126 *In St. Louis*: Nevins, *War for the Union*, vol. 1, 309–10.

126 *Frémont leased a*: Meigs, *Copy of Private Journal*, September 18, 1861.

126 *Meigs permitted McKinstry*: Weigley, *Quartermaster General*, 221, 187–88.

127 *He wrote Frank Blair*: *Official Records*, ser. 1, vol. 3, 463–65.

127 *Despite Frémont*: Strong, *Diary of the Civil War*, 173.

127 *While making their*: Weigley, *Quartermaster General*, 187.

128 *Those reviews provided*: *Official Records*, ser. 1, vol. 3, 540–49.

128 *All the spending seemed to do*: Ibid., 73–78.

128 *The White House resolved*: Meigs, *Copy of Private Journal*, September 10–18, 1861.

128 *Montgomery Blair sent*: Montgomery Blair to Lincoln, September 14, 1861, www.loc.gov.

129 *Meigs described Frémont*: Meigs, *Copy of Private Journal*, September 18, 1861.

129 *Frémont knew trouble*: *Official Records*, ser. 1, vol. 3, 549.

129 *Congressional overseers, along*: "A Near Fatal Attack on Representative Charles H. Van Wyck of New York," House of Representatives Office of History, history.house.gov.

130 *His committee's mandate*: *Journal of the House of Representatives*, July 8, 1861, memory.loc.gov.

130 *They collected two thousand*: *Congressional Globe*, House, 37th Congress, 3rd Session, 1550–51.

130 *In the rush to*: House of Representatives, Report No. 49, 37th Cong., 3rd Session, 1–170.

130 *Lincoln himself dismissed*: Lincoln order, January 28, 1863, Collected Works of Abraham Lincoln, http://quod.lib.umich.edu.

130 *The contracting committee*: Weigley, *Quartermaster General*, 198, 238.

131 *Van Wyck gave*: *Congressional Globe*, House, 37th Congress, 2nd Session, 710–11.

131 *With his encouragement*: Ibid., 3rd Session, 952.

CHAPTER 21: "HARD WORK AND COLD CALCULATION"

132 *The challenges facing*: Quartermaster Department Annual Report, fiscal 1862, *Official Records*, ser. 3, vol., 2, pt. 1, 786–809; Wilson, *Business of Civil War*, 2–15.

132 *Much has been written*: Creveld, *Supplying War*, 1.

132 *"The great part of"*: Meigs letter to John Meigs, November 8, 1861, in Giunta, *Civil War Soldier*, 122–23.

132 *Regulations mandated that*: *Official Records*, ser. 3, vol. 2, 806.

133 *The department had changed*: Risch, *Quartermaster Support*, 332–34.

133 *New recruits learned*: *Official Records*, ser. 3, vol. 1, 682.

133 *Meigs often complained*: Wilson, *Business of Civil War*, 70.

133 *Congress saw that something*: *The Military Laws of the United States*, 5th ed. (Washington, DC: US GPO, 1917), 276–77.

134 *He even pushed back*: Meigs letter to Lincoln, December 21, 1861, Abraham Lincoln Papers at the Library of Congress, http://memory.loc.gov; Meigs letter to Mary Lincoln, October 4, 1861, *Letters Sent by the Office of the Quartermaster General,* June 9–December 31, 1861, roll 36; Wilson, *Business of Civil War*, 65.

134 *The surge in spending*: Wilson, *Business of Civil War*, chart, 38; *Historical Statistics of the United States*, pt. 1, Bureau of Census (Washington, DC: US GPO, 1975), 165.

134 *Quartermaster employees needed*: *Official Records*, ser. 1, vol. 19, pt. 1, 100.

134 *He wrote later*: Ibid.

134 *To be sure, Federals had*: Nevins, *War for the Union*, vol. 1, 145, 252–57, 342; Bureau of the Census, *Manufacturers of the United States, 1860* (Washington, DC: US GPO, 1865).

135 *New technology helped*: Amy Breakwell, "A Nation in Extremity: Sewing Machines and the American Civil War," in *Textile History*, May 2010, 98–107.

135 *The quartermaster system*: Wilson, *Business of Civil War*, 2, 78; Nevins, *War for the Union*, vol. 1, 290.

135 *As historian James McPherson*: McPherson, *Battle Cry of Freedom*, 325.

136 *Though Meigs's portfolio*: Meigs, *Copy of Private Journal,* July 29, 1861.

136 *At the same time*: *Official Records*, ser. 3, vol. 2, 803–4.

136 *"The nation is in extremity"*: Nevins, *War for the Union*, vol. 3, 291.

136 *Waste compounded Meigs's*: *Official Records*, ser. 3, vol. 2, 804.

136 *He adopted the pragmatic*: Ibid., vol. 4, 901–2.

137 *Adjusting his view did not*: Ibid., 224–25.

137 *Gray, wool, and warm*: Ibid., vol. 2, 483.

137 *In something of an*: Ibid., 804.

137 *Though undeniably creative*: Ibid., vol. 1, 582–83.

138 *"Should the Board"*: Ibid., 583.

138 *"[If] the conditions in"*: Ibid., 378–79.

138 *Meigs standardized contracting*: *Report of the Joint Committee on the Conduct of the War*, pt. 1, 222.

139 *Meigs even found*: *Official Records*, ser. 3, vol. 3, 264.

139 *"There never was an army"*: *Report of the Joint Committee on the Conduct of the War*, pt. 1, 138.

139 *Even as Meigs surmounted*: *Official Records*, ser. 3, vol. 1, 866.

CHAPTER 22: "THE WAR CANNOT BE LONG"

140 *McClellan came from*: George B. McClellan, *McClellan's Own Story* (New York: Charles L. Webster, 1887), 13, 52.

140 *"The war cannot be"*: "Presentation of a Sword to Major General McClellan," *Sunbury American* (Pennsylvania), November 9, 1861.

140 *McClellan showed no inkling*: Meigs, *Conduct of the Civil War*, 298.

141 *At the same time*: McClellan, *McClellan's Own Story*, 147.

141 *It was the president*: Meigs Pocket Diary, January 10, 1862.

141 *"General, what shall I"*: Meigs, *Conduct of the Civil War*, 292.

141 *"Send for them"*: Ibid.

141 *Lincoln agreed and*: Ibid., 292–93; Irvin McDowell notes in William Swinton, *Campaigns of the Army of the Potomac* (New York: Charles Scribner's Sons, 1882), 67–72.

142 *"You are entitled"*: McDowell notes in Swinton, *Campaigns of the Army of the Potomac*, 73.

142 *Meigs moved his chair*: Meigs, *Conduct of the Civil War*, 292–93.

143 *He urged the*: McClellan, *McClellan's Own Story*, 148.

143 *He nevertheless offered*: Meigs Pocket Diary, January 14, 1862.

143 *"It is clearly a"*: Draft passage of War Department Annual Report at Freedman and Southern Society Project, www.freedmen.umd.edu.

143 *The war had given*: *Official Records*, ser. 3, vol. 4, 893–94.

143 *The quartermaster general*: Ibid., vol. 2, 809.

144 *He had an*: Welles, *Diary of Gideon Welles*, vol. 1, 15.

144 *"The army will move"*: *Evening Star* (Washington, DC), January 20, 1862.

144 *Meigs's disapproval soon*: Meigs, *Conduct of the Civil War*, 293.

144 *A physician was called*: Carmen Brissette Grayson, "Military Advisor to Stanton and Lincoln: Quartermaster General Montgomery C. Meigs and the Peninsula Campaign, January–August, 1862," in William J. Miller, ed., *The*

Peninsula Campaign of 1862: Yorktown to the Seven Days, vol. 2 (Campbell, CA: Savas Woodbury, 1995), 84.

145   *A War Department clerk*: Charles F. Benjamin, "Recollections of Secretary Stanton," *Century 33,* March 1887, 764, http://digital.library.cornell.

145   *He told Meigs*: Weigley, *Quartermaster General,* 213.

145   *To ensure that Stanton's*: *Official Records,* ser. 1, vol. 5, 41.

CHAPTER 23: GUNBOATS

147   *The story of that*: *Official Records,* ser. 3, vol. 2, 792–93; Myron J. Smith, Jr., *The USS* Carondelet (Jefferson, NC: McFarland, 2010), 3–14.

148   *Meigs put out a*: Nevins, *War for the Union,* vol. 2, 70–73.

148   *He sold the idea*: Smith, Jr., *USS* Carondelet, 6.

148   *On August 7, Eads*: *Official Records,* ser. 3, vol. 2, 817–20; Meigs letter to Lincoln, February 28, 1862, http://memory.loc.gov.

148   *Work began almost*: *Official Records,* ser. 1, vol. 22, 314–16.

148   *It took Foote and Meigs*: Ibid., vol. 8, 367.

149   *Though these wrinkles irritated*: Smith, Jr., *USS* Carondelet, 31.

149   *With improvisation*: Nevins, *War for the Union,* vol. 2, 71.

149   *The black-painted boats*: Smith, Jr., *USS* Carondelet, 35–36.

150   *The* Essex *soon drifted*: Meigs letter to Lincoln, February 28, 1862.

150   *After just over an*: *Evening Star* (Washington, DC), February 8, 1862.

150   *"Whenever you need"*: Weigley, *Quartermaster General,* 243.

150   *Meigs told Stanton*: *Official Records,* ser. 3, vol. 2, 797.

150   *He shared his thoughts*: Meigs letter to Lincoln, February 28, 1862.

151   *With preparations under way*: *Evening Star* (Washington, DC), "The Official Dispatches," March 10, 1862.

151   *At least 240 Union men*: McPherson, *Battle Cry of Freedom,* 376.

151   *The president, Stanton*: Welles, *Diary of Gideon Welles,* vol. 1, 100.

151   *On March 9 he ordered troops*: *Official Records,* ser. 1, vol. 7, 79.

152   *Day after day*: Ibid., vol. 5, 46.

152   *Department officers under*: Risch, *Quartermaster Support,* 415.

152   *"The magnitude of the"*: *Official Records,* ser. 1, vol. 11, pt. 1, 158.

153   *While planning the*: William J. Miller, "'Scarcely Any Parallel in History': Logistics, Friction and McClellan's Strategy for the Peninsula Campaign," in *The Peninsula Campaign of 1862: Yorktown to the Seven Days,* vol. 2, ed. William J. Miller (El Dorado Hills, CA: Savas, 1995, 2013), 129–88.

153   *One of his senior*: *Official Records,* ser. 1, vol. 11, pt. 1, 13–14.

153   *"I beg to assure"*: Ibid., 15.

CHAPTER 24: "HIS BEST NAME IS HONESTY"

154   *The quartermaster general met*: Grayson, *Military Advisor to Stanton and Lincoln*, 88.

154   *Lincoln secretary William Stoddard*: William O. Stoddard, *Inside the White House in War Times* (New York: Charles L. Webster, 1890), 103.

155   *Meigs became Stanton's*: Grayson, *Military Advisor to Stanton and Lincoln*, 87.

155   *Stanton turned to Meigs*: *Official Records*, ser. 1, vol. 11, pt. 3, 57–58.

155   *Meigs did so*: Ibid., pt. 1, 27–28.

155   *"You will retain"*: Ibid., pt. 3, 176–77.

156   *Meigs convinced the president*: Ibid.

156   *At eleven at night, Major*: Ibid., vol. 12, pt. 1, 525.

156   *"The secretary will be"*: Ibid., vol. 51, pt. 1, 628.

156   *Meigs played an important*: Ibid., vol. 12, pt. 3, 216–17; Grayson, *Military Advisor to Stanton and Lincoln*, 94.

156   *Meigs expressed "hope"*: Ibid.; *Official Records*, ser. 1, vol. 12, pt. 3, 219.

156   *"This is a crushing"*: *Official Records*, ser. 1, vol. 12, pt. 3, 220.

156   *But "the lack"*: Peter Cozzens, *Shenandoah 1862: Stonewall Jackson's Valley Campaign* (Chapel Hill: University of North Carolina Press, 2008), 4.

157   *The army consumed six hundred thousand*: *Official Records*, ser. 1, vol. 11, pt. 1, 159; ibid., ser. 3, vol. 2, 806.

157   *Every horse needed to*: Ibid., ser. 3, vol. 2, 798.

157   *All together, the animals*: Ibid., ser. 1, vol. 11, pt. 1, 157–59.

157   *At the beginning of*: Risch, *Quartermaster Support*, 379–82.

158   *But the department eventually got*: *Official Records*, ser. 1, vol. 46, pt. 3, 850.

158   *To keep the army*: Ibid., vol. 11, pt. 1, 157–59.

158   *They naturally blamed*: Regis De Trobriand, *Four Years with the Army of the Potomac*, trans. George K. Dauchy (Boston: Ticknor, 1889), 216.

158   *Still, the quartermaster officers*: *Peninsula Campaign: Robert Lee and the Seven Days*, Civil War Trust, www.civilwar.org.

159   *Instead of one well-organized*: Risch, *Quartermaster Support*, 425.

159   *"A struggle for the"*: John D. Billings, *Hard Tack and Coffee; or, The Unwritten Story of Army Life* (1887; repr., Old Saybrook, CT: Konecky & Konecky, 1888), 356.

159   *Like a growing number*: Charles Royster, *The Destructive War* (New York: Alfred A. Knopf, 1991), 232–95.

159   *"In the mean time"*: Weigley, *Quartermaster General*, 250–51.

160   *To clarify matters*: *Official Records*, ser. 1, vol. 11, pt. 3, 340–41.

160   *Though McClellan claimed*: *War for the Union*, vol. 2, 158.

160   *"I who am not"*: Michael Burlingame and John R. Turner Ettlinger, eds., *Inside*

Lincoln's White House: The Complete Civil War Diary of John Hay (Carbondale: Southern Illinois University Press, 1999), 191.

160 *"President thinks I tried"*: Meigs Pocket Diary, July 5, 1862.

161 *Lieutenant Colonel Rufus Ingalls*: *Official Records*, ser. 1, vol. 11, pt. 3, 326–27.

161 *"They cling to him"*: Meigs letter to Louisa, July 31, 1862, in Grayson, *Military Advisor to Stanton and Lincoln*, 104.

161 *In July Major General*: Meigs, *Conduct of the Civil War*, 294.

161 *"The success of these"*: *Official Records*, ser. 3, vol. 2, 796.

161 *To the end*: Meigs, *Conduct of the Civil War*, 296.

162 *He acknowledged responsibility*: Grayson, *Military Advisor to Stanton and Lincoln*, 97.

162 *But he held McClellan*: Meigs, *Conduct of the Civil War*, 295–97; Grayson, *Military Advisor to Stanton and Lincoln*, 97.

CHAPTER 25: "VAST IN QUANTITY"

163 *"To Quarter Master"*: "Stuart's Raid," *Dayton (OH) Daily Empire*, January 3, 1863, 4.

163 *"As [rebel] resources"*: Stoddard, *Inside the White House in War Times*, 208.

163 *Lee understood the*: Royster, *Destructive War*, 35.

164 *They skirmished with*: *Official Records*, ser. 1, vol. 12, pt. 2, 12–17.

164 *On August 24, Jeb*: Ibid., 641–48; Nevins, *War for the Union*, vol. 2, 175–77.

164 *"The hungry, threadbare"*: McPherson, *Battle Cry of Freedom*, 527.

164 *Jackson's report to Richmond*: *Official Records*, ser. 1, vol. 12, pt. 2, 644.

164 *With flames leaping into*: Nevins, *War for the Union*, vol. 2, 177.

165 *In response to a*: Peter Cozzens, *General John Pope: A Life for the Nation* (Champaign, IL: University of Illinois Press, 2000), 161–62; Hay, *Inside Lincoln's White House*, 37.

165 *While the president pondered*: Hay, *Inside Lincoln's White House*, 37.

165 *Chase privately called McClellan*: Welles, *Diary of Gideon Welles*, vol. 1, 103.

165 *"Unquestionably he has acted"*: Hay, *Inside Lincoln's White House*, 39.

165 *The president told Welles*: Welles, *Diary of Gideon Welles*, vol. 1, 113.

165 *"The purpose, if discovered"*: *Official Records*, ser. 1, vol. 19, pt. 2, 590–91.

165 *"The army is not"*: Ibid.

166 *Questions about supplies arose*: Ibid., 592.

166 *"I shall endeavor"*: Ibid., 596.

166 *Lincoln complained that*: Welles, *Diary of Gideon Welles*, vol. 1, 113.

167 *The army's problem*: *Official Records*, ser. 3, vol. 4, 888.

167 *They carried every kind*: Ibid., vol. 2, 799; Billings, *Hard Tack and Coffee*, 353.

167 *In a stern letter*: *Official Records*, ser. 1, vol. 19, pt. 3, 225–26.

168 *Soldiers dubbed the*: Risch, *Quartermaster Support*, 360.

168 *The quartermaster pegged the*: *Official Records*, ser. 3, vol. 2, 798.

168 *"The extra wagons, now"*: Ibid., ser. 1, vol. 19, pt. 3, 225–26.

168 *In a related push*: Ibid., vol. 25, pt. 2, 489–91; Edward Hagerman, *The American Civil War and the Origins of Modern Warfare: Ideas, Organization, and Field Command* (Bloomington: Indiana University Press, 1988), 70–72.

168 *A year later, in*: *Official Records*, ser. 1, vol. 25, pt. 2, 487.

169 *"The nation is rapidly"*: Strong, *Diary of the Civil War*, 253.

169 *"God bless you, and"*: *Official Records*, ser. 1, vol. 19, pt. 1, 53.

169 *On September 13*: Ibid., 603.

169 *"I have all the"*: Ibid., pt. 2, 281.

170 *By sunset, the death*: Ibid., pt. 1, 200, 813.

170 *McClellan claimed later*: Ibid., 70–71.

170 *"This army is not"*: Ibid., 70.

170 *"The country is becoming"*: Ibid., pt. 2, 394–95; see also *Report of the Joint Committee*, pt. 1, 43–47.

171 *One depot in Washington*: *Official Records*, ser. 1, vol. 19, pt. 1, 21.

171 *McClellan's well-provisioned*: Ibid., pt. 2, 633.

171 *"I am sick, tired"*: Ibid., ser. 3, vol. 2, 703.

171 *"[T]he Quartermaster-General would"*: Ibid., ser. 1, vol. 19, pt. 2, 521.

172 *Though Lincoln did*: McPherson, *Battle Cry of Freedom*, 502.

172 *He hoped they would*: Miller, *Second Only to Grant*, 177.

CHAPTER 26: HOPE WANES

173 *On November 5, 1862, Lincoln*: *Official Records*, ser. 1, vol. 19, pt. 2, 557.

173 *Everyone felt that swift*: Ibid., 565.

173 *Their plan was subverted*: James M. McPherson, *Tried by War: Abraham Lincoln as Commander in Chief* (New York: Penguin Press, 2008), 143–44.

174 *As one historian*: E. B. Long with Barbara Long, *The Civil War Day by Day: An Almanac*, unabridged paperback ed. (New York: Da Capo Press, 1985), 296.

174 *"For the failure"*: *Official Records*, ser. 1, vol. 21, 67.

174 *"My Dear General"*: Ibid., 916–18.

175 *"Every day weakens"*: Ibid.

175 *In January 1863*: *Congressional Globe*, Senate, 37th Congress, 3rd Session, January 15, 1863.

175 *"A question has been"*: Ibid.

176 *The numbers in play*: *Official Records*, ser. 3, vol. 4, 888.

176 *At the beginning*: Ibid., vol. 2, 799.

176 *Enough were available even*: Risch, *Quartermaster Support*, 374.

176 *For many months*: *Official Records*, ser. 3, vol. 5, 220–21.

177 *To Meigs, horses*: Ibid., ser. 1, vol. 12, pt. 3, 60.

177 *Given the number of*: Ibid., vol. 19, pt. 1, 71.

177 *Meigs wrote a testy*: Ibid., pt. 2, 424.

177 *"Major-general Rosecrans complains"*: Ibid., vol. 20, pt. 2, 328.

177 *"General Halleck informs me"*: Ibid.

178 *"It will take some"*: Ibid., 332.

178 *"Your dispatch received; thanks"*: Ibid., 333.

178 *"Cheap horses for service"*: Ibid., vol. 23, pt. 2, 271.

179 *"Inspection by faithful cavalry"*: Ibid., 272.

179 *Rosecrans received 18,450*: Ibid., 301.

179 *Finally, fed up about*: Ibid., 300–304.

179 *"Such marches destroy"*: Ibid., 301–2.

179 *"[N]ever to pass a"*: Ibid., 303.

CHAPTER 27: "FRET HIM AND FRET HIM"

182 *He recognized the*: *Official Records*, ser. 1, vol. 27, pt. 3, 881.

182 *In contrast, the rebels*: Bell Irvin Wiley, *The Life of Johnny Reb,* rev. ed. (Baton Rouge: Louisiana State University Press, 2008), 113–15.

182 *"We are too much"*: Joseph E. Johnston letter to brother, May 7, 1863, in *Journal of the Military Service Institution of the United States*, vol. 50 (Governors Island, NY: Military Service Institution, 1912), 319.

182 *"Never, as long as"*: Royster, *Destructive War*, 242.

182 *The enemy seemed to*: *Official Records*, ser. 1, vol. 27, pt. 1, 36.

182 *"Fight him, too"*: Ibid., 35.

183 *He moved to ensure*: Ibid., pt. 3, 120.

183 *Meigs also focused*: June 20, 1863.

183 *"God does not intend"*: Weigley, *Quartermaster General*, 286–87.

184 *"Last fall I gave"*: *Official Records*, ser. 1, vol. 27, pt. 3, 378–79.

184 *The note troubled Ingalls*: Ibid.

184 *Rumors asserted that Gettysburg*: Robert L. Bloom, "'We Never Expected a Battle': The Civilians at Gettysburg," in *Pennsylvania History* 55, no. 4 (October 1988): 171–72, https://journals.psu.edu/phj/article/view/24708/24477.

185 *Drawing on lessons*: Hagerman, *American Civil War and Origins of Modern Warfare*, 73.

185 *Baggage and tents*: Official Records, ser. 1, vol. 27, pt. 1, 221–24.

185 *"That man Haupt has"*: Risch, *Quartermaster Support,* 396; McPherson, *Battle Cry of Freedom,* 527.

186 *He addressed this apparent*: Official Records, ser. 1, vol. 27, pt. 1, 22–24; Daniel Carroll Toomey, *The War Came by Train* (Baltimore: Baltimore & Ohio Railroad Museum, 2013), 175.

186 *Haupt estimated that 150 cars*: Official Records, ser. 1, vol. 27, pt. 3, 511–12.

186 *"These men are not"*: Ibid., 512.

186 *"They began the fight"*: Ibid., 503.

187 *"Let nothing interfere"*: Ibid., 523.

187 *"Withdraw all your construction"*: Ibid., 696.

187 *Captain W. Willard Smith*: Ibid., 568–70.

187 *People came in "swarms"*: Royster, *Destructive War,* 248; John H. Brinton, *Personal Memoirs of John H. Brinton* (New York: Neale, 1914), 240–45.

187 *Some took guns, bayonets*: Official Records, ser. 1, vol. 27, pt. 3; W. Willard Smith letter to Meigs, August 7, 1863, Gettysburg Library; D. Scott Hartwig, *Quartermaster's Tale,* The Blog of Gettysburg National Military Park, https://npsgnmp.wordpress.com.

187 *"I told him if"*: Hartwig, *Quartermaster's Tale.*

188 *More than 24,000 muskets*: Official Records, ser. 1, vol. 27, pt. 1, 225–26.

188 *"Against any but the"*: John Meigs letter to Don Piatt, June 28, 1863, Giunta, *Civil War Soldier,* 179.

188 *Garrett assigned three hundred of*: Alan R. Koenig, "Ironclads on Rails" (dissertation, Lincoln: University of Nebraska, 1995).

188 *John Meigs named them*: Toomey, *War Came,* 177.

188 *Schenck sent John Meigs*: Official Records, ser. 1, vol. 27, pt. 3, 571–72.

188 *"I am not afraid"*: Ibid., 607.

189 *"Remember that the duty"*: Ibid., 608.

189 *John also wrote to*: Giunta, *Civil War Soldier,* 184.

CHAPTER 28: "EXHAUSTION OF MEN AND MONEY"

190 *Far from Gettysburg*: Grant, *Grant Memoirs,* 381; McPherson, *Battle Cry of Freedom,* 636–37.

190 *In an overview of*: Official Records, ser. 3, vol. 3, 599–605.

190 *He praised Grant's reliance*: Ibid., 601.

190 *Most of all, he*: Ibid., 602.

190 *A Vicksburg woman*: Dora Richard Miller, "A Woman's Diary of the Siege of

Vicksburg," ed. George W. Cable, *Century Illustrated Monthly* 30, no. 5 (September 1885), 775.

191 *"The National Government"*: Official Records, ser. 3, vol. 3, 605.

191 *Still, Meigs warned Seward*: Ibid.

191 *His emotions flared*: Montgomery Meigs in letter to father, August 25, 1863, Meigs Papers, LOC, shelf 18,202, reel 16.

192 *On August 28, 1863*: Meigs Pocket Diary, August 28, 1863.

192 *On his return to*: Official Records, ser. 1, vol. 29, pt. 2, 154–55.

192 *First, he was redirected*: Ibid., vol. 30, pt. 3, 479.

192 *In Louisville*: Meigs Pocket Diary, September 20, 1863.

192 *A ferocious battle*: Nevins, *War for the Union*, vol. 3, 195–98.

193 *Bragg's men cut*: W. S. Rosecrans, "The Campaign for Chattanooga," *Century Illustrated Monthly* 34 (May 1887), 129–36; Bruce Catton, "The Miracle on Missionary Ridge," *American Heritage* 20, no. 2 (February 1969), www.american heritage.com.

193 *Meigs saw that*: Official Records, ser. 3, vol. 4, 879.

193 *For two days, Stanton*: Hay, *Inside Lincoln's White House*, 85–86.

194 *Working through the night*: Official Records, ser. 1, vol. 29, pt. 1, 155–59.

194 *For the answer, Stanton*: Edwin A. Pratt, *The Rise of Rail-Power* (Philadelphia: J. B. Lippincott, 1916), 23–24, 30–36.

194 *He had already worked*: E. G. Campbell, *United States Military Railroads, 1862–1865, Journal of the American Military History Foundation*, vol. 2, 1938, http://penelope.uchicago.edu.

194 *His mission now involved*: Pratt, *The Rise of Rail-Power*, 24; Benjamin, *Recollections of Secretary Stanton*, 767; Official Records, ser. 1, vol. 29, pt. 1, 155–59.

194 *Meigs served as*: Ibid., 150.

195 *"A thousand thanks"*: Ibid., 162.

195 *Any shade disappeared*: Rosecrans, *Campaign for Chattanooga*, 137.

195 *It seemed inhuman*: Ibid.

195 *They joked with one*: Official Records, ser. 1, vol. 30, pt. 4, 101–2.

195 *They dueled with songs*: Joseph S. Fullerton, "The Army of the Cumberland at Chattanooga," in *Battles and Leaders of the Civil War*, vol. 3, ed. Robert Underwood Johnson and Clarence Clough (New York: Century, 1884), 719.

196 *The army, with enough*: Official Records, ser. 3, vol. 4, 880.

196 *"Your very interesting reports"*: Ibid., ser. 1, vol. 30, pt. 4, 78.

196 *"Hold Chattanooga at all"*: Ibid., 479.

196 *"We will hold the"*: Ibid.

197 *Meigs arranged for delivery*: Ibid., ser. 3, vol. 4, 880.

197 *"Their joy at seeing"*: Risch, *Quartermaster Support*, 414.

198 *"It was a surprise"*: Montgomery C. Meigs, "The Battle of Chattanooga: Official Account by Quartermaster General Meigs," *The Indiana State Sentinel,* December 7, 1863.

198 *"At nightfall sky cleared"*: Meigs, "Battle of Chattanooga."

198 *They feared if they*: *Official Records,* ser. 1, vol. 31, pt. 2, 201–3.

198 *"What so often"*: Ibid., 263–64.

199 *"Total defeat; they"*: Meigs Pocket Diary, November 25, 1863.

199 *Meigs collected war*: Peter Cozzens, *The Shipwreck of Their Hopes: The Battles for Chattanooga* (Chicago: University of Illinois Press, 1996), 359.

199 *Then he rode off*: Meigs Pocket Diary, December 2, 1863.

CHAPTER 29: "A BEAUTEOUS BUBBLE"

200 *The cold nights, daily*: Miller, *Second Only to Grant,* 216.

200 *The administrative demands*: Lincoln to Edwin Stanton, February 1, 1864, *Collected Works of Abraham Lincoln.*

201 *In any event, the*: Walt Whitman, *The Uncollected Poetry and Prose of Walt Whitman,* vol. 2 (Garden City, NY: Doubleday, Page, 1921), 31–33.

201 *Meigs also visited*: Meigs Pocket Diary, February 13, 1864.

202 *It would culminate*: Grant, *Grant Memoirs,* 512.

202 *The numbers associated*: *Official Records,* ser. 1, vol. 36, pt. 1, 276–79.

202 *They deployed 4,300*: Ibid., vol. 33, 853–56.

202 *Grant later estimated*: Grant, *Grant Memoirs,* 523.

203 *Grant tells us in*: Ibid.

203 *He was in a*: Nevins, *War for the Union,* vol. 4, 25; Royster, *Destructive War,* 325.

203 *He requested 5 million*: *Official Records,* ser. 1, vol. 36, pt. 1, 3.

203 *James McPherson, the great*: McPherson, *Battle Cry of Freedom,* 733; Hay, *Inside Lincoln's White House,* 195.

204 *At one rebel depot*: *Official Records,* ser. 1, vol. 36, pt. 1, 777.

204 *Now there was rain, day*: Ibid., 5.

204 *"To give some idea"*: Ibid., 1094.

204 *Civilians on both sides*: Strong, *Diary of the Civil War,* 453.

204 *After a month, the*: McPherson, *Battle Cry of Freedom,* 733.

204 *It enabled the crossing*: Huston, *The Sinews of War,* 227.

205 *In the first six*: *Official Records,* ser. 3, vol. 4, 889.

205 *Meigs aimed to*: *Harper's Weekly,* June 11, 1864.

205 *In Fredericksburg, men lay*: Leech, *Reveille in Washington,* 401.

205 *Stanton ordered Meigs*: *Official Records,* ser. 1, vol. 36, pt. 2, 829.

205   *The ability to*: Leech, *Reveille in Washington*, 401.

206   *A stench drifted over*: Robert M. Poole, *On Hallowed Ground: The Story of Arlington National Cemetery* (New York: Walker, 2009), 57.

206   *Care of the dead*: *Official Records*, ser. 3, vol. 1, 498.

206   *That mandate was*: Ibid., vol. 2, 2.

206   *In July 1862*: Michelle A. Krowl, " 'In the Spirit of Fraternity': The United States Government and the Burial of Confederate Dead at Arlington National Cemetery," *Virginia Magazine of History and Biography* 111, no. 2 (2003): 155, www.jstor.org/stable/4250101.

206   *On May 13 a cemetery*: *Official Records*, ser. 3, vol. 4, 903.

206   *Another 2,000 had*: Ibid., 904, 892.

206   *Meigs knew already*: Poole, *On Hallowed Ground*, 58–63; "The Beginnings of Arlington National Cemetery," National Park Service, www.nps.gov/arho /learn/historyculture/cemetery.htm.

206   *The land was put*: Poole, *On Hallowed Ground*, 55.

206   *The burials at Arlington*: Ibid., 59–60.

207   *In a brief letter*: Montgomery Meigs to Edwin Stanton, June 15, 1864, copy, Arlington National Cemetery archives.

207   *With Stanton's approval*: Montgomery Meigs letter to D. H. Rucker, June 15, 1864, copy, Arlington National Cemetery archives.

207   *As he wrote*: Montgomery Meigs letter, April 11, 1865, Meigs Papers, LOC, shelf 18,202.1, reel 6; Poole, *On Hallowed Ground*, 65.

207   *"How appropriate that"*: "The Arlington Estate," *Big Blue Union* (Marysville, KS), July 9, 1864.

207   *The number of burials*: *Official Records*, ser. 3, vol. 4, 904.

208   *Twenty-six graves soon*: Joseph E. Stevens, "The North's Secret Weapon," *American History*, April 2002, 42–48; *Beginnings of Arlington National Cemetery*, National Park Service, www.nps.gov/arho/learn/historyculture/cemetery .htm.

CHAPTER 30: A VULNERABLE CAPITAL

209   *In June, as Grant*: *Official Records*, ser. 1, vol. 27, pt. 1, 346.

209   *Lincoln himself*: Lincoln, *Memorandum on Possibility of Not Being Reelected*, Abraham Lincoln Papers at the LOC, http://memory.loc.gov.

210   *On July 4 the*: Leech, *Reveille in Washington*, 408.

210   *More than 50 forts*: *Official Records*, ser. 1, vol. 21, 902–16.

210   *Some of these men*: Ibid., vol. 37, pt. 2, 98.

210   *Early advanced north*: Ibid., pt. 1, 347–49.

210   *He delayed the*: Ibid., 191–92.

211   *On July 4, 1864*: Ibid., ser. 3, vol. 4, 878.

211   *On the same day*: Meigs Pocket Diary, July 4, 1864.

211   *Though pleased on both*: Ibid.

211   *The next day, Meigs*: *Official Records*, ser. 1, vol. 37, pt. 1, 254–55.

211   *He argued that even*: Montgomery Meigs letter, July 19, 1891, copy, Meigs family papers, courtesy of Louisa Watrous.

211   *The officer accepted*: *Official Records*, ser. 1, vol. 37, pt. 2, 236.

211   *By now, Early's footsore*: John G. Nicolay and John Hay, *Abraham Lincoln: A History*, vol. 9 (New York: Century, 1890), 169–72.

211   *On July 11 they*: *Official Records*, ser. 1, vol. 37, pt. 1, 347–49.

212   *Two houses smouldered*: Welles, *Diary of Gideon Welles*, vol. 2, 72.

212   *Meigs admired the fields*: *Official Records*, ser. 1, vol. 37, pt. 1, 258–59.

212   *As they cleared*: Welles, *Diary of Gideon Welles*, vol. 2, 72–73.

212   *The president stood on*: Nicolay and Hay, *Abraham Lincoln: A History*, vol. 9, 169–73.

213   *"Get down, you damn fool"*: Oliver Wendell Holmes letter, June 14, 1922, at the Shapell Manuscript Foundation, www.shapell.org.

213   *The Union had*: *Official Records*, ser. 1, vol. 36, pt. 1, 28.

213   *As of July 5*: Ibid., vol. 37, pt. 1, 259; Meigs Pocket Diary, July 11, 1864.

213   *In the war's*: *Official Records*, ser. 1, vol. 38, pt. 1, 59–85.

213   *The supply line began*: Ibid., ser. 3, vol. 5, 987.

214   *The supply line later*: Ibid., 987.

214   *When clergy and others*: Royster, *Destructive War*, 270.

214   *The mill enabled them*: *Official Records*, ser. 3, vol. 5, 234.

214   *One of them, over*: Ibid., vol. 4, 957.

214   *They made an even*: Ibid., ser. 1, vol. 52, pt. 1, 573.

214   *Rail lines in the*: Ibid., ser. 3, vol. 4, 883.

215   *On September 2 Sherman took*: Ibid., ser. 1, vol. 38, pt. 5, 777.

215   *Sherman calculated that*: Sherman, *Memoirs of Gen. W. T. Sherman*, 890.

215   *"Bridges have been built"*: *Official Records*, ser. 1, vol. 38, pt. 1, 83.

215   *More than a dozen*: Ibid., 87.

215   *Federals under Phil Sheridan*: "Official War Bulletin," *Evening Star* (Washington, DC), October 10, 1864; P. H. Sheridan; *Personal Memoirs of P. H. Sheridan*, vol. 1 (New York: Charles L. Webster, 1888), 464–68.

215   *Though still green*: Sheridan, *Personal Memoirs*, vol. 1, 467.

215   *John and two aides*: Giunta, *Civil War Soldier*, 249–56.

216   *The exact details of*: Sheridan, *Personal Memoirs*, vol. 2, 49–52.

216   *"And so has perished"*: Meigs Pocket Diary, October 3–7, 1864.

216 *Sheridan ordered his men*: Sheridan, *Personal Memoirs*, vol. 2, 51–52.

216 *The next day, Lincoln*: Meigs Pocket Diary, October 8, 1864; Lincoln Log, October 8, 1864, www.thelincolnlog.org.

217 *"Dear Mont grieves for"*: Louisa Meigs letter, November 27, 1864, Giunta, *Civil War Soldier*, 245–46.

217 *Among those in his*: Weigley, *Quartermaster General*, 336.

217 *He thought of the*: Montgomery Meigs letter, October 6, 1864, Meigs Papers, LOC, shelf 18,202, reel 16.

217 *Decades later, Mosby disputed*: "The Meigs Killing," *Baltimore Sun*, October 7, 1895.

CHAPTER 31: THE REFIT AT SAVANNAH

218 *As the story went*: Sherman, *Memoirs*, 626.

218 *Sherman would send all*: *Official Records*, ser. 1, vol. 34, pt. 1, 35–36.

218 *He wanted to crush*: Royster, *Destructive War*, 35.

218 *Grant consented*: *Official Records*, ser. 1, vol. 34, pt. 1, 36.

218 *Then his army, some*: Nevins, *War for the Union*, vol. 4, 157.

219 *Sherman encouraged his men*: *Official Records*, ser. 1, vol. 44, 13.

219 *"This may seem"*: Ibid.

219 *It fell to Meigs*: Ibid., 568.

219 *"The handwriting of"*: *Scientific American*, January 30, 1892, vol. 66 (New York: Munn, 1892), 71; East, *Banishment of Captain Meigs*, 118; *Vincent Meigs*, 268.

219 *Meigs summoned a special*: *Official Records*, ser. 3, vol. 5, 215.

220 *They had waded through*: Nevins, *War for the Union*, vol. 4, 163.

220 *They left friends along*: *Official Records*, ser. 1, vol. 38, pt. 1, 716.

220 *And now they received*: Ibid., vol. 44, 637; Ibid., ser. 3, vol. 5, 214–15.

220 *He was especially taken*: Ibid., ser. 1, vol. 44, 807.

220 *"I beg to assure"*: Ibid.

220 *"To his admirers"*: Royster, *Destructive War*, 366.

220 *On January 5, 1865*: Meigs Pocket Diary, January 5, 1865 (transcribed extracts courtesy of Louisa Watrous); Abbot, *Memoir*, April 1893.

221 *Congress had formed*: National Academy of Sciences, *History*, www.nasonline.org.

221 *The next day, he*: *Official Records*, ser. 1, vol. 47, pt. 2, 18–19.

221 *Meigs was most concerned*: Ibid., vol. 42, pt. 3, 3.

221 *Grant's siege force*: Ibid., ser. 3, vol. 5, 293.

221 *The cost of shipping forage*: Ibid., 216.

221 *Those vessels comprised*: Ibid., 229.

221 *He urged Sherman*: Ibid., ser. 1, vol. 47, pt. 2, 180.

221 *Union leadership decided*: Ibid., ser. 3, vol. 5, 215.

222 *The army pushed on*: Sherman, *Memoirs*, 778.

222 *To help prepare for this refit*: *Official Records*, ser. 3, vol. 5, 227.

222 *Every soldier received*: Ibid.

222 *With the Confederacy*: Ibid., ser. 1, vol. 47, pt. 3, 4.

222 *Meigs joined the army*: Ibid., vol. 5, 227–28.

222 *Then came word*: Grant, *Grant Memoirs*, 697.

222 *Lee declared that Five*: *Official Records*, ser. 1, vol. 46, pt. 1, 52.

222 *Leaders fled as soldiers*: "From Richmond," *Evening Star* (Washington, DC), April 6, 1865.

222 *Meigs boarded a boat*: Weigley, *Quartermaster General*, 316.

223 *In Washington, War Department*: "Extra," *Evening Star* (Washington, DC), April 3, 1865.

223 *Meigs heard the best*: Meigs Pocket Diary (transcribed extracts), April 11, 1865.

223 *For the first time*: Ibid., April 12, 1865.

223 *He hoped that*: Montgomery Meigs letter, April 11, 1865, Meigs Papers, LOC, shelf 18,202.1, reel 6.

223 *He chose instead*: Meigs Pocket Diary (transcribed extracts), April 12, 1865.

223 *Meigs also visited*: "The Accident to Secretary Seward," *Evening Star* (Washington, DC), April 6, 1865.

223 *He made the rest*: Minerva Rodgers letter, April 17, 1865, Meigs Papers, LOC, hard copy.

223 *"The country is drunk"*: Meigs Pocket Diary (transcribed extracts), April 14, 1865.

223 *That night, as Meigs*: Minerva Rodgers letter, April 17, 1865.

224 *Seward's son Frederick*: Meigs Pocket Diary (transcribed extracts), April 14, 1865; Leech, *Reveille in Washington*, 485–86.

224 *Stanton asked Meigs*: Welles, *Diary of Gideon Welles*, vol. 2, 285–86.

224 *Lincoln breathed slowly*: Ibid., 287.

224 *The eyes of everyone*: McColloch, *Men and Measures*, 225.

224 *A rainstorm*: *Illustrated Life, Services, Martyrdom, and Funeral of Abraham Lincoln, Sixteenth President of the United States* (Philadelphia: T. B. Peterson & Brothers, 1865), 209, http://quod.lib.umich.edu.

224 *At midnight, on authority*: *Official Records*, ser. 1, vol. 46, pt. 3, 756.

225 *"The murderers have"*: "Meigs Pocket Diary (transcribed extracts), April 14, 1865.

225 *On Tuesday, April 18*: *Illustrated Life*, 216.

225 *The next day, as*: Meigs Pocket Diary (transcribed extracts), April 19, 1865.

225 *Instead of demanding*: *Official Records*, ser. 1, vol. 47, pt. 3, 245.

226 *The apparent presumption*: Ibid., 263–64.

226 *"No better officer"*: Meigs Pocket Diary (transcribed extracts), April 22, 1865.

CHAPTER 32: THE JOURNEY HOME

227 *To mark the North's*: Royster, *Destructive War*, 408; *Official Records*, ser. 1, vol. 46, pt. 3, 1171 and 1181–82.

227 *Soldiers bivouacked in*: *Official Records*, ser. 3, vol. 5, 231.

227 *The Army of the*: *Grant Memoirs*, 768.

227 *In forty days, some*: *Official Records*, ser. 3, vol. 5, 217.

227 *Others passed through*: Ibid., 231.

227 *By winter, a second*: Ibid., 233, 1033.

227 *The government sent*: Ibid., 233.

228 *Not long after Grant*: Drew Gilpin Faust, *This Republic of Suffering* (New York: Alfred A. Knopf, 2008), 190–91.

228 *On June 7, under Special*: *Official Records*, ser. 3, vol. 5, 317–23.

229 *The next assignment*: Ibid., 319.

229 *"[A]ll of them candidly"*: Ibid., 320.

229 *With help from records secretly*: National Park Service, Dorence Atwater, www .nps.gov/ande/learn/historyculture/DORENCE_ATWATER.htm.

229 *News about the*: Ibid., 321; "Clara Barton and Andersonville," National Park Service, www.nps.gov.

230 *"Nothing has been destroyed"*: *Official Records*, ser. 3, vol. 5, 322.

230 *Commanders had not*: Ibid., vol. 2, 2.

230 *In the fall of*: *The Army Reunion: with Reports of the Meetings of the Army of the Cumberland; the Army of the Tennessee; the Army of the Ohio; and the Army of Georgia, Chicago, December 15 and 16, 1868* (Chicago: S. C. Griggs, 1869), 227.

230 *"To ask"*: *Army Reunion*, 241.

231 *"It revealed the"*: Ibid., 243.

231 *By late 1866*: *Official Records*, ser. 3, vol. 5, 1037–38.

231 *"I do not believe that"*: Montgomery Meigs, *Congressional Globe*, May 8, 1872, House, 42nd Congress, Second Session, 3220.

CHAPTER 33: "DOGS TO THEIR VOMIT"

232 *"I must be permitted"*: *Official Records*, ser. 1, vol. 52, pt. 1, 692.

232 *He had to move*: Ibid., ser. 3, vol. 5, 1031–33, 1045.

233   *"Poor woman she"*: Weigley, *Quartermaster General*, 325.

233   *Meigs spurned him*: Ibid., 324.

233   *"The emancipation of"*: Ibid., 338–39.

233   *In his frustration*: Weigley, *Quartermaster General*, 341.

233   *In early 1867 Meigs*: Report of the Quartermaster General, October 20, 1868, in *Message of the President of the United States to the Two Houses of Congress*, 40th Congress, Third Session (Washington, DC: US GPO, 1869), 444.

234   *"The prevailing opinion"*: Seward letter, May 28, 1867, letter in Henry B. Meigs, *Record of the Descendants*.

234   *Now he was responsible*: Quartermaster General report, October 20, 1868, 445.

234   *"As a measure of humanity"*: Ibid., 456.

234   *He eventually oversaw*: Report of the Quartermaster General, October 19, 1871, in *Report of the Secretary of War, Being Part of the Messages and Documents Communicated to the Two Houses of Congress*, vol. 1, 42nd Congress, Second Session (Washington, DC: US GPO, 1871).

234   *All through the postwar*: Quartermaster General report, October 19, 1871, 135–37.

235   *In the meantime*: Ibid., 136.

235   *The standard markers now*: National Park Service, National Register of Historic Places, *Civil War Era National Cemeteries*, August 31, 1994, E10–E13, copy, www.nationalregister.sc.gov/MPS/MPS045.pdf.

235   *He let his imagination*: Pamela Scott, "Montgomery C. Meigs and Victorian Architectural Traditions," in *Building of the Nation's Capital*, 64.

235   *It had a simple*: General Montgomery Meigs House, LOC, Prints & Photographs Online Catalog, Historic American Buildings Survey, Engineering Record, Landscape Survey, www.loc.gov; Weigley, *Quartermaster General*, 351.

235   *The house became*: Louisa Taylor oral history and memoirs, Meigs Papers, LOC, shelf 18,202.1, reel 20, 7.

236   *In 1870 he sought*: History and Development of the National Cemetery Administration, National Cemetery Administration, US Department of Veterans Affairs, www.cem.va.gov.

236   *One of the first*: Official Records, ser. 3, vol. 5, 241; Battleground National Cemetery, Most Endangered Place for 2005, D.C. Preservation League, www.dcpreservation.org; Battleground National Cemetery, National Park Service, www.nps.gov; Civil War Defenses of Washington newsletter, National Park Service 1, no. 1, March 2010.

236   *Dozens of the lodges*: Mark P. Slater, *Historic Structure Assessment Report, Superintendent's Lodge: Memphis National Cemetery*, National Cemetery Administration, US Department of Veterans Affairs, January 2011, www.cem.va.gov.

236 *In another collaboration:* Annual Report of the Quartermaster-General to the Secretary of War (Washington, DC: US GPO, 1872), 17; John Kleber, ed., *The Encyclopedia of Louisville* (Lexington: University Press of Kentucky, 2001), 740.

236 *He also had a:* Michael Mills, "Commissary Sergeant's Quarters, Building 42, Fort Myer, Virginia," in *Building of the Nation's Capital,* 112–19.

236 *In 1877:* Smithsonian Arts and Industries Building (Museum Building) Historic Building Survey, National Park Service, HABS no. DC-298.

236 *Meigs attended the Centennial:* James D. McCabe, *The Illustrated History of the Centennial Exhibition, Held in Commemoration of the One Hundredth Anniversary of American Independence* (Philadelphia: National, 1876), 816.

236 *The board of regents:* Report of the U.S. *National Museum*, in Annual Report of the Board of Regents of the Smithsonian Institution, June 30, 1903, United States National Museum (Washington, DC: US GPO), 238–42.

236 *His plans called for:* Report of the U.S. *National Museum*, 246–48.

236 *It had an open:* Smithsonian Arts and Industries Building (Museum Building) Historic Building Survey; *Arts and Industries Building,* National Register of Historic Places Inventory—Nomination Form, National Park Service, www .nps.gov.

237 *It is still considered:* Smithsonian Arts and Industries Building (Museum Building), Historic Building Survey.

CHAPTER 34: "SOLDIER, ENGINEER, ARCHITECT, SCIENTIST, PATRIOT"

238 *In 1875, on special:* Annual Report of the Quartermaster-General to the Secretary of War, fiscal 1875 (Washington, DC: US GPO), 19.

238 *Meigs described the typewriter:* Montgomery Meigs letter, July 19, 1891, copy, Meigs family papers, courtesy of Louisa Watrous.

238 *We learn from his:* Montgomery Meigs letters, September 1875, Meigs Papers, LOC, shelf 18,202.1, reel 20.

239 *"It is impossible":* Ibid., September 17, 1875.

239 *Meigs thought that:* Weigley, *Quartermaster General,* 355.

239 *On February 6, 1882:* Abbott, *Memoir,* 315; Meigs, *Cullum's Biographical Register.*

239 *Others had waited:* Washington Post, editorial, February 8, 1882.

239 *"The corps has seen":* Abbott, *Memoir,* 323–24.

240 *The federal Pension Bureau:* National Register of Historic Places—Nomination Form, *Pension Building* (National Park Service), www.nps.gov.

240 *By the early 1880s*: Linda Brody Lyons, *A Handbook to the Pension Building, Home of the National Building Museum* (Washington, DC, National Building Museum, 1989), 26.

240 *Meigs's design drew on*: Nomination Form, *Pension Building*, section 8a.

240 *Plans showed a building*: Annual Report on the Construction of the New Pension Building, September 3, 1887, *The Executive Documents of the House of Representatives*, 50th Congress, First Session, 1887–1888 (Washington, DC: US GPO, 1889), 1345.

241 *Just as he did*: Nomination Form, *Pension Building*, 4; Lyons, *Handbook*, 14–17.

241 *He documented each*: Lyons, *Handbook*, 23.

241 *His theory about the space*: Annual Report on the Construction of the New Pension Building, 1343–44; Nomination Form, *Pension Building*, 4.

241 *Meigs took care to*: Kathryn Allamong Jacob, *Testament to Union* (Baltimore: Johns Hopkins University Press, 1998), 63–68.

242 *For the building's west entrance*: Jacob, *Testament to Union*, 67.

242 *Still others joked*: "Little Known Story of Meigs Barn Told," *Washington Post*, March 6, 1964.

242 *Sherman or Sheridan*: Jacob, *Testament to Union*, 67. Note: This quote remains apocryphal, but it captures the skepticism about the building at the time.

242 *by 1985, the great*: Paul Goldberger, "Museums Set the Tone in Architecture," *New York Times*, September 8, 1985.

242 *Meigs continued to crackle*: Memorial Record of M. C. Meigs.

242 *The request came in*: McClellan, *McClellan's Own Story*, 154.

243 *Meigs did not want*: Montgomery Meigs letter, May 24, 1888, Meigs Papers, LOC, shelf 18,202.1, reel 20.

243 *"Many military names"*: Meigs, *Conduct of the Civil War*, 299.

243 *Meigs did not get*: Louisa Taylor oral history and memoirs, 12.

243 *In a habit begun*: Montgomery C. Meigs Papers, National Museum of American History, Archives Center, Collection no. 881, box 17.

244 *"The idea of that"*: Louisa Taylor oral history and memoirs, 13.

244 *Early on January 2*: "Gen. M. C. Meigs Dead," *Evening Star* (Washington, DC), January 2, 1892.

244 *Honorary pall bearers*: "At Rest at Arlington," *Evening Star* (Washington, DC), January 5, 1892.

244 *"The Army has rarely possessed"*: General Orders No. 2, Headquarters of the Army, January 4, 1892, *General Orders and Circulars, Adjutant General's Office 1892* (Washington, DC: US GPO), 1893.

244 *"M. C. Meigs"*: McColloch, *Men and Measures*, 269–70.

INDEX

About the Author

Robert O'Harrow Jr. is a reporter on the investigative unit at the *Washington Post*. He is author of *No Place to Hide* and *Zero Day: The Threat in Cyberspace*, an ebook produced by the *Post*. He lives in Arlington, Virginia, with his wife and children.